# LAUGHING IN THE FACE OF DANGER

## World War True:
Real People, Real Heroes, Real Funny…

Foreword: R.J. Hillier,
General
Chief of the Defence Staff

### By: Scott Haskins

**Author and Editor**
SCOTT HASKINS

**Published By**
TMH Marketing Inc.
TAMARA HASKINS
PO Box 32092
2331-66 Street
Edmonton, AB
T6K 4C2

Phone: 780-642-7987
Fax: 780-642-7859
Email: scott@scotthaskins.ca
Web: www.scotthaskins.ca

**Interior layout and cover design**
DEAN PICKUP
Dpict Visual Communications
4817 44 Ave, Beaumont, AB T4X 1G5
Phone: 780-929-8169
Email: dpictcom@telus.net
Web: www.dpict.ca

**Cover photograph**
MELISSA PICKUP
Dpict Visual Communications

**On The Cover**
Veteran Patrick Sparrow and graphic designer Dean Pickup share a laugh during a photo shoot for the cover of this book at Patrick's home in Drumheller, Alberta.

Copyright © 2006 TMH Marketing Inc.
All rights reserved. No part of this publication may be reproduced, stored in a retrieval system, or transmitted, in any form or by any means, electronic, mechanical, recording, or otherwise, without the prior written permission of the publisher, except in the case of a reviewer.

Printed in Canada by Friesens Corporation, Altona, Manitoba.

Library and Archives Canada Cataloguing in Publication

Haskins, Scott, 1957-
  Laughing in the face of danger : world war true : real people, real heroes, real funny-- / written by Scott Haskins ; forword: Rick Hillier.

Includes index.
ISBN 0-9781227-0-4

  1. World War, 1939-1945--Personal narratives, Canadian. 2. World War, 1939-1945--Veterans--Humor. 3. World War, 1939-1945--Humor. I. Title.

D768.15.H365 2006          940.54'8171          C2006-904680-8

Chief of the Defence Staff     Chef d'état-major de la Défense

National Defence Headquarters
Ottawa, Ontario
K1A 0K2

Quartier général de
la Défense nationale
Ottawa (Ontario)
K1A 0K2

## Foreword – Laughing in the Face of Danger

By nature, conflict and war are not humorous by any means. They change the course of lives, create orphans, cause famine, destroy infrastructure, and deplete economies. The loss of lives, property, and the damage to social and economic structures incurred is such that nations, if they continue to exist at all, require decades to recover from the consequences.

Of wars and conflicts are also born heroes; brave men and women who answer the call to duty and choose to defend their country, their rights and their freedom. During the course of the Second World War, one out of every 11 Canadians answered that call, the vast majority voluntarily. They fought to protect the values that Canadians stand for, they fought to protect our freedom, and they fought to protect our way of life; for that, we must be forever grateful.

In historical textbooks, war is often recorded in the form of statistics, with an emphasis on overall military and political strategies. Amid all that information, it is sometimes easy for people to forget the very human and personal side, and the effect on people. And yet, every person involved has his or her own personal story – of triumph, despair, sorrow, or courage – that is worth sharing.

As we have seen, the number of Second World War veterans dramatically diminished in the last few years, therefore recording their stories now is more important than ever. We must not forget that they fought to protect the freedom we have today, a freedom often taken for granted.

We have much to learn from these brave veterans. Not only do they serve as the purest examples of honour, bravery, courage and modesty, but they also embody the true spirit of resolve. Faced with adversity, bearing witness to countless horrors, tested physically, emotionally and psychologically, they found a way to soldier on.

When I was offered the opportunity to provide a foreword to this book, I did not hesitate, for I truly admire the intent of this work. The stories contained in the next pages are great examples of the triumph of the human spirit over adversity. They are proof that no matter what faces us, the human spirit finds a way to survive, sees humour, and reminds us of what it is we are fighting for.

On behalf of today's men and women in uniform, I wish to thank, from the heart, our veterans for providing us the opportunity to live in freedom and democracy, for inspiring us to emulate your bravery, and for sharing these wonderful stories.

R.J. Hillier
General
Chief of the Defence Staff

# ABOUT GENERAL RICK HILLIER

Born in Newfoundland and Labrador, General Rick Hillier joined the Canadian Forces as soon as he could. Having enrolled in 1973, he graduated from Memorial University in Newfoundland in 1975 with a Bachelor of Science Degree.

After completing his armour officer classification training, he joined the 8$^{th}$ Canadian Hussars (Princess Louise's) in Petawawa, Ont. Subsequently, he served with and later commanded the Royal Canadian Dragoons in Canada and Germany.

General Hillier has had the privilege and pleasure of commanding troops from the platoon to the multi-national formation level within Canada, Europe, Asia and the United States. He has worked as a staff officer in several headquarters, first at the Army level in Montreal and later at the strategic level in Ottawa.

In 1998, he was appointed as the first Canadian Deputy Commanding General of III Corps, US Army, in Fort Hood, Texas. In 2000, he took command of the NATO stabilization force's Multi-national Division (Southwest) in Bosnia-Herzegovina.

In May 2003, General Hillier was appointed as Commander of the Army and subsequently, in October 2003, he was selected as the Commander of the NATO-led International Security Assistance Force in Kabul, Afghanistan.

He assumed his current duties as the Chief of the Defence Staff on Feb. 4, 2005.

General Hillier and his wife Joyce have two sons, Chris and Steven, a daughter-in-law, Chris' wife Caroline and a grandson, Jack, who has already learned to salute his grandfather. He enjoys most recreational pursuits but, in particular, runs slowly, plays hockey poorly and golfs not at all well.

# About the Author

Scott Haskins grew up in the tiny village of Lion's Head, Ont. His respect for soldiers and interest in war history began with his grandfather Sterling, a veteran of the First World War.

His goal was to reach the National Hockey League but, because he didn't score many, it would have to be as a sports writer. After attending Chesley District High School, he left home at the age of 17 to take (but not necessarily learn) journalism at Georgian College in Barrie, Ont.

Even before graduation, he had landed a job at the *Barrie Examiner*, becoming – at the time – Canada's youngest-ever sports editor of a daily newspaper. Which begs the question, What the hell happened to him?

In 1979, he joined the *Edmonton Sun*. Within three years, he had indeed reached the NHL – covering the Flames for the *Calgary Sun*. He even had the audacity to call it work.

A 30-year veteran of the newspaper wars, he was named sports editor of the *Edmonton Sun* in 1985. Thirteen years later, he left the position to write a column about anything … and sometimes nothing. His 'Real Life' was twice selected by readers as the newspaper's most popular column.

In 2005, he left Sun Media after 26 years to follow his heart with this project. His reasoning? "Soon there will be no one left to speak for the men and women who blew up toilets and drank way too much during the Second World War."

He and his wife Tamara live in Edmonton, Alberta. He has four children – daughter Glenys and sons Ryan, Sean and Jaden. He plays golf often but not worth a damn. His handicap is stupidity.

# Introduction

y grandfather was not a big man, but he was a giant in my eyes. Even slumped in his old rocking chair, the ravages of cancer taking a terrible toll, he stood tall.

He is my hero and the impetus for this book.

Sterling Haskins was a man of quiet dignity. He didn't say much at the best of times. Of the worst of times, he would say nothing at all.

When Canada was called to war in June of 1914, he was one of the first to answer that call. "Why, grandpa?" a young boy wondered. "Why did you go? Did you kill the Germans, grandpa?"

It wasn't until years later, long after he had died, that I finally got my answer from men who had fought other battles. These men had different names and different birth dates, but it was like they replied with one voice. "When your country needs you, you go. You do your part."

Sergeant Sterling Haskins fought in the First World War. The Great War, they called it. The only thing great was the end of it. They said it was the war to end all wars, but that wasn't true, either.

He fought at Passchendaele, in the trenches, in the mud and the blood, where John McCrae penned *In Flanders Fields*. Such a beautiful poem for such a terrible place and high price. You'd think mankind would be smart enough never to go there again.

My grandfather was one of the 172,950 Canadians who were wounded. A mortar shell landed in the bombed-out foundation four men shared. He came home with three pieces of shrapnel in his left shoulder. The other three, including his best friend, are listed among the 66,655 Canadians who gave their lives in the service of their country.

Between June 28, 1914 and Nov. 11, 1918, more than 65 million men from 30 countries bore arms. More than 10 million died. It is not just a number. It is a number with faces and names. And next of kin.

By the time it was over, this country had sent 619,636 men into battle. From Ypres to Vimy Ridge to Mons, Canadian heart became legendary. Our insignificant colony became a proud nation.

* * *

If you learn nothing from history, you are doomed to repeat it.

Just 21 years later, on the morning of Sept. 1, 1939, the German armies swept into Poland and the world stepped over the brink again. Two days later, Britain and France declared war. On Sept. 10, Canada followed suit. This has never been a nation to sit idly by.

We didn't have much more to offer than a pitchfork and a propeller when the Second World War began, but that would change. In September alone, 58,337 men and women enlisted.

By the end of the war, Canada boasted an army of six divisions. From France, Belgium, Holland and Germany, to Sicily, Italy and Hong Kong, the Canadian soldier was renowned for his bravery and professionalism. A country of only 11 million people enlisted more than one million men and women to fight in the name of freedom. Ours was a young nation, but we still knew the difference between right and wrong.

The Royal Canadian Navy began the war with a mere 13 ships and 3,000 men. Six years later, Canada boasted a fleet of 373 ships and more than 90,000 men. To say nothing of our merchant fleet.

If the transformation of the navy from laughingstock to world power was impressive, the achievements of the Royal Canadian Air Force were both astounding and remarkable. In 1939, it was stretching the truth to even suggest we had an air force. By 1945, Canada could lay claim to the fourth largest air force among all the Allied countries.

In all, 250,000 Canadians served in the air and on ground crews. In addition, thousands more served with Britain's Royal Air Force. From Lancaster and Halifax bombers to Hurricane and Spitfire fighters, and everything in between, Canadians served with distinction. In Bomber Command alone, more than 10,000 Canadians gave their lives.

It is not insignificant to point out that Canada was at war for 27 months before the Japanese forced the United States to act with the Dec. 7, 1941 attack on Pearl Harbour. And yet Hollywood would lead you to believe John Wayne won the war all by himself.

For a time, I did believe that. History didn't teach the Germans anything and history class didn't teach me very much. I was too busy doodling tanks and airplanes on the back of notebooks. I sketched American stars and German swastikas and hurried home to read *Sgt. Rock* comic books and watch *The Rat Patrol* on television.

It was all cozy and convenient for me, but the Second World War was six years of hell. Millions of people died in a conflict beyond imagination. In the Soviet Union alone, 13 million military personnel would perish, plus another 7.7

Sterling Haskins

million civilians. In China, 10 million civilians lost their lives. The totals are staggering, with more than 50 million military and civilian war dead before the merciless ending in 1945. Canada lost 45,000 men and women. Another 55,000 were wounded.

Necessity is the mother of invention, but the development of the atomic bomb must be regarded as the mother of all mistakes. It would be one thing if dropping Fat Man and Little Boy on Nagasaki and Hiroshima was the end-all, but Korea proved that would not be the case. We're a lot of things, but mostly we're slow learners.

Only five years later, Canada would send 27,000 men and women to battle communism in the war between North and South Korea. When the call comes, we answer.

Wars are caused by greed, corruption and lust, by religious differences and ridiculous obsession. They can be fought on land or in the sky, on the oceans and under them, but they all have one thing in common – human error. Or they wouldn't have started in the first place.

For a little boy, it was all very glamorous. A trip upstairs to grandpa's attic was always thrilling. "There's nothing up there," he would say, but he never convinced me. I didn't know what I was looking for, but I knew when I had found it.

I opened a ragged, old chest and found his uniform. It didn't fit, but I put it on anyway. I stood in front of an old mirror and saluted myself. Then I hit the mother lode. There was an old grenade that had been defused. There was a bayonet and two rifles he had somehow smuggled home. And there was the Luger, the sidearm only German officers carried.

I closed my eyes and saw the whole thing. Sgt. Haskins storming out of the trench, piercing the German General with his bayonet, shooting him with his rifle, then ripping the weapon out of his cold hand as the bullets whizzed by and mortar shells exploded around him.

Or something like that.

My hero was horrified when I came downstairs, diving behind a couch for protection, blasting imaginary enemies. My grandfather never said how he got it, but he did tell me to put it back where I found it.

In the parks and out behind Michael Bruin's house, we whittled guns out of tree branches and skulked behind boulders and bushes. "Bang, you're dead." Except for the odd skinned knee, there was no bloodshed. And, at the end of the day, everybody went home for dinner.

"How was your day, Scott?"

"Great, mom. I killed Pat. Blew him to smithereens."

After a good night's sleep in a warm bed, we were back at it. That was the beauty of my war. Nobody stayed dead for long.

In the little village of Lion's Head, on the shores of Ontario's magnificent Georgian Bay, the only invasion came in the summertime when the population exploded from 407 into the thousands. The cliffs on both sides offered protection from the storms of November, and their caves made a damn fine headquarters in July and August.

The peace talks began promptly at 3 p.m. and a settlement was usually reached by 3:04. Then we went swimming.

What did I know about the real thing? *The Battle Of Britain* was a movie, not a heroic stand.

Because of the sacrifices of our armed forces, then and now, little boys still play war in parks and on PlayStations. The worst casualty is still the odd skinned knee, but real men and women died in the name of democracy and freedom.

\* \* \*

This is about memories. The heroes from the First World War have no voice today. An 18-year-old boy in a trench in France in the last days of that war would be an old man of 106 today. My grandfather didn't speak of his war, and there is no one left to speak for him.

I wondered about my other grandfather, Bert Sutter. Why didn't he fight in WWI? Where was he when WWII broke out?

I got my white hair from him. He is the man who handed me a shotgun when I was 13 and told me to make sure I kept it tight against my right shoulder, then laughed when I didn't. He cleaned my rock bass and we played war – the card game.

Grandpa Sutter was 21 when the First World War began . He, too, answered the call immediately. While in England, however, before he could be sent into battle, he got sick and was sent home. During the Second World War, in his 40s, with a family at home, he didn't go to Europe, but he did guard German prisoners in northern Ontario.

I've always considered myself a war aficionado. It interests me certainly. What I lack in knowledge, I make up for with a healthy respect. And that's the thing old soldiers deserve most.

How can I possibly know how it feels to cross an ocean when there are hundreds of U-boats waiting? How can I understand the courage it must take to run on to Juno Beach? How can I fathom the fear that comes from fending off an enemy fighter in the tail of a Lancaster bomber?

"I'm not going to tell you about the horrors of war," Joe Dyck says. "You would never believe it. Unless you were there."

But he will tell you about bobbing for apples in a galvanized tub filled with wine after the Canadians had taken Ortona. And he will tell you about the German shell that landed right beside him and failed to explode.

Bert Sutter

"If blood's yellow, I've been shot," he said to himself.

The men and women of the Second World War have cried their tears of pain. They deserve a good laugh. "I always said there were more Canadians wounded or hurt badly coming back from pubs that there were in the war," Ed Hayes says. "And that's a fact."

Harry Trimbee was born in Toronto. Today, he lives in Enderby, B.C., with his wife Margaret. Every weekday morning, he makes the 20-minute trip into Salmon Arm to play pool at the Legion. "I'm a hooker," he says. "I'm lucky. I've had a lifetime of living."

Every morning, the first thing he does is count his blessings. "At my age, when you can wake up and put your arms around your wife, that's the most important thing," he says. He is 87.

"I wanted to go, but I was an old man. I was 26," he says. There is an emptiness that remains to this day for the old flight instructor. "I don't feel like I did my part," he says.

\* \* \*

I was driving home from a golf course when a most unusual thing happened. I had a good idea. It was August, 2001 and I was a columnist employed by *The Edmonton Sun*.

Twenty-four years earlier, I had told my parents I was headed to this strange, far-away place for one year, two at the most, to get some experience. That was two wives, four children and a million laughs ago.

I don't know why this idea popped into my head, but I must have been thinking about how good life was. I had lived my dream of covering a National Hockey League team, the Calgary Flames.

There's a book in that, too, but not yet. Most of the guys are still married. Doug Barclay, the old Detroit Red Wing, worked the Flames' radio broadcasts at the time. He liked his poker. He had lost an eye during his playing days, but not his sense of humour.

We were hard at it one night in his hotel room when he plucked his glass eye out and placed it on the table. "I have to go to the can, boys," he said. "Keep an eye on my cards."

I spent 13 years as a sports editor and another six writing a column about anything I wanted to write about. But there was nothing left that I wanted to write about. My favourite subjects had been older people who had lived a full life. They have insight, experience and intelligence.

For some reason, I thought of old soldiers. Books about the horror and heartbreak of war are everywhere, but there had never been a book written about the humour of war.

An old family expression came to mind – "Laugh … I thought I'd die." But too many did die during the Second World War. There is nothing funny about that, but it is the essence of *Laughing In The Face Of Danger*. There was fun to be had. There were lighthearted moments.

The more men and women I met, the more respect and admiration I had for them.

Canada was just emerging from the Great Depression, another period in our history that was anything but great, when the Second World War began. There were no wrinkles and no white hair back then, but there was undeniable courage. I salute these people for that and thank them for all they did for us. I admire their valor and thank them for their candor.

My oldest son is 20. In another time, he would be in another place. He would be Sal Polito. Or Harold Hague. Or Ross Tunbridge. Instead, thanks to these men and thousands more just like them, he dreams of becoming a golf pro. Nobody shoots back.

There was only one place to find these Canadian heroes – the Royal Canadian Legion. We're all so good at taking, but this was about giving back, too. A portion of the proceeds from this book will be returned to the Legion.

War is a testament to the human spirit as much as human frailty. It is not something to be made fun of, but there was fun to be had. It is with respect and admiration that I present the other side, the bright side.

Scott Haskins
Edmonton, Alberta

# Table Of Contents

**Fleaing The Scene**
Ross Tunbridge — 14

**A Rare Bird Indeed**
Patrick Sparrow — 20

**To Hell And Back**
Joe Dyck — 25

**'Get The Hell Outta Here'**
Alan Sunley — 30

**'I'd Like To Shake Your Hand'**
Frank Ball — 33

**One In A Million**
Bradley Anderson — 38

**'We Could Do It All'**
Hank Planger — 42

**Rum A Dumb-Dumb… Thump**
Harold Hague — 47

**'It Was In My Blood'**
Alex Sim — 51

**The Boy Becomes A Man**
George Evans — 58

**'I Didn't Want To Miss Anything'**
Al Trotter — 65

**'I'll Have That Rum Now'**
Norbert Todd — 72

**'Not A Day Goes By'**
Barb Uttley — 76

**'It Could Be Worse'**
Newman Pratt — 80

**Friends For Life**
Roy Armstrong — 84

**Taking A Swing At It**
Norm McIver — 89

**Look Before You Leap**
Gordon Bregoliss — 93

**Friends And Enemies**
Banff Boys — 98

**Where There's Smoke**
David Dickson — 106

**'A Bit Of Mischief'**
Tom Ford — 112

**'A Tin Can On Wheels'**
Fred Burton — 117

**Of Dogs And Craps**
Albert Threatful — 120

**'Six Square Meals A Day'**
Brewster & Wilson — 124

**Two For The Show**
Guthrie & Kochanski — 131

| | | | |
|---|---|---|---|
| **'Anybody Want A Roll?'**  <br>Murphy & McGlynn | 134 | **History In The Making**  <br>Ivan Lockhart | 190 |
| **Love And War**  <br>Ethyl Julseth | 139 | **Robbery Victim Would Be Proud**  <br>Elmer Phillips | 196 |
| **Tanks For The Memories**  <br>Sal Polito | 144 | **The Luck Of The Draw**  <br>Jim Miller | 200 |
| **'It Was Like… Hallelujah'**  <br>Ed Hayes | 148 | **The Making Of A Man**  <br>Donald Kohl | 204 |
| **'I Came Back With Two Prisoners'**  <br>Les Garnham | 151 | **It's A Mad, Mad World**  <br>Bert Madill | 209 |
| **To Sea The World**  <br>Harry Urwin | 156 | **Love At First Flight**  <br>Jim Brownell | 212 |
| **Whine But No Whining**  <br>Robert Weskett | 161 | **Just Call Him Lucky**  <br>Hugh Rayment | 218 |
| **Lady Chatterley's Lover**  <br>Fred Gilbert | 166 | **More Power To Him**  <br>Cliff Power | 223 |
| **The Devils, You Say**  <br>Rector & Peppard | 170 | **Madcap And Englishman**  <br>Jim Kelly | 226 |
| **Not Exactly Ship Shape**  <br>Jack Tiernay | 171 | **'Missed It By That Much'**  <br>Ken Linklater | 231 |
| **To Dieppe… And Back**  <br>Bill Orser | 182 | **The Champagne Breakfast**  <br>Willis Roberts | 234 |
| **In The Swim Of Things**  <br>David Bowman | 186 | **Acknowledgements** | 239 |

# Fleaing The Scene

'Fighting for my country was the right thing to do.'

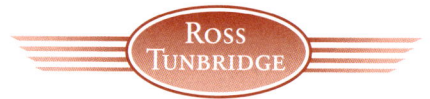

Ross Tunbridge

Even at the age of 83, Ross Tunbridge still refers to himself as "a jock." A good hockey player and a better baseball pitcher in his younger days, he is still at it. Not going strong, exactly, but still going.

He's not trying to recapture anything. He never lost it, steadfastly refusing to put away the pucks and balls of his youth.

It may be a claim to fame, but it is not what he is most proud of. "I guess I'm a patriot," he says. "I was happy to do my part. Fighting for my country was the right thing to do."

Growing up in Toronto, life revolved around sports. Not that it was the gravy train it is today. Rocket Richard was the best hockey player on the planet at the time. He made $7,500 a year.

At 15, Ross was already playing Junior hockey and was on the protected list of the Boston Bruins. The National Hockey League, he thought, was his calling. Until he heard the call of his country.

Two weeks before his 18th birthday, in March of 1941, Ross walked into the air force recruitment office with aspirations of becoming a fighter pilot. "I wanted to fly a Spitfire," he says.

Doctors, however, determined he had a wonky shoulder. "They wanted me to be member of the ground crew. To hell with that." So he wandered over to the army recruitment office. "I made the mistake of breathing when I went in there," he laughs.

He was sworn in immediately and sent to Petawawa for artillery-survey training, amazing even himself with his aptitude. By Christmas, he was on his way to England aboard the French ship *Andes*.

"Ours was the first troop ship that wasn't part of a convoy," he says. "It was fast and, because it was winter and the German submarines couldn't travel on the surface, we could easily keep ahead of them. We zig-zagged our way there."

But not before dealing with what he calls a "stuffy Lieutenant who wasn't nearly as important as he thought he was."

The ship had an open deck and when one of the soldiers put his pack down, the Lieutenant came over and said he couldn't put it there. The soldier dropped the pack somewhere else. The Lieutenant came over and said he couldn't put it there.

"So he walked over to the side of the ship and tossed it over. Then everyone else walked over to the side and threatened to do the same thing," Ross laughs. "A Major came over and said, 'What the hell is going on here?' It wasn't the lowly soldier who caught hell."

The next 18 months were spent in southern England. Artillery recalibration, elevation, surveying and co-ordinance became his specialty.

He remembers his baptism by fire this way.

"There were about 75 guys standing on one side of a brick building, lining up for food, when a Messerschmitt came over and opened up. Mess tins were flying everywhere as guys ran and dove for the other side of the building. He came around for another run and everybody scrambled back to the original side. The pilot didn't hit a soul. He ran out of bullets and went home."

Ross Tunbridge. A young man ready to take on the world.

Ross holds a picture of himself and a buddy in the living room of his house in Bobcaygeon, Ont.

Assigned to the Third Field Regiment, Baker Troop, First Division, 19th Battery, Ross Tunbridge arrived in Sicily on July 10, 1943.

"There were barrels of wine in every house, all the way up through Italy," he says. "But you didn't want to get drunk… and lost. With all those numbers, you'd never find your way back to the proper outfit."

He had many jobs, but the most important one was the procurement of wine. "I got good at it," he says. "Italian champagne was the elite, but wine didn't work quickly enough, so we set up our own distillery. Peach brandy or any other fruity stuff went into the still and what came out the other end worked… quickly."

But it also led to inevitable bad judgment. Like the time they were brought out for a rest along the Adriatic coast.

"We were billeted in an old Italian naval barracks. It had a beautiful beach and someone came up with the bright idea of placing empty jerry cans out in the water and having a contest with the Bren guns to see who could sink them first," he says.

It wasn't long before an officer pulled up in a jeep and put an end to the shenanigans. The bullets were skipping off the water and hitting a peninsula where another group was supposed to be enjoying some R and R.

It was during a creeping barrage that Ross thought he was a goner. They were supposed to advance 100 metres behind their own artillery fire, but one of the shells landed right beside him and his signaler. "I felt this stinging in my behind and I thought, 'Oh, God, I've been hit.' I put my hand back there and it was wet, but there was no pain. I thought it was just my adrenalin, but there was no pain when I got up," he laughs sheepishly. "I got hit all right – with a chunk of mud."

Strangely, it's the memory that cost him most of the hearing in his left ear that is the clearest. It was during the massive shelling barrage of Monte Casino. "Supposedly it was the largest ever. It lasted 24 hours, with 2,000 guns. It sounded like a dozen freight trains right over your head and it was so bright you could have read a newspaper," he says. "The sound was just amazing. It was unbelievable."

He was a treasure hunter. Once. "We were at a rest camp near Salerno when we heard from one of the locals that they used to hide in some nearby caves to avoid the bombs and artillery shells," he says. "Four of us decided to take a look. We thought the people might have left some things behind.

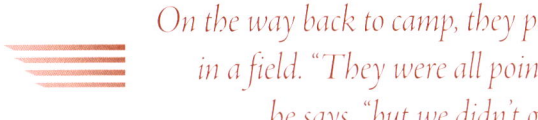

*On the way back to camp, they passed women working in a field. "They were all pointing and laughing," he says, "but we didn't give a damn."*

"Another bright idea," he laughs. "The caves were just huge – 75 metres high and 100 metres wide. They went on forever. There was straw on the ground, but we never found anything worthwhile."

Instead, something found them. Fleas. "They were all over us. We took off our pants and shirts, even our underwear, and threw it all away. All we had on were our boots and our belts."

On the way back to camp, they passed women working in a field. "They were all pointing and laughing," he says, "but we didn't give a damn. The guard noticed us as we got close to camp and pretty soon everybody was out there laughing at us. I didn't care. The only thing that mattered was getting into the shower."

The welcome in Rotterdam, Holland, is something that will stay in his mind and his heart until the day he dies. "We rode into town on these Bren gun carriers and the crowd was just unbelievable. They set up this huge dance floor in the middle of town," he says. "Three guys invited us for beers and they dug up three huge barrels they had buried to keep it away from the Germans. It was three days later, but we caught up to our boys. We found out later they were members of the Heineken family."

This was during the late stages of the war, when most of the fight had been taken out of the Germans.

"We were in this little town near Rotterdam when we got word there were 10 or 15 of them who wanted to surrender," Ross says. "A couple of us went to pick them up and there turned out to be about 500 of them. Pretty good haul."

It's hard to say how many times and how close he came to being killed. But it was at least once. Twice if you count the clump of mud on his backside.

"We were dug in on one side of a canal and the Germans were on the other side," he says. "Every once in a while, one side would take a pot shot at the other side just to tick them off. They were in towers, so the air force was called in. They fired these typhoon rockets that knocked the towers down, but it didn't get everybody.

 *"You did things you thought you couldn't do, because you had no choice."*

"This Limey bigwig showed up. We could see a German dug in and this guy said he had never fired a 50-calibre machine gun. 'Mind if I have a go at Jerry,' he said. He fired and missed. He fired and missed. He fired and missed again. There was a shot that hit the plaster right beside his head. 'What the hell is that?' he said."

Ross didn't miss a beat. "They do shoot back, you know."

It was usually the reinforcements getting killed. "If you lasted 30 days, you had a 50% chance of making it home," he says. "If you made it 60 days, you had an 80% chance of making it home. If the bullets sounded like bees, they missed you by three feet. If they sounded like somebody snapping their finger in your ear, they were within a foot and it was time to duck."

He was a boy when he left home and a man when he returned. War will do that to you. "You did things you thought you couldn't do. Because you had no choice."

He helped bury his friends. "Every soldier carries a blanket," he says. "It's like carrying your own casket. It is what you get buried in."

When Ross Tunbridge arrived back in Canada, his plan was to resume his budding hockey career, but a case of malaria overseas zapped him of much of his energy. He wasn't back on the blades in a big way until the winter of 1946. The Bruins offered him $2,300 a year. "A princely sum," he laughs.

In the meantime, he spent two months surveying on behalf of Ontario Hydro in Northern Ontario. He had plans to marry Doreen, too, and pro hockey wasn't the sure-fire, strike-it-rich game it is today.

"I could go to university free of charge on the government," he says. So he turned his back on fame and went to the University of Toronto. The rest is family history.

Doreen and Ross married and had three children – Craig, Doug and Jane. They have seven grandchildren and lived happily in Bobcaygeon, Ont. Doreen died in May.

Ross held down various jobs in various departments during a 37 year career with Ontario Hydro. "It all worked out for the best," he says.

Thank-you, all the people in the war have given us peace, freedom, speach and right Thanks to all of you now we can play sports, Go to school and even play on the computer. Now we have more phillvages then other countries which is really cool. This is a long way of seying THANK-you

—Alison

Patrick Sparrow: You don't have to be crazy, but it helps.
He is a man of many voices… and faces.

# A Rare Bird Indeed

'Rank? yeah a lot of times on our way back to the ship.'

PATRICK SPARROW

"Patrick Charles Sparrow at your service, sir." Serial number? He begins … "8232. No, wait. That's my phone number." The devilish look on his face is that of a young boy up to no good.

"Rank? Yeah, a lot of times on our way back to the ship."

This man spent three years in the navy, 10 years at a county jail, 25 years at the penitentiary in Drumheller, Alberta, and 16 years with the RCMP.

"Working," he points out. "It seems like I've been locked up my whole life."

It's amazing that nobody threw away the key.

This 79-year-old local icon with a million faces and half a dozen accents is a special individual. He never got married. "Could never afford to," he laughs. And yet he loves children. Don't blame them for their wicked ways. "Blame the parents who baby and spoil them. Too much television, not enough discipline."

Patrick Sparrow's voice booms even when he's whispering. When he walks into Royal Canadian Legion Branch 22, the stage is his. He would have made a good actor. He has always been a bit of a bad actor.

"My dad (Frank) was the infield announcer for 45 years at the Calgary Stampede. Now that was a voice. '*Coming out of chute 4 …*' " He suddenly stops and looks very sad. "He had a tough life," Patrick says. "He had me."

He cups his hands around his mouth and produces a perfectly-pitched siren wail. It was good enough one day to make the visiting firefighters at the Legion drop their beers and race for the truck outside. As they were scrambling out the door, Patrick nonchalantly walked in. Oh look, free beer.

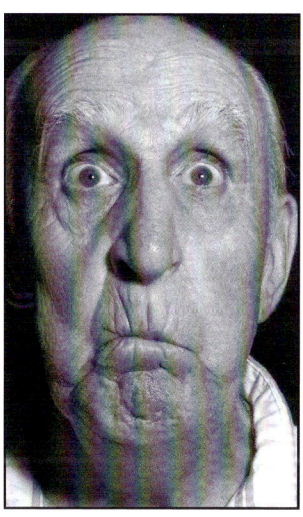

Let's face it, Patrick is no ordinary gentleman.

"Bad," he says proudly. Necessity is the mother of invention. The man was thirsty. And a thirsty man will do … well, obviously just about anything. This has been proven many times.

Bear in mind that Patrick was only 16 when he went against his father's wishes and joined up. It wasn't the age thing that bothered his dad. Frank had been in the Royal Canadian Air Force in the First World War and two of Patrick's sisters had followed him there. "I had to be different," he says. "I was a swimming instructor, so I joined the navy."

It was easier than it should have been.

A lawyer in town who was a Colonel in the First World War, Leo Casswell, told him that if Patrick cleaned his office, he would "type something up" for the recruitment officer in Calgary. It was eight pages long and not worth the effort to read, so they just gave it the stamp of approval. It was 1942.

Young and stupid is a dangerous combination in wartime. In one sense, his mouth has always gotten him into trouble. In another, it's what makes him unique. You have to try very hard not to like Patrick Sparrow.

"Little things were always happening to me," he says of the 909 days he spent serving his country. "I was always volunteering for things. I didn't know any better. I thought it was macho." He shakes his head. "Nuttier than a fruitcake."

As a youngster stationed in England, it was his job during one leave to find the lads four bottles of scotch and sneak them back on board the ship. He met the "salesman" on a dark corner, had a sip to authenticate the quality and proudly returned a hero… with what turned out to be four bottles of tea.

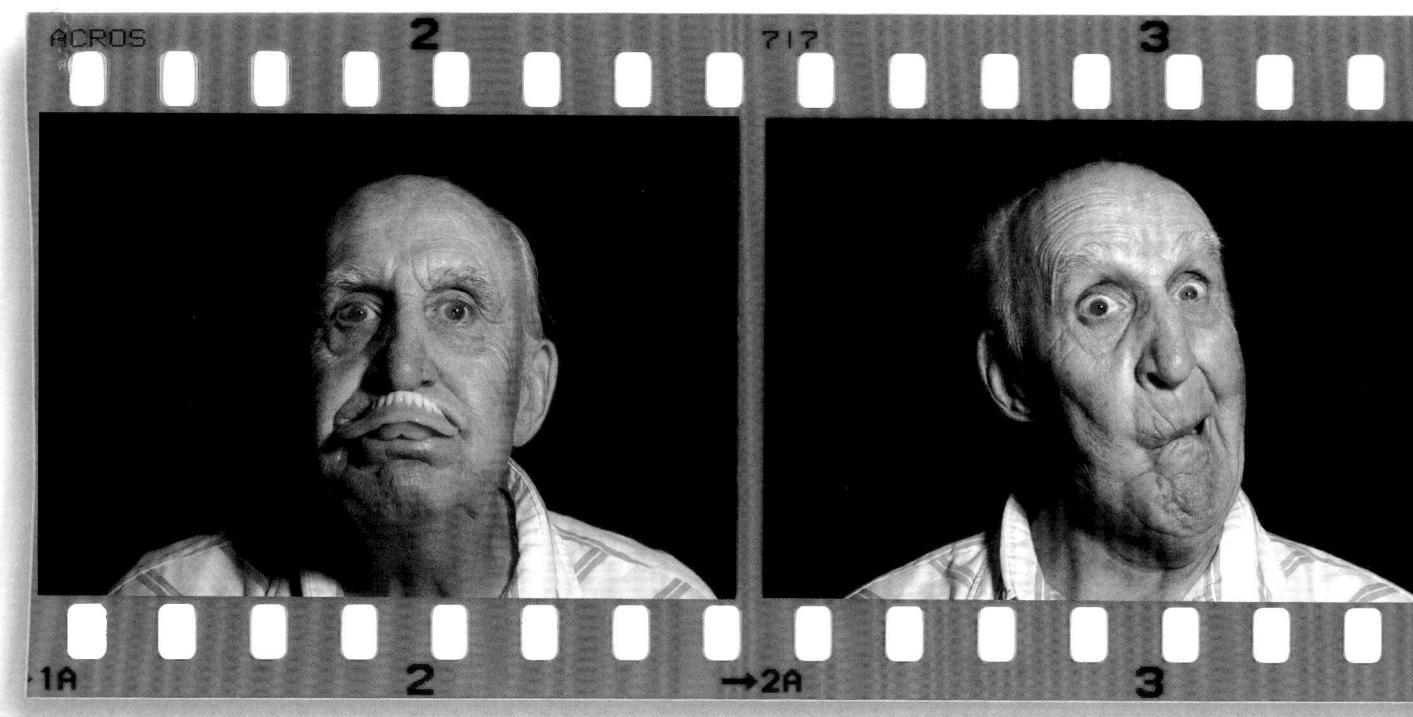

"That was the closest I came to dying," he says.

This is a man who battled and beat cancer in 1974. On Nov. 1, he weighed 210 pounds. On Nov. 30, after 30 radiation treatments, he weighed 160 pounds.

This is a man who volunteered – "Like I said, young and stupid." – to be first off the landing craft on June 6, 1944, D-Day, to swim to shore and hold a rope the others could use to pull themselves in. He was literally swimming in a minefield, where one wrong stroke would have meant certain death.

"It wasn't until the tide went out and I saw all the mines that I got scared," he says. "My whole life has been lucky." Especially the part about never getting married. There's no telling how much a character like this might have paid in alimony by now.

But it is said that luck is a residue of hard work. Patrick has never shied away from getting his hands dirty. He has never been afraid to go the extra mile in order to make a difference, whether it's to help a fellow soldier or make a child smile.

If there's one thing he's not short of it's ingenuity.

"Late again," he says, beginning the story.

While on leave, he missed the last boat back to his ship. No problem. He swam back. Which did turn out to be a problem. He was wet behind the ears – and everywhere else – when he was discovered by an officer. "Twenty days without pay and 20 days without leave." In the navy, you don't sit around playing solitaire. He was put in charge of the paint locker, which wouldn't have been so bad if that didn't include painting the deck.

It gets worse. And funnier. He discovered the officers' stash of rum.

Patrick returned to the ship with four bottles of tea. 'That was as close as I came to dying'

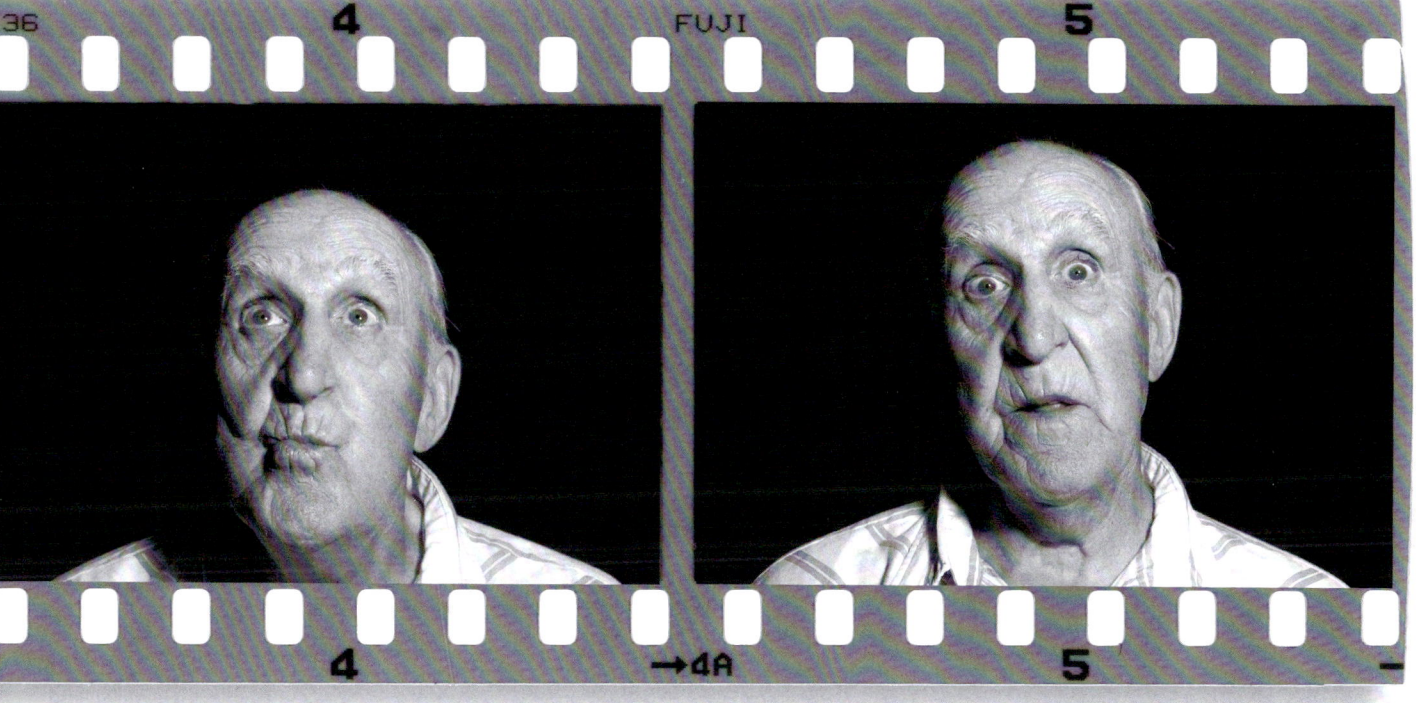

A young Patrick. He was not as innocent as he looks.

"Nelson's blood," he calls it. So close, but yet so far. It was locked up, but he could reach the bottles with a syringe. He painstakingly went about his work, removing the rum from the bottles and replacing it with tea.

It was all in good fun until the toast was made. It was a watery grave. Another 60 days without leave and pay."

Patrick isn't sure if he finds trouble or trouble finds him. Either way, they are best friends and enemies. Like the night while drinking with 400 of what he calls "dockyard meanies." There were 12 sailors, and one of them was in worse shape than the others. This man had a poor sense of humour. He thought it would be funny to kick the crutches out from under the guy who ran the place, a man with two wooden legs. You have to understand their adversaries had hooks they used for carrying boxes and crates.

Patrick has the scar on his arm to prove the first cut is the deepest. It went right to the bone. "All hell broke loose. We had to fight them all the way back to the ship. Booze makes smart people do stupid things. It was the most harrowing experience of my life," he says. "The first thing I did when I got back on board was change my shorts."

As a young teen, he dressed up as a Keystone Cop and roamed the streets of Drumheller selling war bonds.

On many occasions, for more parades and special events than he can count, or remember, he has been an Indian chief. Every December, he becomes Santa Claus.

"There's nothing like putting a smile on a youngster's face," he says.

Which is why he has a motorized dog at his home. With something called a moosesparrowtaurasaurs in his yard. And a pterodactyl, complete with moving wings. There's a sound box in the mouth he can start from inside when a child walks by. Drumheller does, after all, bill itself as the dinosaur capital of Canada.

"I love the look on their little faces when it starts to talk," he says.

He looks up, suddenly deadly serious. "Do you know the cause of depression? Some men borrow from Peter to pay Paul. That makes Peter sore." There is a pause. "And you can't do business with a sore Peter."

# To Hell And Back

The enemy could not break this man's spirit

JOE DYCK

At the age of 83, they don't come much more full of life than Joe Dyck. Or full of something else, for that matter. It is a compliment.

"That's Dyck (as in dike)," he stresses, clarifying the pronunciation for a good reason. "I have a cousin named Harry."

Joe and Gladys have been married 55 years and were preparing for a move from Edmonton to Chilliwack, B.C. What has life been like living with this old soldier, this remarkably funny and candid character.

"Entertaining," she says with a smile. Gladys smiles often and easily. It is her only defence. There is much love in this home.

Joe Dyck was only 17 when he lied about his age and signed up with the infantry to fight for his country. The family had moved from Swift Current, Sask., to Nelson, B.C., where his father was a grave digger. It was one of few steady jobs during the Depression years.

School wasn't an option. "I quit in the fourth grade," he laughs. "It was embarrassing. My father was only a grade ahead of me."

Work wasn't an option. There was no work.

He comes from a family of eight. Miraculously, in the summer of 2005, all eight are still alive. "My mother was hard of hearing," he says, explaining all the children. "My father would say, 'Do you want to go to sleep or what?' And my mother would answer, 'What?'"

In June of 1940, the only thing for a healthy, young man to do was go to war. "The doctor who examined me knew how old I was," Joe says. "He knew I was doing the right thing. He didn't say a word."

His war was fought in Italy, with the Seaforth Highlanders, the 2$^{nd}$ Brigade, 1$^{st}$ Division of the Princess Patricia's Canadian Light Infantry. It was one of the most bitter battles waged during the Second World War. When it finally ended after a hellish 20 months, total Canadian casualties in Sicily and Italy numbered 25,264. Fifty-nine hundred Canadians lost their lives.

The eyes are old, but not tired. The things they have seen. While there is grudging respect for the German soldier – "The best in the world," he says. – the day of total forgiveness has not yet arrived. Decades have dulled the anger and hatred, but there is still resentment that the world had to be taken to the brink of destruction.

"We had a guy in camp with a great German accent. He'd crack us up. 'You will stand and you will listen. Otherwise, you will go in the oven and come out popcorn.' He'd say." He does not make light of the barbarism of the enemy, but there were times when laughter literally kept him alive.

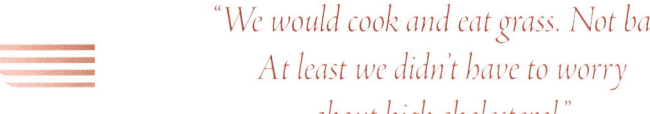

*"We would cook and eat grass. Not bad. At least we didn't have to worry about high cholesterol."*

When Joe Dyck says camp, he doesn't mean a cozy barracks in England or even a hole dug into the ground far away from the front. He means a German prisoner-of-war camp, one of the most hellish places on earth.

"One small potato, a slice of black bread and little chunk of blood sausage," he says. That was fine dining at Mooseburg. "People were so hungry they would draw pictures on the wall of a roast turkey or a steak. We would cook and eat grass. Not bad," he says. "At least we didn't have to worry about high cholesterol."

Joe battled the fear, the mental and physical torture, and the hunger pains with humour. In a place where the outlook was bleak, he still managed to look on the bright side. This, despite the fact his weight plummeted from 170 pounds to 90 pounds in 11 months. Others had it worse.

He will have no hero talk. "My heroes are under the ground over there," he says. Asked about his medals, he shrugs. "I ate the most Spam."

When Joe Dyck hit the beach in May of 1943, there was really no fear. Even when the front of the landing craft came down. "The best thing was not to think about what might happen," he says.

The front line was ever-changing in one sense as the Canadians surged forward, north to Ortona. But the shelling never changed. It came all day, almost every day. "It was like wiping your ass with a hoop. There was no end to it. The Germans would counter-attack with tanks … we had rifles. We were like brothers." Only closer. "We lost a lot of heroes on the Hitler Line."

On one occasion, 325 Canadians attacked and 158 came back "It was like walking into a wall of steel. The bullets whizzing by sounded like bees." Combat turns a boy into a man in a hurry. "It's amazing how fast you can run when the bullets are nipping at your heels."

He remembers the night he was sent back to the rear with a message. "I was walking along a trail when a German shell landed right beside me." Even then, or at least even now, he manages to see the humour. "I remember looking down," he laughs. "I remember thinking, 'If blood is yellow, I've been shot.' A rabbit couldn't have caught me after that." The happy life he has lived since, you could say, has been a dud.

"I remember the day after we took Ortona. We had this big galvanized tub full of wine and apples and we were bobbing for apples. Some of the guys had their head right at the bottom."

Late in 1944, Joe Dyck was captured. It seemed like the first step would last forever. He and thousands of his comrades were marched 1,000 miles to a prison camp just outside of Munich. "When I got there, I had no bottoms

Joe Dyck and his better half, Gladys. Life has been a lot of things but never dull.

on my shoes. Two guys tried to escape into an open field. They never got 100 yards." He pauses, knowing it sounds crass. "Stupid!"

He is in the middle of a serious conversation when he interrupts himself. "Did you hear about the Japanese kamikaze pilot on his third mission?" Joe just shakes his head when he sees a veteran licence plate on the back of a Japanese-made vehicle.

There were 30,000 people in the prison camp, all ranks and nationalities. Suddenly his eyes well up.

"Young people today, they should never forget," he says. "It can never happen again. Thousands of people under the age of 20 – nurses, medics, soldiers, sailors … If you forget, these people will have died in vain. I speak at schools, but I don't tell them about the horrors of war. They wouldn't believe me."

There was no sitting around. Joe was regularly sent to help a local farmer. Although still under armed guard, "one day, the old man managed to sneak me downstairs. He was supposed to give everything to the army, but he had a stash. We locked the door. There were barrels of beer and endless sausage. It was good." The Allies kept blowing up the train tracks and the Allied prisoners kept rebuilding the train tracks. Joe Dyck shrugs his shoulders. "We made a lot of mistakes."

By May of 1945, even the Germans knew the last days of the war were at hand. The Red Cross was delivering packages to the prisoners of war, and the Germans had even allowed some of them to reach their intended destination. "Guys would literally eat the box.

"One day, I came around a corner on the way back to camp from the pick-up zone and ran right into the American 4th Army. The next day, I was in England. If I had stumbled upon the Brits, I'd still be there, filling out papers."

Joe Dyck remembers the endless shelling and the bombing of nearby Munich almost every night. "We were miles away and the ground still shook." He remembers men lying in their bunks, shaking. Even the sound of friendly fire was terrifying. "A lot of guys came back half spiny."

Joe Dyck interrupts himself again.

"Did you hear about the Lufthansa pilot who crashed into the ocean? He was very calm. He ordered everyone who could swim on to the right wing and everyone who couldn't swim on to the left wing. To the people on the right wing, he said, 'Now swim for shore.' To the people on the left wing, he said, 'Thank you for flying Lufthansa.'"

He has a million of 'em. If the enemy was intent on breaking this man's spirit, they failed miserably.

On Remembrance Day, 2005, I had the privilege and honour of

accompanying him to Edmonton's University of Alberta Butterdome for the city's main ceremony. He can't help but notice the bus from a local funeral home parked outside. "Wishful thinking," he says. "If they're looking for business, this is probably a good place to be."

On our way inside, a mother and young daughter stop to hand him a hand-made thank you card. "Dear veteran," it reads. "Thank you for keeping our country peaceful. Also, thank you for making our country free."

He reaches down and gives her a warm hug. "Isn't that beautiful," he says. The tears well up in his eyes. It is the first of many times this day. It is the Year Of The Veteran. Shouldn't every year be the Year Of The Veteran?

A painful hip keeps him from marching, but a crisp salute greets each parade group as it passes his position. His thoughts and memories of fallen friends are his own.

His legs balk, but his heart beats strong. It is the heart of a country. After the ceremony, it means so much when another youngster, this one a boy, hands him another card. "Thank you, soldiers, for risking your family time to go to the war. And we feel sorry if you lost some of your family."

Joe Dyck doesn't say a word. He offers the boy only a crisp salute.

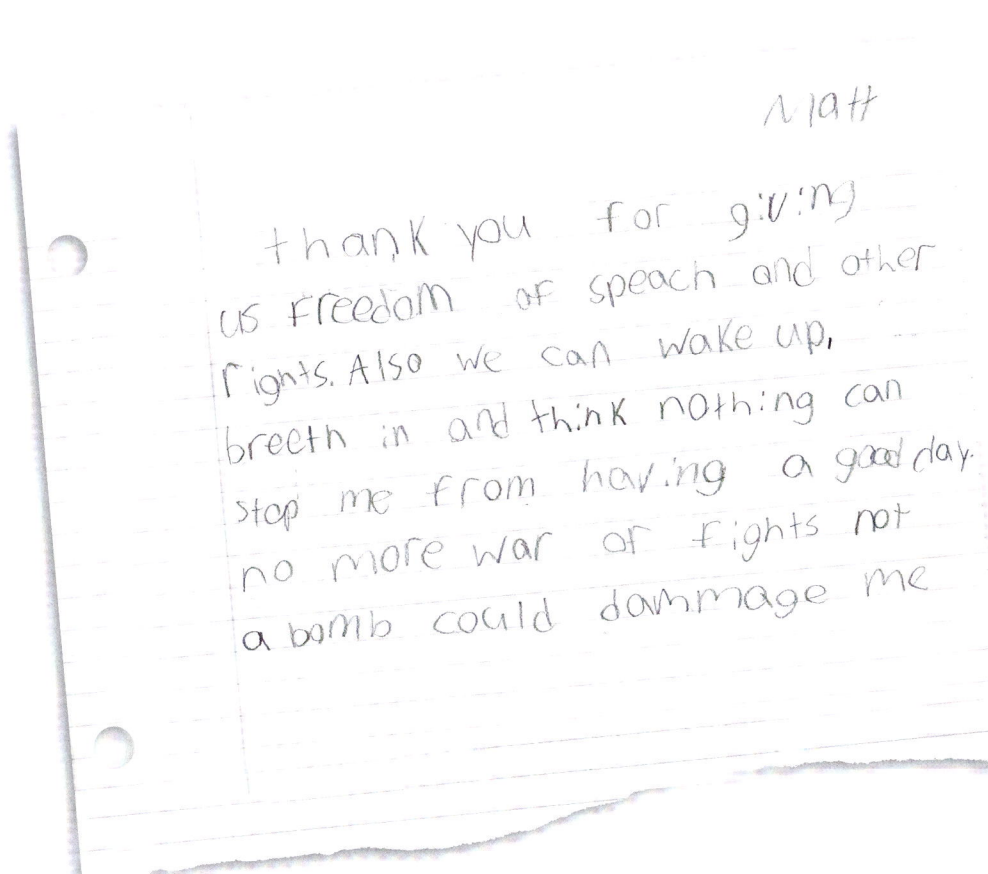

# 'Get The Hell Outta Here'

### Sometimes it's better to be lucky than smart

Alan Sunley

Alan Sunley is not at all happy to see the video camera show up at his front door. "What the hell is that?" he says. "You're not taking my picture with that thing."

And he isn't thrilled with the line of questioning. A humorous side of the Second World War? His look could cut through steel.

"There is nothing funny about war," he says. "War is a serious thing. The humour is usually at someone else's expense. It's very sadistic."

Practical jokes can be like war itself. "Beware of escalation," he says. "Someone always has to get even."

But the 84-year-old native of tiny Stenen, Sask., is quick to help attach the microphone to his shirt. All bark, no bite. A keen sense of humour is intact, but it is hidden under mounds of scars. There are stories to be told by Canada's war heroes, whether they manned the guns or filled the gas tanks. Some were more hazardous than others, of course, but every job was important.

Serial number? He laughs, so he is starting to get the idea. "R85139," he says. "You think I'd forget that?"

One by one, every veteran rhymes off their serial number like it is etched on the brain. In a sense, it is a part of their essence. No one who fights for their country is unchanged by the experience.

A proud Canadian? "You're damn right," Al says. "I have a great sense of pride. We did what had to be done." Which is why he often speaks to school kids. "They ask me if I was ever scared. How do you tell them the grim reality?" He would like more of them to join the armed forces. "For a good education. You learn a lot about yourself."

As a youngster, there was no question what he wanted to do. At 16, he joined the militia. In 1940, at 18, he joined the air force. "I wanted to be a pilot, but I was colour blind," he says. He ended up in England with Coastal Command, 407 squadron, as part of the ground crew.

Al Sunley is a serious fellow, but he couldn't help but laugh the night some joker dropped a flare down the chimney into a barracks stove. It wasn't a bright idea, but it sure brightened up the building.

"It was like Christmas came early," he chuckles. "Looking back, though, the whole place could have caught on fire. We never did find out who was responsible. There would have been hell to pay."

You could usually count on the new guys for a laugh. Or two, if they lasted that long.

During one German attack, a new replacement was enthralled by the flares. Or what he thought were flares. He stood in the open, admiring the show, until Al grabbed him. "That's jerry shooting at us," he said. "Get the hell outta here."

Another time, during an attack, the same guy dove for cover … under a fuel truck. Miraculously, proving once again that good luck can be every bit as important as good sense, Al believes he made it through the war in one piece. "Not that he deserved to," he says.

The only thing predictable about war is its unpredictability. Every second could be your last.

A young Alan Sunley. Does this boy look like he's ready to do a man's work?

Which bullet or bomb has your name on it? "You get used to it," Al says. "When is it your turn to say bye-bye?"

The best part of the experience, of course, was leave. But even that could be dangerous. "I crashed my bike into a brier patch," he says. "I was all scratched up. That was my worst injury." He enjoyed the shows in London, the dances, the fun, the pub crawling. "For some guys, it was mostly crawling."

Al never lost his love of the sky. In the summer of 2005, he still owned half a share in a glider. "There's nothing like the whistle of the wind," he says. He worked for General Electric as an engineer for 40 years following the war, raising three sons. This year marks Al and Florence's 60th wedding anniversary.

With all the travelling he did, life was often hard. But it was always good. He has been a curler and a golfer, a gardener and an amateur astronomer. Most importantly, he was someone who answered when his country called.

— 🍁 —

Alan: "I have a great sense of pride. We did what had to be done."

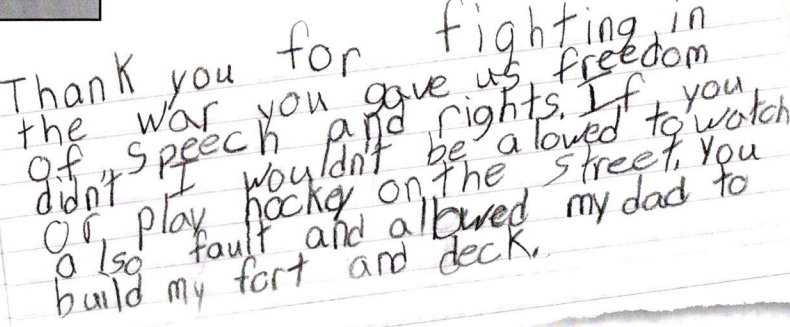

Thank you for fighting in the war you gave us freedom of speech and rights. If you didn't I wouldn't be aloved to watch or play hocky on the street. You also fault and alowed my dad to build my fort and deck.

# 'I'd Like To Shake Your Hand'

'The kids are so wonderful.
In a way, we were fighting for them.'

FRANK BALL

"It's not the size of the man. It's the size of the fight in the man."

Frank Ball could be Exhibit A when it comes to that old saying. If they measured his heart, they'd find something almost as large as his contribution during the Second World War.

At 87, the years having ganged up on him, he still stands proudly as a testament to the courage and commitment it took to defeat a terrible enemy.

He is both a proud Englishman and a proud Canadian. One of his greatest joys these days is speaking to school children in and around the southern Ontario towns of Chesley and Tara.

"I had this little boy come up to me," he says. "He didn't have a question about the war. He just said, 'I'd like to shake your hand.' " A tear forms in the corner of his eye. "It was really beautiful," he says. "The kids are so interested, so wonderful. I guess, in a way, we were fighting for them."

Without men like Frank Ball, there's no telling what their future might hold.

Born in Bristol, England, on May 29, 1918, he was 21, already in what was known as the Territorial Army and working as a customs clerk in a meat importer's office, when all hell broke loose in 1939.

On Sept. 1, when the "weekend soldiers" were mobilized, he could have claimed an exemption because the company was taken over by the Ministry of Food, but he never even considered it. On Sept. 2, he was on guard duty at the barracks door when war was declared. "Suddenly it wasn't all fun and games," he says.

Frank, because of his size – or lack thereof – was assigned to the 44th Battalion, Royal Tank Regiment. "I didn't even have to duck when I went inside," he laughs.

He got used to the air raids. So much so, that he didn't even bother looking for cover. His introduction to Canadians came one night when a bomb blew out the windows of the pub he was visiting. Nobody received as much as a scratch, but it was still a horrible thing. "A Canadian got to his feet and cried in disgust, 'The dirty so-and-so upset my beer.' "

 *"The Germans threw everything at us. I swear I saw a kitchen sink go by."*

During another raid, a lady had been enjoying a bath when a bomb hit and the side of the house fell off. The bathtub was hanging by the plumbing. "Complete with occupant," he says. "I saw a double-decker bus sitting upright on top of a three-story building."

Frank Ball's war was fought in North Africa, against legendary German tank commander Erwin Rommel. He arrived in Alexandria on his birthday – May 29, 1941.

There were tough times, but there were also times when it was impossible not to laugh.

"We were fighting with the 4$^{th}$ Indian Division against Italian troops with German officers," Frank says. "Our guys were scary to look at." They must have been. "The Italians threw down their rifles and ran away, with the Indians chasing them, slapping them on the ass with their bayonets. We took 200 prisoners that day. The Italian officers were very helpful. They guarded their own men for us."

Frank's regiment was only supposed to be in Africa one year, but things change during war. Especially plans. He was still there on his next birthday. And, come hell or high water, he was going to celebrate.

"I had a can of pears I had been saving. We were being shelled at the time, but that didn't matter. My CO (commanding officer) was with me and he was going to share my pears and tea. I dug a hole in the sand and poured gasoline in to make a fire for the tea. Just then, a shell came in and blew everything all to hell."

Not that a little bad luck was going to stop them.

They were boiling up more water for the tea when another shell came in. "The same thing happened. Blew it all to hell."

Frank found more water on an abandoned German truck. They made their tea and sat it on top of the truck. Another shell came in and blew the mugs off the top of the truck. "But we ate the pears," he says proudly. As birthday parties go in the middle of a war, it could have been a lot worse.

There was the funny and the sad. And sometimes it was impossible to tell them apart.

"We were in our tank during one battle when we must have been blown 50 feet in the air. I don't know how we survived," Frank says. "We didn't know what or who we were or where we were. I didn't know it at the time, but sometime during the night, the guy who had been in the tank with me wandered off in the direction of the German front line." They turned him around and sent him back. "That's how out of it he was. They didn't even want him as a prisoner."

Desert warfare was hell. There were times when the two sides were so close to each other he could see the Germans loading artillery shells. "We were in the desert for a year. You could take a fix on a series of sand dunes, then the wind would come up and it would be completely changed. We never knew where we were."

Rumours of Frank Ball's demise were greatly exaggerated at least once ...

"We were out on patrol and came across some of our infantry trapped in a minefield. The officer said he had spotted German tanks through the gap. He radioed in for tanks, but was told none were available for at least two or three days," Frank says. "We were commandeered and I was ordered to man the machine gun inside the tank. I wasn't allowed to sleep or even go to the bathroom. When I fell asleep, somebody would shake me. On the second day, they started giving me shots of rum. If it was supposed to keep me awake, it didn't work. I

Small but mighty. After the war, Frank Ball came to Canada "determined to make a go of it."

A man with a ready smile, Frank Ball is always willing to talk to school children.

passed out. Thankfully, when I came to, the other tanks had arrived and we set out to find our own unit."

Lost, in the middle of an ever-changing desert, surrounded by enemies. "Scared the hell out of me," he readily admits. "It was three weeks before we found our way back. We had already been listed as missing and presumed dead."

Sometimes fate smiles on you. Sometimes it kicks you in the groin.

A unit doesn't spend more than a year in the desert. For Frank Ball, the magic date was supposed to be May 30, 1942, one day after his feast of pears on his birthday. Instead, June 1, 1942 turned out to be the tragic date.

Their last job before heading back to Cairo was to help free an infantry unit that had been surrounded. It was a battle that lasted four days. "The Germans threw everything at us," he says. "I swear I saw a kitchen sink go by."

At 8 a.m. on June 1, the message was delivered that it was every man for himself. His tank disabled, Frank joined others on the trek through a minefield. "We came over a rise and found a line of German troops with their guns at the ready," he says. "I was a prisoner of war."

The Germans, he says, "were firm and at times tough, but they were also decent." The Italians, on the other hand were crude and vicious. He remembers an Italian Sergeant taking all the wedding rings off the prisoners' fingers. "When someone told an English-speaking German officer what had happened, he made the Italian empty his pockets, then he shot him."

Moved from camp to camp in Italy and eventually into Germany, there were good and bad times. "I didn't lose much weight because I didn't have much to lose," Frank says. "One time, a German guard let an attack dog loose in the compound next to ours where they kept the Russians. They all ran into their hut and the dog followed. The next morning, the dog's fur and bones were piled neatly by the gate." That's good eatin.'

His final stop was a camp near Hanover. "We watched our bombers come over in waves," he says. "A British fighter came over and dipped his wings. We waved back."

It was well into 1945 by this point. One morning, during a march to who knows where, they awoke to find themselves on their own. The German officers and guards had run away during the night.

"We heard the sound of tanks coming. They were American," he says. Frank Ball, a prisoner for two years, 10 months and eight days, was a free man.

Upon returning to England, he learned that his mother had died while he was in captivity. "It all seems so senseless now," he says. "I remember it, but it can't be true."

Frank returned home to Bristol, but didn't like the direction his life was taking. In 1947, he came to Canada to start a new life. "I had relatives here. I was determined to make a go of it."

He fell in love almost immediately. With the country and with a young woman named Ivadelle. They met in a car owned by a mutual friend, on his first holiday – a trip from Toronto to Huntsville. They met in August, got engaged in October and were married in February.

"Best thing that ever happened to me," he says.

She is gone now, but there is plenty to remember her by. They had four children. He has 12 grandchildren and two great grandchildren. He worked for Ford in Oakville for 25 years. His home, like the man himself, is warm and comfortable.

He lives in Chesley, but is a proud member of Royal Canadian Legion Branch 383 in Tara.

"This country has been very good to me," he says. "I volunteer for this and that and I love talking to the kids. I lost a lot of friends, but I have made a lot of new ones."

# One In A Million

He grew, up but that doesn't necessarily mean he matured

BRADLEY ANDERSON

It has been said that it takes all kinds. If that's true, it only stands to reason that every once in a while you're going to run into someone who can only be considered one of a kind.

That would be Bradley Anderson.

While the man's level of sanity may be open to debate, there is no disputing his character. He is one.

You can't judge a man by the clothes he wears, but his licence plates can give you a pretty good idea. On the back of his rusty old '87 Bronco is a veteran's plate. On the front is a plate that reads, "Horn not working. Watch for finger." He laughs about the first time he tried Viagra. "I didn't sleep all night," he says. "I didn't have enough skin left to shut my eyes."

Bradley grew up in the tiny Saskatchewan farming community of Rockglen. Which was near Little Woody. Which was near as you can get to nowhere. "If you were driving through town and your brakes failed, you ended up in Montana," says the 81-year-old resident of Pincher Creek, Alberta.

He grew up, but that doesn't necessarily mean he matured. He's putting that off as long as possible.

"I had nothing as a kid and I have even less now," he says, pointing out that a divorce will do that to you. "I never had a million dollars." But he has had a million laughs.

He recalls a recent drive to Edmonton. "Everything was fine until I got to Red Deer," he says. "Then I saw a sign – *Edmonton Left*. So I turned around and came home."

It was during this same trip that he saw another sign – *Clean Bathrooms Ahead*. He shakes his head sadly. "It took me two days," he says. "They were a real mess."

By the fall of 1941, with his country at war, he couldn't sit on the sidelines any longer. While you had to be 18 to join the army or the air force, Canada's budding navy would gladly take you at 17, as long as he had a parent's consent.

"The crazy Swede," he says of his dad Henry, "was away at work." And his mom, Augusta, "would sign anything because she didn't know how to read."

So it was that he found himself at a naval training centre in Regina. Straight off the farm. And straight off the boat, so to speak. "I was in the navy and I had never been on a ship. Hell, I was from Saskatchewan. I had never been more than 30 miles from home. I didn't have a clue."

The first thing he learned was that you salute your superiors. And, since he figured that included just about everybody, he wasn't taking any chances. "I spent the first two weeks saluting the milkman," he says.

Bradley started out as an ordinary seaman. He proudly announces that he ended his military career as an able seaman and anti-aircraft gunner. It may not be original, but that doesn't make it any less apt. "The older I get," he says, "the more rank I get."

His first assignment was aboard a minesweeper, out of Halifax. Up until then, his only oceanic experience was a ferry ride while stationed in B.C. There were worse places to fight the war than Bermuda, even if their prey was German U-boats. "They were basically giving away rum," he says. "You could get a quart for $1."

Bradley Anderson: The boy would become a man in the navy, but he retained his childishness.

Bradley: Older and wiser, but not exactly well behaved.

Getting it and keeping it down were two different things, however. "I fed a lot of fish the first few weeks," he says. To make matters worse, he was a young boy far from home. "I was homesick," he admits.

He returned to Halifax and boarded *HMCS Guelph*, completing the treacherous North Atlantic trip to England 10 times in order to protect convoys. It's not what happened, it's what could have happened. Every second brought the possibility of a U-boat attack.

It was during the worst times that Bradley was at his best. He took it as a personal challenge. This guy, more than most, knows the value of a good chuckle. "It's the best medicine so I can usually come up with something," he says. "I can get anybody to laugh."

Leaves were usually a drunken, gambling fiasco. "It says right in the Bible that you're supposed to raise cane as long as you're able." The height of ridiculous was going to see a movie. Or trying to see a movie.

"Sunday nights in Halifax were movie nights," he says. Trouble is, the men were issued condoms and they blew them up and bounced them around the theatre. "You couldn't even see the screen, there were so many of them. Most of the guys were so young, I guess they didn't know what they're supposed to be used for."

The closest he can to dying, he believes, was at the dinner table. "We had a cook who couldn't cook," he says. "He was so bad that we'd steal canned goods."

As we visit at Royal Canadian Legion branch No. 43, where he is a past president, former infantryman Woody Riley makes the mistake of sitting down and relating a story about MV stew. "The MV stood for meat and vegetables, but we always thought it meant mostly vomit," Woody says.

Now 80, he, too, is sharp as a tack. But you don't get into a battle of wits with Bradley Anderson around.

"We ate all sorts of things," Woody says. "In Italy, I remember eating donkey."

Bradley can't help himself. "Did you get a good piece of ass?"

Since he worked for Shell Oil for 31 years after the war – as a part time shift supervisor and a full time party organizer – it seems like an obvious question to ask if he gets free gas. Anderson goes into hysterics.

"Only when I eat beans," he says.

There was a lot of fun to be had, but there was also serious work to be done. "Fighting for your country is something to be proud of," he says.

So, when the war in Europe ended, he was fully prepared to head off and fight the Japanese, too.

"Never got the chance," he says, "but I'd do it all over again."

It's that responsibility that he talks to area school kids about. He is a life member of the Legion and he has delivered more eulogies than he cares to remember. "Whatever I can do to help," he says.

He readily admits his drinking cost him his marriage. But not before he produced six children. He now has 13 grandchildren and one great grandchild. He has a new lady friend, Barbara. What he never has these days is a drink.

Here's to you, Bradley.

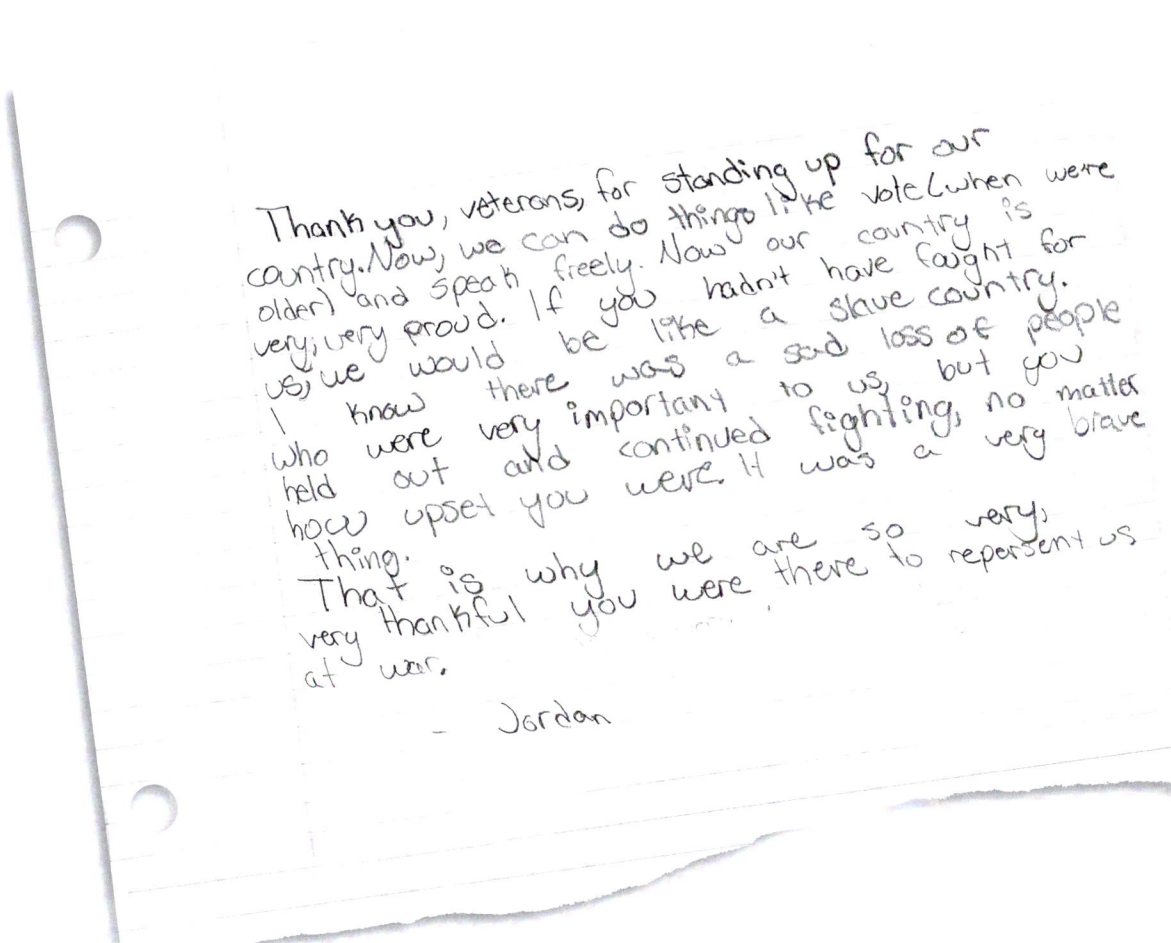

Thank you, veterans, for standing up for our country. Now, we can do things like vote (when we're older) and speak freely. Now our country is very, very proud. If you hadn't have fought for us, we would be like a slave country. I know there was a sad loss of people who were very important to us, but you held out and continued fighting, no matter how upset you were. It was a very brave thing. That is why we are so very, very thankful you were there to represent us at war.

— Jordan

# 'We Could Do It All'

## The men of First Special Service Force were special indeed

HANK PLANGER

**W**hy is it that men who are true heroes don't consider themselves the least bit heroic? Funny how that works. And so sad that it often works the other way around.

Hank Planger scoffs at the notion that he did anything special. "We just did our job," he says. To think he would have missed out on the experience of a lifetime if he had just done a little better in school.

When duty called in 1940, the 21-year-old resident of Pincher Creek, Alberta, called the air force. He wanted to fly fighters. Instead, he would become one of legendary proportions.

"I only had a Grade 8 education. They said they couldn't use me, that I was too damn dumb," he says. So he joined the infantry. "They'd take you as long as you had a pulse."

And the rest is history, even if the Hollywood version of the First Special Service Force didn't let the facts get in the way of a good story. "I wouldn't have missed it for the world," he says.

Even today, at the age of 87, the former Staff Sergeant is a mountain of a man. His good friend Bradley Anderson describes him as "a tough old bastard." It is, for a soldier, a great compliment.

After basic training in Brandon, Manitoba, Hank volunteered for a special project and was sent to Calgary for an interview.

"Can you kill somebody?" he was asked.

"Yes," he said.

"You're in," he was told.

Together, 1,000 Canadians and 1,000 Americans represented the toughest of the tough. It was a collection of lumberjacks, forest rangers, miners and the like that would grow into a cohesive, one-of-a-kind unit the enemy would dub The Black Devils.

"We were like two nations that became one," he says.

The Special Force was officially activated on July 20, 1942. The Canadians travelled south from Lethbridge to meet their American comrades for extensive training at Fort Harrison, just outside of Helena, Montana. As a sign of respect and admiration, that road between the two cities was renamed the First Special Service Force Memorial Highway in 1999.

How extensive was their training? These men would become capable of everything and anything. They were and still are family, like brothers. Stealth tactics, hand-to-hand combat, amphibious warfare, rock climbing, demolition, parachuting and explosives. All of that, plus mountain fighting and skiing. No job would be too big, too perilous. Special jobs called for special men.

"I guess," Hank says, unimpressed by himself, "we could do it all."

In 1968, Hollywood would call them "The Devil's Brigade," and honour their accomplishments on film. William Holden and Cliff Robertson starred but, in reality, it was people like Hank Planger and Tommy Prince, Canada's most decorated Aboriginal soldier from the Second World War, who were the stars.

"I saw the movie, but there were parts of it I never experienced," Hank says with a chuckle. The beginning of the movie focuses on the infighting and the all-out hatred between the men from the two countries. In reality, there was an instant camaraderie and respect among the men. Not that

Hank Planger: Ready to take on the world.

The accomplishments of The Black Devils were immortalized with a Hollywood movie.

there wasn't the odd incident.

"If you gave somebody a cigarette, you had a friend for life," Hank says. "We're still that way. We got along good. Those Americans have the same blood."

They have met every year since the war to honour each other and relive the glory days. Not that looking for glory is something they would ever do. The get-togethers become much sadder every year as the number of survivors dwindles. There used to be hundreds, then 100, or 90. "This year (2005)," he says, "there were very few."

Hank Planger's war story isn't gut-splitting funny, but it is most worthy of attention. And boys, even the elite boys, will be boys. "It becomes harder and harder to find humour."

Theirs, for the most part, was serious business.

There are people who consider actors and athletes worthy of special attention. Because they speak well or because they can shoot a puck, they are placed on a pedestal. Silly.

"I met the actors from the movie," Hank says. "They're the same as anybody else." There may be respect and admiration, but hero worship is something reserved for those who genuinely deserve it. It doesn't take a lot of guts to storm an enemy position when the bullets aren't real and the dead body beside you will be buying that night in the bar.

The danger was real. You had to look hard to find the humour, but you could still find it.

"I remember one night, we were going through a corn field and one of the guys kept stepping on the stalks. He was making a lot of noise and I said, 'You want to go back? I think you missed one.'"

Of course there were dances and drink. "We had a lot of spirit and sometimes too much spirits," he says. It wasn't all work and no play. "And any time a shell missed you was reason to celebrate.

"The most dangerous thing in the army is a Lieutenant with a map," Hank says only half jokingly. The unit's first mission was supposed to be Project Plough. They were to parachute into Norway and knock out strategic targets such as hydroelectric plants, but it was scrubbed.

"They thought we had a spy in our midst," Hank says.

In October of 1943, The Devil's Brigade earned its nickname. At Monte la Difensa, in the dead of winter, the unit wiped out what was thought to be an impenetrable enemy defensive position high atop a mountain that was surrounded by steep cliffs. That mission would become the basis for the motion picture. The casualty rate was a staggering 77%.

Still, members weren't looking to make their own great escape. There was no place they'd rather be than with each other. While Hank Planger came through unscathed, he did spend time in hospital with a severe case of diarrhea. All he thought about was getting back.

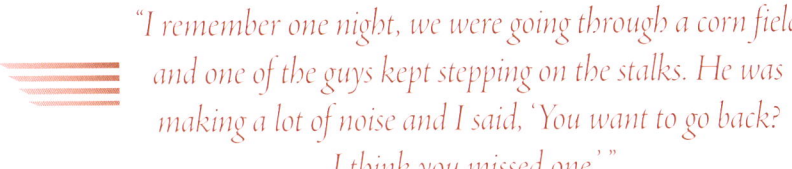

*"I remember one night, we were going through a corn field and one of the guys kept stepping on the stalks. He was making a lot of noise and I said, 'You want to go back? I think you missed one.'"*

"I missed the fellas," he says. "I didn't want to let them down."

It was during Operation Shingle, in Anzio, Italy, in February of 1994, that the Special Force was dubbed The Devil's Brigade. A diary was found on a dead German. In it was the following passage: *The black devils are all around us every time we come into the line.*

The enemy soldier referred to them as black because members of the unit smeared their faces with boot polish.

He can laugh as the memories come flooding back. "The Germans could never understand how someone at the back end always went missing when they went out on patrol. We didn't hate them, but we did get pissed off when they killed one of our friends."

During Shingle, they fought for 99 days without a break, pushing an enemy that had been less than 80 metres away back more than three kilometres. "We never retreated. We backed up to a more strategic location," Hank laughs.

They rode horses, donkeys and oxen. They ate whatever they could find. A nearby farmer could usually count on counting a few less chicken in the morning if they were around. Pigs also mysteriously went missing. After all, they were trained in stealth. They were good scroungers. Especially when it came to wine.

"We found (stole) a five-gallon cask one night," Hank says. "There was some falling down the next day. The trail was a little more slippery than usual."

> Thank you for the freedom of speach. Not being able to say what you want when you want. is like say girls have to where a dress everyday. By fighting in the war Canada is a hole diffrent place. You have the right to chose your job and are aloud to marrie who you want to marrie. I want to thank these soiders for doing what they did
>
> Thanks
> Mackenzie

The Devil's Brigade was the first unit sent into Rome, securing seven bridges the retreating Germans were intent on blowing up. The next day, when the Allies were treated as conquering heroes and had their picture taken for the world to see, the unit that actually liberated the city was gone, chasing the fleeing Germans. These were men who didn't sit around waiting for accolades.

With Italy secured, Hank Planger and The Devils Brigade were sent into France, paving the way for the Rhineland Campaign that would eventually end the war. Their intelligence work behind enemy lines is credited with saving countless lives.

The unit was officially disbanded Dec. 5, 1944. Most of the Canadians would become replacements for the 1st Canadian Parachute Battalion, while the Americans were sent to Airborne divisions.

Their bond, however, is everlasting. During the war, the unit accounted for more than 12,000 German casualties and captured more than 7,000 prisoners. After the war, The Black Devils template would be used to establish Delta Force and the Navy SEALs in the U.S. In Canada, today's elite JTF2 military unit is modeled after the Devils of the Second World War.

Hank Planger is clearly unimpressed by himself, but he is justifiably proud. Just days before this interview, he was called to Calgary and presented with the United States' Combat Infantry Badge by American Gen. Phillip R. Kensinger Jr.

"We did our job," he says with a shrug.

# Rum A Dumb-Dumb... Thump

For a Prairie boy, being in the navy was a sickening experience

HAROLD HAGUE

Harold Hague knew exactly what he was going to be when he grew up – an ace.

"Billy Bishop the second," he says of Canada's legendary First World War pilot. A recipient of the Victoria Cross, Bishop had 72 confirmed German kills. He even tangled with the celebrated Red Baron on one occasion. When he returned home, it was as a national hero.

OK, so Harold's story didn't turn out exactly the same. He turned out to be a bit of a joker. And there was no parade.

Instead, Harold ended up being sick. "Puked my guts out," he says. War will do that to you. Considering what would transpire later in life, you might even say the air went out of his dream and the shoe wound up on the other foot.

Earl Grey was a little town just north of Regina. "A grain elevator and a post office," he says. But at least it was close to the Regina Flying Club. "I spent most of my time there. I had a great love of the air." He built model airplanes and he dreamed.

Capt. Del Hay, an RCAF pilot who flew in the First World War, was his hero and mentor. "He would sneak us up," Harold says. "I learned the fundamentals from him. He let me take the controls when I was 16."

When war broke out and a buddy joined the air force, one look at the spiffy uniform sent Harold on a dead run to the recruiting office. It was 1940. He was still just 17.

Cyril Malone was the recruiting officer. He looked at the application and the baby face in front of him and decided this boy was a far cry from 18. "So you want to be a fighter pilot," he said. "Unless my eyesight is gone, you are not the age you say you are." Plus, he didn't have his high school matriculation.

Cyril lacked a sense of humour and Harold lacked the necessary facial hair. He was told the air force needed tail gunners. "That wasn't my cup of tea," he says. "I was so disappointed."

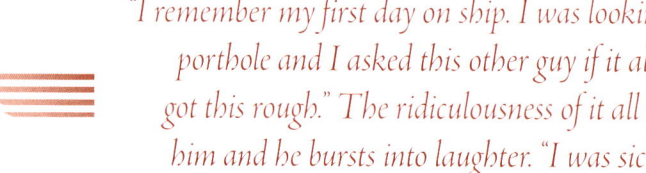

*"I remember my first day on ship. I was looking out the porthole and I asked this other guy if it always got this rough." The ridiculousness of it all strikes him and he bursts into laughter. "I was sick as a dog and we were still tied up to the dock."*

Then he saw another buddy who had joined the navy. "The girls flocked to him," he laughs. "I figured I may as well join the navy. And I had never even been in a rowboat."

Harold went to boot camp in Halifax and signal school in Quebec, learning Morse code, lights and flags. He became a signalman and was assigned to the Corvette *HMCS Sudbury*.

He was the very definition of a landlubber. "I remember my first day on ship," he says. "I was looking out the porthole and I asked this other guy if it always got this rough." The ridiculousness of it all strikes him and he bursts into laughter. "I was sick as a dog and we were still tied up to the dock."

Most of the men considered the shot of rum they received every morning to be one of the best parts about being in the navy. In Harold's case, it was one of the worst things. So seasick, he staggered to the bridge at the captain's request and was presented with a ladle of rum. He wanted to be one of the men even if he was still a boy. Down it went.

"And down I went, flat on the deck. I was out cold."

The captain was not impressed. "Send me up another signalman," he said, "not another god-damn kid."

"He was a tough old bastard," Harold says. "I hated him." To this day, the smell of rum leaves him nauseous.

He did, however, get some good advice from an old engineer who took pity on him. "If you feel something hairy and fuzzy in your mouth," he said, "don't spit it out. That's your ass——."

The first part of the war was uneventful, mostly screening for German U-boats in the triangle between Newfoundland, New York and Trinidad. "You tried not to think about what might happen," he says.

Harold thought he might like to grow a beard. Easier said than done, though. His nickname was Sonny, for obvious reasons.

"I was still only 17," he says. "I requested to grow a beard and the captain didn't even answer me." It was, he admits, a ridiculous notion.

By D-Day, he was a seasoned seaman serving on a minesweeper near Omaha Beach. "I will never forget the slaughter," he says quietly. "It was terrible, just terrible." The mines were so thick you could almost walk on them. "We used hooks to push them away from us. There had to be thousands of mines." He saw one ship get hit. It went down in four minutes. There was no way to save the crew.

Things like that stick with you. Harold Hague grew up during the Second World War. He became a man. He has a great sense of pride and accomplishment, and rightfully so. He learned to do his job well.

The reunions are something he looks forward to, because he knows it

Harold Hague: The baby-faced boy who became a man during his time at sea.

could have all worked out differently. "Ron Wilson worked with me at the telegraph office before the war. We were like brothers. He was lost at sea. To this day, we don't know what happened to him."

He fondly recalls his captain, Kenneth Hall, on the minesweeper *HMCS Cowichan*. "A great guy," he says. "He wasn't traditional navy, but he was a great seaman … and a hardnosed drinker." He'll never forget his nights in New York City, the nights when the non-drinker had to play the role of adult for his friends.

When the war in the Atlantic ended, he was fully prepared to head to the Pacific. Obviously the Japanese were afraid of him. "They surrendered," he says.

Harold Hague raised two girls and a boy. Son Kelly became a pilot. A touch of irony there. Harold Hague went into the shoe business.

"I had this buddy, Don Smith, who couldn't get into the service. Skinny, glasses. After the war, I went to work for him at the Reward Shoe Company in Toronto. The smell of leather got to me."

He ended up returning to Regina and going to work for Loggie's Shoes, taking over the business in 1975. He sold it to his son recently, but he's still there most days, even at the age of 84.

"I had heart bypass surgery and I spent some time sitting around feeling sorry for myself," he admits. "Being here, helping out, it's the best thing for me. It keeps me going."

Life, he says, has been good. And, through his efforts, he has made many lives better. In Regina, he is often referred to as Mr. Committee. When we talked in the fall of 2005, he was preparing for Remembrance Day. He has held virtually every office in the Royal Canadian Legion, from sports commissioner and president of the Saskatchewan Command to vice-president of Dominion Command.

"It's a sign of respect," he says. "The men of the first World War paved the way for us. As someone who took part in the Second World War, I feel it is my responsibility to continue to create awareness. We owe a lot to these men."

Harold Hague is not one to sit on the sidelines. He has been on or headed virtually every board and association in Regina over the years.

We owe a lot to this man.

# 'It Was In My Blood'

From the time he was a little boy, he was itching for a fight

ALEX SIM

Alex Sim was seven years old when he decided that if there was any fighting to be done, he'd be the one to do it. He didn't realize at the time there would be so many people telling him he couldn't.

"My parents bought me a little sword and an imitation army helmet one year for Christmas," he says. "I always wanted to be a soldier."

And he wouldn't take no for an answer. Getting there may not have been half the fun, but it was at least three-quarters of the hassle.

Alex was born in Calgary in 1925. So, if you're any good at all at math, you know he was only 14 when the Second World War began. He wasn't about to let a little thing like a birth certificate get in the way. In fact, a birth certificate would eventually play an integral part in his story. He counted the days … and then multiplied by two.

Not that his childhood was something he wanted to escape. "It was a great time. I chased a lot of cattle," he says of life on a ranch south of the city. He came from a military background. His grandfather was with the Mounted Police during the 1885 Northwest Rebellion, and his father and uncles had fought in the First World War.

"I guess it was in my blood," he says. At the age of 12, he joined the Alberta Institute Military Cadet Corps. And he waited. By 1941, still only 16, he could wait no longer.

"I tried to join the air force. For some strange reason, I wanted to be a tail gunner." It was the most dangerous place on a Lancaster bomber, but he never considered the consequences. "That was stupid," he says.

"Just like a lot of guys. I guess I thought I was bulletproof."

He never considered the possibility that Lady Luck would conspire against him. Who you know can help, but it doesn't always work that way.

A huge redheaded fellow was sitting, head down, at a desk when he walked into the air force office in Calgary. Alex knew he was grounded as soon as the man raised his head. "It was Dick Watson, one of my old school teachers," he says.

"What are you doing here, young Alex?" he asked. Young being the key word.

"I want to join the air force," I said. "He asked how old I was. I said 18. He said, 'No, you're not. You're 16. Get out of here.'"

Dejected and wondering where to go from here, he

Alex Sim, second from the left, and three buddies.

wandered the streets for a while before noticing an army recruitment office. "A Calgary Highlanders Staff Sergeant was sitting there in his dress uniform from the First World War. He looked at me a little funny when I told him I was 18. 'You have to be 18½ to go overseas,' he said. Then he said, 'Why don't you go outside, take a walk around the block and think about that.'

"So that's what I did. Then I walked back inside. 'Good morning, sir,' the old guy said. 'What can I do for you?' I told him I was there to join the army and he asked how old I was. I told him I was 18½. 'That's better,' he said."

He was in the army now. At least for the time being. When it came to smooth sailing, you could say this man missed the boat.

His uncles told him to avoid the infantry at all costs, so he opted for the artillery. "One Major laughed like hell. He said we had shells that weighed more than me. I was all of 116 pounds, but I talked them into it."

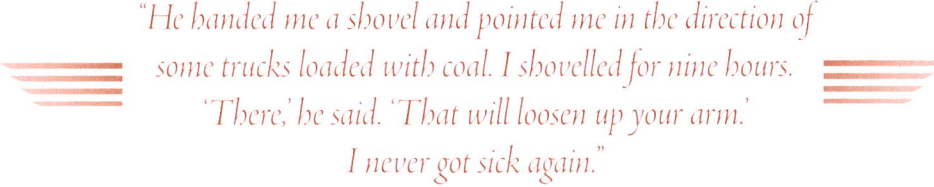

*"He handed me a shovel and pointed me in the direction of some trucks loaded with coal. I shovelled for nine hours. 'There,' he said. 'That will loosen up your arm.' I never got sick again."*

Alex took his basic training in Grande Prairie, Alberta, learning quickly that the last thing you want to do was go on sick parade.

"They gave us an inoculation and my arm swelled up," he says. "One of the old guys told me to ask for sick parade and I walked up to the Sgt. Major and handed him this piece of paper. I expected him to tell me to go back to the barracks, but he told me to get my coveralls and report back to him. He handed me a shovel and pointed me in the direction of some trucks loaded with coal. I shovelled for nine hours. 'There,' he said. 'That will loosen up your arm.' I never got sick again."

On leave, before moving on to Shilo, Manitoba, in January of 1942, he stopped by the house to tell his parents he was alive and well.

"I wanted to surprise them so I showed up at home and knocked on the door," he says. "My sister came out and said, 'Hey, dad, there's a soldier here.' " His father tried to talk him out of it, but Alex would not be swayed. "I told him I would just run away and enlist somewhere else so he left it alone."

It was his aunt Sue who applied the brakes. She wrote to Ottawa, explaining that this man they were readying for war was still just a boy of 17. That was the end of Alex Sim's military career. Kind of.

What he lacked in size, he made up for in determination. One way or the other, he was going to war. "I didn't want to miss it," he says.

Desperate times call for desperate measures. He was already going out with future wife Dina at the time. Her family had a typewriter and he had an idea. By 1942, those volunteering to enlist had to show a birth certificate. Ever resourceful, Alex sent away for his young brother's birth certificate. A little forgery goes a long way … all the way to Europe.

"I found out you could remove the ink from a birth certificate with wet white bread," he says, still proud of his ingenuity. "We erased the last two numbers of his date of birth and Dina typed in a new number that made me – or him – old enough." In a matter of minutes, Alex Sim became William Sim, soldier. A lot of men tried hard to get out of the army, but very few tried so hard to get into the army.

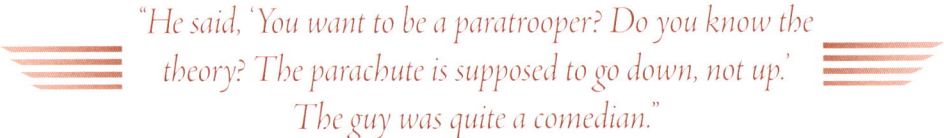

*"He said, 'You want to be a paratrooper? Do you know the theory? The parachute is supposed to go down, not up.' The guy was quite a comedian."*

He joined the Alberta Reconnaissance Regiment and found himself in Nanaimo, B.C., in July of 1942. A month later, he volunteered to join the First U.S.-Canada Special Service Force that would come to be known as the Black Devils.

He went to Calgary to meet the brass. It was a short meeting. "The Major took one look at me and said I was too small," Alex says. "He said, 'You want to be a paratrooper? Do you know the theory? The parachute is supposed to go down, not up.' The guy was quite a comedian. I thought I was never going to get to see this war."

They sent him back to Vancouver Island and put him to work. "We did armoured car patrols on the inside of the island." The idea was to thwart a Japanese attack. The absurdity didn't strike him till years later. "If there was going to be an attack it would come on the west coast," he said. "We did a lot of dumb things."

By the end of 1942, still anxious for action, he was transferred to an anti-tank regiment in Saskatchewan. There wasn't a lot of fighting to be done there, either, so he celebrated the day they boarded the train for Halifax. In July of '43, he found himself on board the *Queen Elizabeth* with 25,000 other troops.

He was well trained by this point, but the regiment broke up and he was sent to tank training school near York. "We were in Shermans," he says. "In six weeks, I had three of them burn up under me. I was almost killed and there wasn't even anybody shooting at me yet."

So, going against the advice of his father and uncles, he asked for a transfer to the infantry. This is the ultimate example of throwing caution to the wind. His commanding officer was shocked. No one had ever done that before, but there was no talking Alex out of it.

At 8:20 a.m. on June 6, 1944, the front of Alex Sim's landing craft crashed down on Juno Beach. "Terrible," he says. Of course there was fear, but you do your job. Instinct and training takes over. "Your friends are going, so you go, too. There wasn't really time to be afraid." Of the 100 men in B Company, only 60 made it safely off the beach as hell rained down on them from Nazi positions above.

Caen, the Battle of Ardens, Leopold Canal. The march through France, Belgium and Holland into Germany was fraught with danger, but Alex Sim survived. "Just a little guy," he says. "I guess I was hard to hit. You say all kinds of prayers and make all kinds of promises. Why do some men live and some men die? Luck."

Of all the harrowing nights, one stands out. "We were near Nijmegen (Holland) and I found this can of carrots," Alex says. "I had heard they were good for night vision so I ate the whole thing. If there were any Germans, I was going to see them."

On guard duty, looking out to the darkness, he noticed movement in the distance. "I kept watching and it kept moving.

Amazing: So many years later. Alex still fits into his uniform.

It kept getting closer and closer." Finally, figuring the entire German army was about to overrun their position, he opened up with his Bren gun. "I fired 28 rounds at the enemy," he laughs. And 28 rounds hit a tree that had been growing there, minding its own business, for decades.

"The guys never let me forget it," he laughs. "They would say things like, 'If you're around Sim, keep moving. He likes to shoot at stationary objects.' "

Alex was wounded in February of 1945, taking shrapnel in his back and leg, and evacuated to a hospital in Belgium. That should have been the end of his wartime experience, but this guy is no quitter. When V-E Day came, he volunteered for the Pacific Force and the occupation army. "I wasn't accepted for either of them," he says.

 *"There has to be a better way to solve our problems than sending people to die. Sometimes, it seems like we haven't learned anything since we crawled out of a cave."*

He wound up back in England, waiting for a ship to take him home to Dina. "I would peel potatoes and go on leave, peel more potatoes and go on leave again." It was April of 1946 before he made it back to Canada. He still hadn't turned 20.

The first thing he did was marry Dina. The second thing he did was realize that civilian life wasn't for him. He tried the railroad in Alberta. No thanks. He tried logging in B.C. No thanks. "I soon realized that the army was the place where I belonged. I regretted getting out.

"I tried to get back into the army in 1947, but they weren't taking married men at the time," he says. Korea changed that. He re-enlisted in 1949 and spent one tour of duty in Korea with the Princess Patricia's Canadian Light Infantry, as part of an anti-tank platoon.

There's just something about the camaraderie of combat that agreed with Alex Sim. "It's like family, even closer than family," he says. "You live and die in the same hole."

He wasn't about to make the same mistake twice. When the Korean War ended, he stayed in the military. "It was my calling," he says.

He retired to Kamloops, B.C., in 1969, as a Master Warrant Officer. He is still just a tiny man, if you don't go by the size of his heart. Even today, he can still shoehorn himself into his Second World War uniform. Alex Sim grew up, but he didn't grow much.

Dina and Alex have a wonderful life in Kamloops. They have two children, a son and a daughter, and four grandchildren. Great grandchild No. 1 is due to arrive in late 2006. Getting started so young, he is still only 81 years old.

He looks back on his experiences fondly, but he often wonders why these aren't better days. "There has to be a better way to solve our problems than sending people to die," he says. "Sometimes, it seems like we haven't learned anything since we crawled out of a cave."

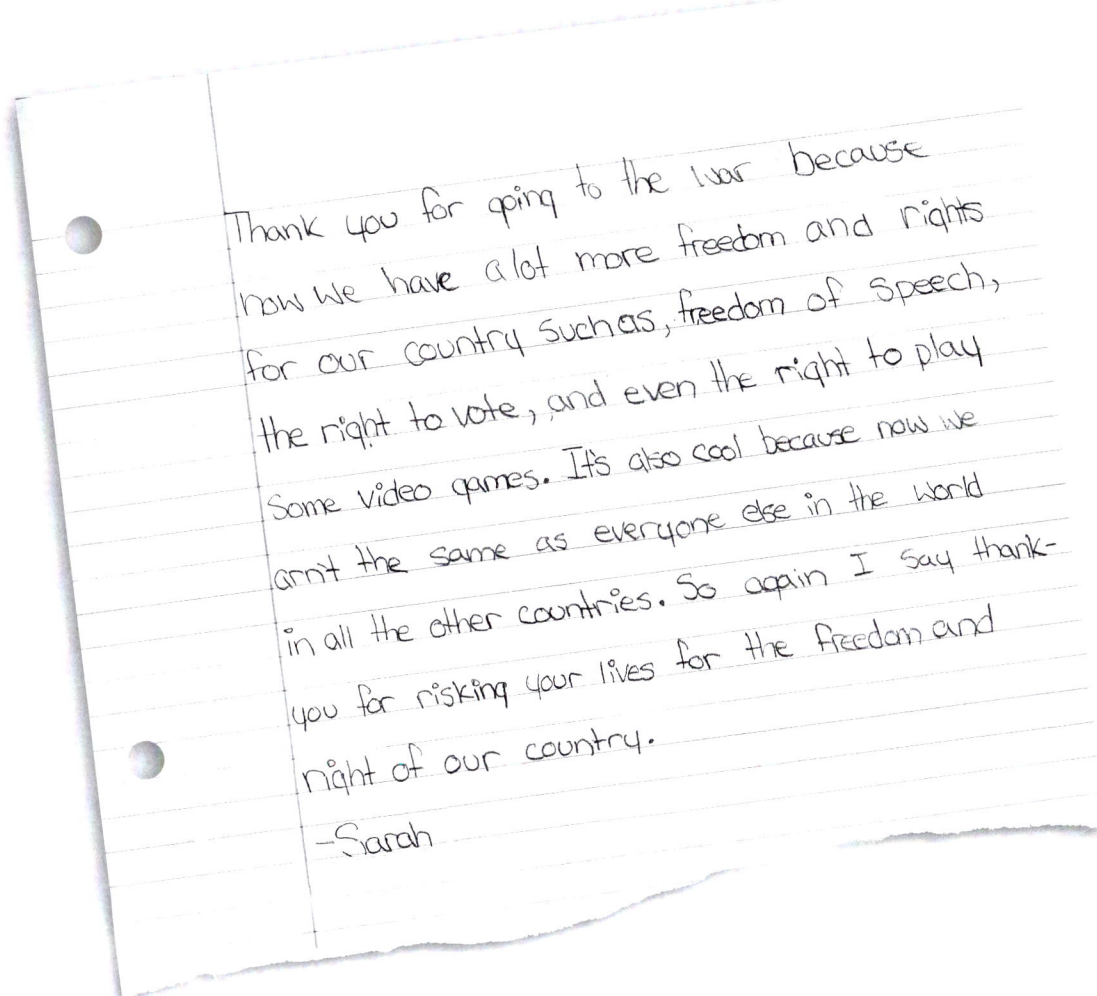

Thank you for going to the war because now we have a lot more freedom and rights for our country such as, freedom of speech, the right to vote, and even the right to play some video games. It's also cool because now we arn't the same as everyone else in the world in all the other countries. So again I say thank-you for risking your lives for the freedom and right of our country.
—Sarah

# The Boy Becomes A Man

One way or the other, he was determined to be part of it.

GEORGE EVANS

As a youngster growing up in St. John's, Newfoundland, there were two constants in the life of George Evans.

The first was water. If it was a weekday, there was a lot better chance of finding him down by the harbour than there was of finding him in a classroom.

"I loved the water. I didn't spend a lot of time in school. Education wasn't that important to me," he says. "I stole a lot of boats, but I always brought them back so you could say I just borrowed them."

And dinnertime was a time for fighting.

The trouble started when he got home, but it had nothing to do with being disciplined. Rowing take a lot of energy so you have to eat. Easier said than done in a house with 14 kids – seven boys and seven girls. You can imagine the chaos when there's one pork chop left on the plate. There was no such thing as leftovers.

"I went to bed hungry a lot of times," he says. "It was tough going for my dad, but he did the best he could. He was a good man."

This was before Newfoundland joined Canada in 1949. Although George has a different take on the union. "I prefer to think that Canada joined Newfoundland," he says.

His favourite times were fishing with his dad. "I was maybe eight years old. We'd be out three or four miles, catching cod or jigging for squid. No compass, no lifejackets. Looking back, it was kind of crazy. We got $2\frac{1}{2}$ cents a pound with the head off."

It was one such trip when he was 15 that changed his life and turned a boy into a man. "The crew of a ship waved us over as we were coming into the harbour." While his dad dickered over the price of fresh cod with the captain of the Norwegian freighter *Einvik*, George boarded the ship in search of something to eat. He figured he had a better chance of finding something on board than he did at home.

"The chief steward took me aft," he says. "When we finished, I cleaned up after myself and the others." It was the least he could do and the smartest thing he ever did. "The cook asked if I'd like to join the crew. Boy, was I excited. I had nothing against being at home, but I wanted adventure. I asked when I could start."

George had tried to join the navy a few weeks earlier, but was told to come back next year. "You won't see me," he said. "I'm not going to wait that long. I'm going to stow away."

George Evans had been at sea his entire life even before he joined the navy.

The war was already well underway in 1941 and he wanted to be a part of it. He needed three things to get on the *Einvik*.

He needed a parent's approval. "No problem," he says.

He needed a letter from his priest. "No problem," he says.

He needed a copy of his birth certificate. "Big problem," he says.

George reported to the ship the next morning, artfully dodging the captain until safely underway as part of a convoy bound for England. When finally cornered, he said his birth certificate had been in his pants pocket when his mother washed them. So it was all her fault. You know how mothers can be.

If there was one thing he was good at, it was coming up with excuses.

59

"I had a million of 'em," he says. Welcome to the Merchant Navy, seaboy.

It was Aug. 28, 1941. His heart beat with excitement. The first few days were calm. He set tables, washed dishes, made coffee and helped the cook peel spuds. When he wasn't working, he was up on the deck, sunning himself. This is the life, he thought. It doesn't get any better than this.

But it did get worse. They blew a bearing in the engine and couldn't keep up. "We became a straggler," he says. "You don't stop a convoy for one ship."

They were at the mercy of the sea now. Even worse, they were at the mercy of the German Wolf Pack. Two days later, on Sept. 5, some of the men were below, talking about the war and their chances of surviving it. "One of the guys came in and said that's the last thing we should be talking about," George recalls. "That's like asking for it."

Bang!

It was 3:30 a.m. when the German torpedo struck the *Einvik*. Thankfully, he says, you don't have time to think. George Evans had been on board for all of nine days. His career could have been over before it began.

There were 22 men in the crew, but there were only 21 in the two lifeboats. "The wireless operator was missing. He had stayed behind to send out an SOS," George says. "We thought we had lost him, then we spotted another lifeboat off in the distance."

They spent nine days in the lifeboats, in the rain and the fog. "You couldn't see your hand in front of your face," he says. It was the loneliest feeling … and then a miracle. They were

A man with a ready smile and a hearty laugh.

spotted by Icelandic fishermen, who gave them coffee and took them in tow. Most 15 year olds would want to run home to mommy at this point. "There was no turning back," he says. George boarded a troop ship bound for Scotland. "The worst part wasn't that my feet were frozen," he says. "So were our wages."

The experience jogs his memory of an experience when he got into a lively barroom debate with a Bomber Command gunner. The fellow scoffed when George said he was on a merchant ship. "That's not the real war," his adversary said.

George didn't miss a beat. "Do you burn fuel in those bombers?" he asked. "How do you think it gets to you?"

 *"We fought for our country and we made the supreme sacrifice just like the others."*

Good point. They toasted each other after that, two men on the same side. Almost all of the men and materials for the Allies arrived in Britain as part of a convoy. The outcome of the war depended on men, munitions and supplies. The first convoy sailed from Halifax with 18 merchant ships just six days after Canada declared war. By the end of 1939, 410 ships had sailed from Halifax. Three didn't make it.

When the war began, Canada had only 38 merchant ships capable of ocean travel, and 1,400 seamen. By the end of the war, there were 10 times that many. Plus all of the other ships and men, like George Evans, who sailed under the flag of another Allied nation.

Seventy-two Canadian merchant ships were lost to enemy action. Between Jan. 1 and July 31 of 1941, 400 Allied ships were sunk by 300 German U-boats estimated to be patrolling the Atlantic Ocean. Of the 12,000 Canadians serving on merchant ships, 1,500, one in eight, were lost. The Battle of the Atlantic began with the firing of the first shot and didn't end until the final shot had been fired on May 8, 1945. There were more than 25,000 crossings.

Make no mistake, people like George Evans paved the way to victory. And yet they were largely ignored and forgotten until winning one last battle in 2003, when the inaugural Merchant Navy Veterans Day was recognized. It is now held every year on Sept. 3.

"It was long overdue," says George, who is the Nova Scotia-Prince Edward Island director for the Canadian Merchant Navy Veterans

Association. "We fought for our country and we made the supreme sacrifice just like the others." His basement in Amherst, Nova Scotia, almost qualifies as a museum, with no end of memorabilia and countless mementos. "I'm proud of the work I did."

George got frozen feet when his ship went down, but he didn't get cold feet. Upon arriving in Dornoch, Scotland, the first thing he did was search for another ship. They were easy to find. He also took a gunnery course. The next time, he wanted to be able to shoot back.

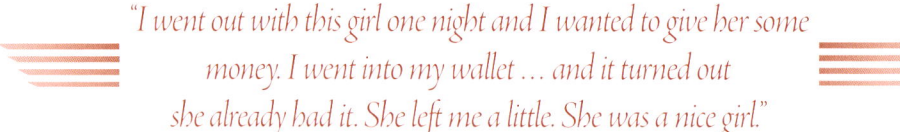

*"I went out with this girl one night and I wanted to give her some money. I went into my wallet ... and it turned out she already had it. She left me a little. She was a nice girl."*

The most harrowing part of the war came while serving on the Dutch freighter *Pieter de Hoogh*. He was on her for more than two years, including two trips to Murmansk, Russia, carrying guns, tanks, munitions and food for the Russian army. He was a part-time gunner and full-time stoker.

"She used 37 tonnes of coal a day and I shovelled all of it," he laughs. "It seemed that way."

The Murmansk Run was the most dangerous of them all. While his ship was only shot out from under him once, he lost track of the close calls. "The Stuka dive bombers would come in out of the sun so we couldn't see them. I just blasted away. I have no idea if I hit anything."

But the Germans certainly did. He saw many ships go down. "It was terrible, but it was important work," he says. "There was no chance of survival if you went into the water. You wouldn't last more than a minute or two."

They used to fly kites above the ship that would snag on the wings of enemy fighters and bring them down. "I remember coming off duty one time and a shipmate was having a helluva time getting a kite into the air," he laughs. "I said, 'What's the matter, son? Can't get it up?' "

It wasn't nearly as funny when he got his hand caught in the rope and ended up flying for a few frightening moments.

"You were always scared. Either that or you had a dangerous lack of intellect," he says. "I guess I was destined to live."

There was no daily shot of rum in the Merchant Navy, but there was rum to be had. "You had to buy it," George says. "I asked the chief steward for a bottle one day and he wouldn't give it to me. He said I had one the day before and asked what the occasion was. I said, 'Today's my birthday.' I had forgotten that I had said the same thing the day before." Hey, there's no crime in asking. Some people have short memories.

His drink of choice? "Whatever they had."

Being at sea was bad enough, but shore leave was no picnic, either. "I missed the boat a few times," he admits. "I blamed it on air raids, but that may not have been the case." Remember, this is a man who knew his way through a maze of red tape.

"I went out with this girl one night and I wanted to give her some money," he laughs. "I went into my wallet … and it turned out she already had it. She left me a little. She was a nice girl."

George Evans was in Halifax when the war ended.

The old sailor salutes his comrades during the First Merchant Navy Veterans Day. Inset, the oldster and the youngster.

"But I didn't start the riot," he says. "All I know, all I remember, is that a buddy showed up with a couple of bottles of rum."

He returned home to Newfoundland and you can probably guess what he did. "I bought a fishing boat," he says. "The sea is home." He literally travelled the world on 11 different ships. From South America to the Suez Canal, from Murmansk to Cuba. And all of this before his 20th birthday.

"I'm very proud of my service to my country," he says. "Nine days at sea and I found myself in a lifeboat. I didn't know how long I was going to last, but it all turned out pretty good. I had a lot of fun."

A couple of years after the war, he joined the navy reserves. He met wife Mary one night at the barracks gate. "We went next door to listen to the jukebox and have a Coke," he laughs. And the rest is family history. They had four children – three boys and a girl. He lost her in 2000, but his life remains full and rewarding.

On the 60th anniversary of the Murmansk Run, he was selected by Veterans Affairs to return to the Russian city with his son. "It was a great experience," he says. "I always wanted to go back."

It looked different, but it brought back a lot of old memories.

George eventually found a home with Canada Customs that would take him off his beloved rock to the mainland. In his latter years, he wrote his own book, *Through The Corridors Of Hell*. It's more a personal memoir than a best-seller, but it says a lot about the man and his accomplishments.

"For a long time, I don't think the Merchant Navy got the respect it deserves," he says. "But I think that has changed." He is now working on his second book – *The Enemy Above And Below*.

George Evans never served on a Canadian ship, but he did serve his country.

# 'I Didn't Want To Miss Anything'

### They had to talk him into becoming one of Canada's finest pilots

"There were a lot of people who did a lot more than I did," Al Trotter says.

This from a man who was one of only 12 Canadians to receive both the Distinguished Flying Medal and the Distinguished Flying Cross during what should be considered a heroic Second World War career.

He was just a 16-year-old kid when the Nazis overran Europe and threatened the rest of the world. "We lived in a little village near Swift Current, Sask., really close to No. 32 air base." He would see the airplanes overhead and dream. The locals were sometimes invited out to the base to meet and talk to the pilots.

Most people would dream of becoming a fighter ace. Al Trotter isn't most people.

"For some reason, maybe it was because I did a lot of hunting as a kid, I wanted to be a wireless air gunner," he says. That's what he joined as when he turned 18. But other people had other plans for him. His mother wasn't at all happy when the base brass came by in an attempt to talk some sense into him. If they couldn't do it, maybe she could. "They told her I would be the first guy to get shot," he laughs.

And she told him a thing or two. Sons don't always listen to moms.

He had never been in an airplane. He had no idea what he was getting himself into. But he would not be swayed. "I gave my mom a choice," he says. "I could be a wireless air gunner or I could run away and join the army.

It was kind of cruel on my part." He had the proper education and all the necessary qualifications. The only thing he lacked was a clue, but he would eventually acquire one.

"They talked me into it. I became a pilot," he says. In fact, he would become one of the finest.

After completing his training, Al Trotter arrived at a bomber base in England in early 1943. Still wet behind the ears, with no missions to his credit, he went to his first pre-flight meeting. He can still hear the commanding officer's voice. "Gentlemen," he said, "we wish you well. Tonight's target is … Berlin." Al jumped, or was pushed, right into the frying pan. Not only that, he was designated as a Pathfinder, marking targets for the other bombers that followed his lead. "I hadn't even seen enemy fire yet."

Not that he had any complains. "The Pathfinders were the glory boys," he says.

His first three missions came and went without serious incident. The scary part is after the briefing, sitting around and waiting for takeoff. "Once you cross the French coast, it's all business," he says. "Adrenalin takes over. There isn't time to be scared."

Al flew with the Royal Air Force. His seven-member Lancaster flight crew was like the United Nations. "We had an Aussie, a Scot, a Syrian, a couple of Englishmen, a Kiwi and me," he says. They were strangers at the beginning, but they would become brothers. "We were closer than family," he says.

It was flight No. 4 that all hell broke loose. As did part, or most, of his airplane. They reached their target and delivered their bomb load despite being harassed by a Messerschmitt. "I always lowered my seat so I couldn't see all the tracers and flak," Al says. "It was unbelievable."

The flak hit them just seconds after their bombs were dropped, blowing out a portion of the fuselage. Another blast ripped off eight feet of a wing tip. To further complicate matters, the Messerschmitt was back.

"The airplane was on it's side but I got it back under control, more or less," Al says. "It was a struggle to keep it in the air. It wanted to roll over. I was sure we were goners." A blast from the Messerschmitt machine gun went right between the pilot and the flight engineer. "It was a mess," the pilot says.

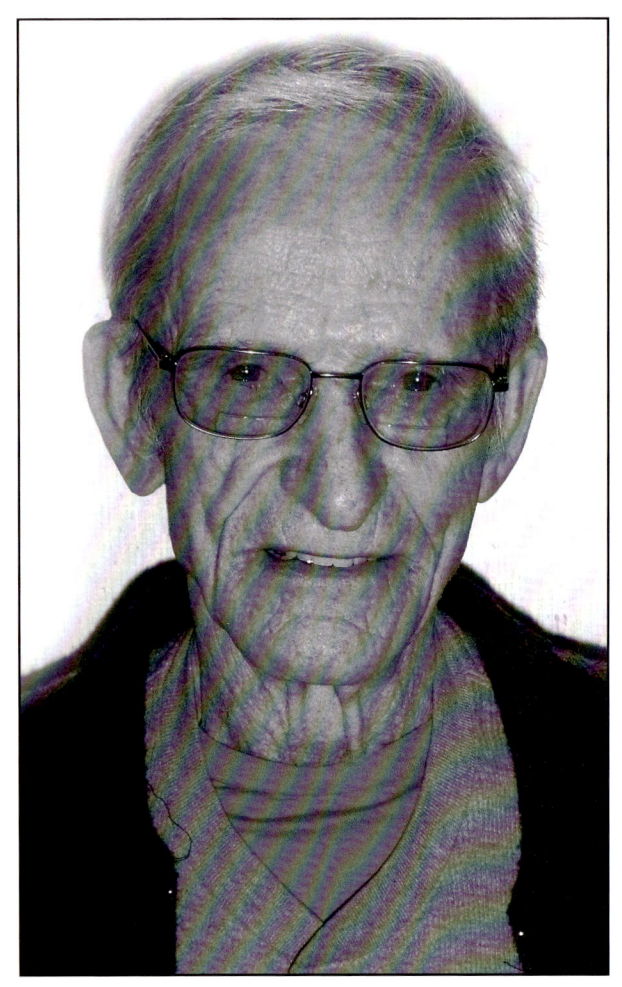

Al Trotter would lower his seat. He didn't want to see what was missing him.

Somehow, he managed to keep it in the air, but the news wasn't all good. The mid-upper gunner was dead and Archie, the rear gunner, hadn't been heard from in a while. "I got the bastard, skipper," he finally reported over the radio, "but I've been hit."

The inside of Archie's flight suit was wet. He was sure it was blood. He reached down inside and felt around. A hole. Oh, God. "He figured he'd been gut shot," Al says with a chuckle. It did turn out to be something to laugh about. "The hole was his belly button."

Somehow, Al Trotter kept his Lanc in the air, limping back to his base. No one had ever seen a plane so riddled with holes, with part of a wing missing, make it back. For doing the impossible, Al Trotter earned the Distinguished Flying Medal. Even more importantly, he earned the complete and total respect of his crew.

A young Al Trotter was determined to be a gunner.

Archie's last name? "Archibald was his last name," Al laughs. "I didn't know any of the first names."

He was a character. "The CO caught the two of us walking down the street on a hot day and Archie had his battle dress open," he says. "Archie didn't take any guff when the CO went after him. He said something like, 'My skipper has more guts in his left leg than you have in your whole body.' For that, he received six weeks hard time."

He would return to Al's crew after his time off for questionable behaviour, but war isn't always about happy endings. Archie would not return from mission No. 44.

"Only two or three per cent of Pathfinders make it to 45 missions, which is a double tour," Al says. "We had been part of the three missions with the highest casualty rates – 73, 79 and Nuremberg with 96 bombers lost."

On Aug. 13, 1944, at 1:30 a.m., near the German-Luxembourg border, their luck ran out. "A Junkers 248 had guns that pointed up at a 45-degree angle so it attacked from below, where we couldn't see it," he says. "We didn't know what hit us."

There would be no great escape this time. In fact, within a matter of days, Al Trotter would wind up in Stalag Luft III, where the legendary Great Escape took place.

 *"I couldn't get out because of the G-forces. The bomb aimer was still sitting there. I guess he couldn't or wouldn't jump. He went down with her."*

"I can't explain it," Al says of the mayhem of those early-morning moments. "I had no control, it was flopping around, there were explosions, both starboard engines were on fire, then they stalled." He ordered the crew to bail out, but he stayed behind. "It goes back to being brothers," he says. "It's a terrible feeling when you know these are the people who count on you." There had been no word from the gunners. He tapped the wireless operator on the shoulder. He was dead. Suddenly, the trusty Lancaster broke in half, plummeting straight down.

"I couldn't get out because of the G-forces," he says. "The bomb aimer was still sitting there. I guess he couldn't or wouldn't jump. He went down with her." Al Trotter fought his way to an opening. When the plane rolled over, he was literally thrown out, hitting his head on the instrument panel as he departed."

His parachute hadn't been done up properly. "You get cocky," he says. "It's never going to happen to you." His dog tag chain had broken back at the airfield. He didn't have his dog tags. If captured, he thought, he would immediately be shot as a spy.

Life and death came down to a matter of inches. From 2,000 feet, the plane fell to 500 feet before he got out. Experts determined that his parachute deployed literally just a few feet off the ground. "I counted one thousand and one … then I hit the trees," Al says.

He hung in the branches, battered and bruised, as the bombers flew home overhead. "Damn them," he thought. It was an empty feeling. He could hear dogs barking in the distance. When he finally cut himself down, he heard what he was sure were German voices. He had no idea where he

Al and Val Trotter on their wedding day. The sky has been good to him. She was a stewardess when they met.

Part of Al Trotter's very impressive medal collection.

was going, but he kept going. On his third day, he came around the corner of a building and found himself face to face with two German civilians. One had a shotgun, the other a rifle. Captured.

"The guy with the shotgun kept pointing it at me. He was drunk and he wanted to shoot me, but the other guy wouldn't let him," Al says. "They took me back to their village and everyone came out to see me. I felt like a monkey in a cage. I tried to give candy to the kids, but they wouldn't let me until I had some myself. They thought it was poisoned."

His first stop was a Gestapo interrogation centre. "Nobody knows if you're alive or dead. If they want to kill you, they can." He was thrown in a tiny cell, with the heat turned on and no ventilation, for nine days. Then the real fun started. "It didn't matter if they took every tooth in my mouth. All they were getting was my name, rank and serial number."

Everybody was smoker back then. Including Al Trotter. "The first thing the officer did was offer me a cigarette, but he would always get mad and take it back before I finished. I got smarter. I asked the questions until it was finished."

He was astonished by what the Germans knew about him. "They knew more about me than I knew about myself," he says. "They knew everything about my parents." He spent 268 days in captivity, including 200 at Stalag Luft III. "I experienced it all. I didn't want to miss anything."

As 1944 turned into the year the war ended, he found himself on the historic and horrific death march west as the Germans escaped the advancing Russians. "The dead of winter, no food. We walked in a daze and slept in snowbanks." At one point, they rode a train, 70 men in a boxcar meant for 30, for three straight days before being allowed out to do their business.

"Bare asses the entire length of the train," Al laughs.

Even then, the air force was trying to kill him. "We got hit by our own planes a few times," he says. "No matter how quickly you got into the ditch, there was always a German guard under you. We were eventually rescued by a British tank brigade. By that time, the Germans were our prisoners. They either gave up or disappeared into the night."

Al Trotter earned his Distinguished Flying Cross for his stellar body of work during the war, but it would be just the beginning of a long, distinguished career.

He got out of the service in 1946, trying the railroad for about five minutes before deciding it wasn't for him. "I weighed 130 pounds soaking wet, so shovelling coal was a bit tough on me." He enrolled at the University of Saskatchewan and wanted to be a lawyer, but his love of flying ate up all his money and then some. "I rented a plane every chance I got," he says.

It only made sense to re-enlist. Now 83 and in good health, he retired after 22 years, as a Lieutenant Colonel. He and wife Val have six children, three boys and three girls, and eight grandchildren. They make their home in Kamloops, B.C. Fittingly, he met her when she was a stewardess. The sky has been good to him.

"I have had the most fantastic career a person could ever have," he says. "I've flown in Saigon, Calcutta, all over the world, and I've loved every minute of it."

It still boggles the mind that he even made it through all those missions, those hellish days in the prison camp, and especially one leave in London when Al Trotter and a buddy came across another "crazy Canuck" who was trying to defuse a bomb. "He had a cigarette hanging out the side of his mouth as he went about his business. We thought he was nuts," Al laughs. "Then we realized we were sitting there beside him."

Any sailor, soldier or airman will tell you the most important thing in war is good luck. "I had plenty of that," he says.

# 'I'll Have That Rum Now'

Juno Beach was enough to drive you to drink

NORBERT TODD

Norbert Todd's war story actually begins in 1919. "I had two uncles in the First World War," he says. They both died shortly after returning to Canada. "Mustard gas."

His father lost his brothers. He did not want to lose his sons.

When the dirty '30s hit, Joe Todd was one of those special men who put others ahead of himself. "He gave money to people who needed it more than he did," Norbert says. "And it wasn't long before he had none left for himself."

Born in the tiny farming community of Hamiota, Man., John Norbert Todd was one of 10 children born to Joe and Helen Todd. He was determined to follow in his uncles' footsteps. Almost as determined as his father was to see that he didn't.

"We were out in the field threshing one day. I was just about to turn 18 and I told my dad I was going to join the army," Norbert says. He will never forget his father's words: 'No, you're not.'

There's a difference between a lie and a fib. Joe told his son he had to be 19 to join the army. Besides, there was work to be done.

"I had to move five huge piles of hay into the barn," Norbert says. It was a four-month project that wasn't completed until January of 1941. By then, there was no stopping him. This time, he didn't wait for permission.

"I rode my bike into town, on the train tracks, in the middle of winter," he says. "It's amazing I didn't kill myself right then and there."

He wrote his father a letter a month later, telling him to come and get his bike. "It was still there. I had enlisted and taken off."

Norbert, whether he liked it or not, was designated as an engineer and sent to Petawawa for basic training. When he suffered an attack of appendicitis, he was dispatched to Ottawa to convalesce.

For anyone ranked as a Captain or below, the first thing they did was take away your uniform. "Everyone was treated the same," he says. "You had to draw a ticket to determine what your job would be while you were there." He became a dishwasher. It was a good gig. "All I had to do was put the dirty dishes in this huge machine and hang them up when they came out the other side. A junior officer drew pots and pans. "Oh, boy, was he hot. He kept trying to bribe me."

He had been in the service for 14 months when a letter arrived from his mom, informing him that he had to return home immediately. "I got my notice," he laughs. "I had to join the army."

 *"I rode my bike into town, on the train tracks, in the middle of winter. It's amazing I didn't kill myself right then and there."*

He took an intelligence test while stationed in England. "It came back that I was an idiot," he says. "That was right before they made me a Corporal."

Norbert was assigned to the 1st Field Squadron and sent overseas in October of 1941. "The most rotten outfit of them all," he says. "The Sergeant may have been an ex-priest, but he wasn't going to heaven. He gave me a gun, no bullets, and made me guard the Captain's quarters every day on the way over to England. The Captain was a good guy, though. He let me come inside and sit down. I spent the rest of the trip sitting on my ass. Good deal."

When D-Day came, Norbert Todd was in one of the first landing crafts to arrive at Juno Beach. "On the way in, our Sergeant was pouring rum," he says. "I didn't drink." A bullet struck a soldier behind him in the helmet. "I'll have that rum now," he said.

Men were screaming for their mothers.

"One guy turned yellow and wouldn't get off the landing craft," he recalls. "The Captain ordered me to shoot him, but I couldn't do it. He was a friend of mine. I threw him overboard and the waves washed him into shore. He became my backup, all the way through France, Belgium, Holland and into Germany. He had no idea how he got to shore until I told him."

Norbert also told him he wouldn't wait for a Captain's orders the next time it happened. And it never did.

It's the heroism and courage Norbert Todd remembers about that fateful day. There is a tear in his eye as he pictures the young man who had his right arm totally shattered by a German shell. "That didn't stop him," he says. "He kept going."

A lot of non-drinkers became seasoned professionals by the end of the war. But not Norbert.

It was just after the fall of Caen that he was offered a drink upon returning from a night patrol. It seemed like a good idea at the time. "Pure alcohol. I could barely make it to my slit trench and when I got there, I couldn't move. I was paralyzed," he laughs. "The Germans hit us hard that night, but I never moved. I couldn't."

Norbert wasn't much of a fisherman when the war began, either. The most important thing, he discovered, is using the proper equipment.

"It was right near the end of the war, when the Germans were dropping their weapons and walking home," he says. "Those potato masher grenades worked really well. Boom! We had more fish than we could carry."

For years, Norbert wouldn't talk about what happened overseas, but the years have dulled the pain. He came home and married a girl named Ethel. The result was seven children, nine grandchildren and a happy, rewarding life.

"Everything I went through," he says, "it was worth it."

The years have dulled the pain and misery of war for Norbert Todd.

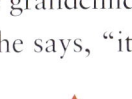

# 'Not A Day Goes By'

'Losing your home is one thing, but I lost my sister.'

BARB UTTLEY

"Laughter," says Barb Uttley, "is the best medicine. It's the only one I take."

Growing up in London, in the days leading up to the Second World War, it was the only attitude to have. The writing was on the wall – in big, bold letters – during her teenage years. The Germans were coming and she wouldn't be on the welcoming committee.

"I wanted to do my part. I wanted to help any way I could."

Barb is a delightful, tiny lady, 84 years young and five-foot-one. "And shrinking," she says. At 17, though, what she lacked in stature she made up for in national pride. "I signed up to be an air raid warden. We were all in it together."

August of 1941 is forever etched in her memory. It was the start of the Battle of Britain and, as it turned out, the beginning of the end for the Nazis. The enemy bombers came in waves, like a deadly tsunami.

"There was no end to them," she says. "The sky was black with planes." It was a Sunday morning. The air raid sirens went off at 11:15 a.m. And life changed forever.

Today, she is a proud Canadian, but Barb is probably right when she says North Americans can't comprehend. The 9-11 terrorist attacks on New York and Washington were hideous, certainly, but imagine that – or worse than that – day after day, night after night, during the Blitz. The enemy could reduce buildings to rubble, but they could not overcome the spirit of the people.

War leaves no one unscathed. Entire neighborhoods were reduced to rubble, but Barb Uttley lost more than most. Her little sister, Jill, was killed

The happy couple. Barb and Arthur Uttley on their wedding day. The happiness wouldn't last.

during one bombing raid. She was only seven. Her aunt had been babysitting. She was lost, too.

"I was mad as hell at God," she says. "It was the worst thing that ever happened to me. Not a day goes by that I don't think about her. Losing your home is one thing, but I lost my sister. We were tough. We had to be."

Barb Uttley had a choice at that point. She could retreat into her own private hell, or she could step boldly, proudly, into the battle. Remember, she was only 17 at the time. She chose the latter, joining the Women's Auxiliary Air Force in 1941. It was a move that would shape the rest of her life.

After training, she was assigned to a radar station near Dover, one of more

Barb and Arthur Uttley hand in hand, but it would not be a stroll in the park.

than 200 scattered along the English coast. It wasn't a glamourous job, but it was the key to victory in the Battle of Britain. Without radar, the Germans probably would have occupied England. Without it, there would have been no staging area for Operation Overlord and the end could have been and probably would have been much different.

"We'd be speaking German. And I didn't take German language classes in school," she says. "I was so young then. Life was good. I loved to dance. We made the best of it."

It was shortly after she was transferred to a station in Northern Ireland that she met Arthur Uttley, a radar mechanic from Ontario, Canada. It was love at first sight. "We danced the night away." And she gave her heart away, calling off one engagement to enter into a new one.

Barb was 98 pounds when she joined the service. "And I was 97 pounds when I got out. I wasn't in it for the food, that's for sure. I lived on lemon curd." Arthur was only five-foot-six, "but he seemed like the alpha male to me. He looked so dashing, so important, in his uniform. Short men like to dance with short women, because it makes them look tall. I guess I fell for him."

They were married in 1943. "A Canadian man and an English woman, married in Ireland, witnessed by a Scotsman. God help us."

V-E Day was a day like no other and, in a strange sense, the end of the good old days. "We were all so giddy," she says. "I was afraid of heights, but I climbed to the top of a water tower. The men were inside, playing water polo."

Barb's mother didn't approve of her choice of a husband. She should have listened to her mother. "I gave up everyone I knew and everything I knew to move to Canada."

English war brides came to

Canada by the thousands. "They played *Here Comes The Bride* on the hospital ship on the way over," she says. To put it mildly, it was not a joyous reunion when she spotted Arthur. It was not exactly love at second sight.

"I felt like jumping overboard. When I saw him in his civilian clothes, I had to look away. He certainly didn't make an impression on me. He looked like a slob."

She was a stranger in a strange land. "I wanted to cry," she says. "The cars were on the wrong side of the road. I couldn't even cross the street. I was scared stiff, but I still tried to make it work."

And she did, for 60 years. Barb worked as a bookkeeper and office manager. They adopted two children and they have two grandchildren. But there would be no happy ending. They went separate ways in 2003. "We drifted apart," she says.

Canada, however, grew on her. "I guess I'm a proud Canadian," she says. "This is my home now."

And Royal Canadian Legion Branch 6 in Owen Sound, Ont., is her second home. "I had to raise hell, because they wouldn't sell me wine by the glass," she says. "I got that changed."

She is a regular volunteer and a past membership chairman. She has also spoken to children about her experiences.

"I'm a lot of things," she says, "but I'm no war hero."

# It Could Be Worse

'We were on leave and there was a little inebriation going on.'

Newman Pratt sees his glass as half full even when it's empty. That's just the way he looks at life. The expression on his face is one of happiness and contentment.

His favourite expression is, 'It could be worse.'

After 63 years together, he and wife Inez couldn't be better. They have lived in the same warm, friendly home for 58 years. Surrounded by their five children, eight grandchildren and a great granddaughter, there is much to smile about.

Right now, he is busting a gut.

"We had this one guy, Bill, who was always saying, 'It could be worse.' It didn't matter how bad something was, that was his attitude," Newman laughs. "Drove us nuts, so we figured we'd get back at him by coming up with a story that couldn't possibly be worse." Something so bad, so fictionally hideous, it would definitely change his tune.

"Did you hear about Jim and Harry? They're dead. Jim picked up this woman in a pub and they went back to her place. It turned out to be Harry's wife and he walked in and caught them in the act. He shot his wife and Jim, then he turned the gun on himself. They're all gone. It was a bloody mess."

There was stunned silence, but only for a second or two. "It could be worse," Bill said.

The others, including Newman, were appalled, of course. "How could it be any worse than that? Two of your friends are dead."

Bill didn't miss a beat this time. "I was there the night before.

That could have been me. It could have been a lot worse."

"We gave up trying after that," Newman says.

Nemwan Pratt, Newmie to his friends, was only 14 in 1939. He would have joined the day after war was declared if they'd let him. He would have joined the day after he turned 18, too, but his dad wouldn't let him. He needed his help as a well driller in and around Durham, Ont. His uncle, a veteran of the First World War, cautioned him. "Don't be too damn anxious," he said. "They shoot back."

He joined when he was 18½, already an excellent marksman thanks to a childhood spent hunting chipmunks and squirrels. "It seemed like a good way to get over and see the old country. My dad was born in England."

Like so many others, he was young and foolish. And very naïve.

"I thought I might be mechanically inclined. I kind of wanted to get into the ordinance end of things, but the officer I went to see said I had three choices. I could join the infantry, the infantry, or the infantry. So I joined the infantry."

It could have been worse. He was assigned to the Lake Superior Regiment. "It was a mobile infantry unit with half-tracks, Bren gun carriers, that sort of thing. At least we didn't have to walk very much."

The money was no hell, even for a gifted sniper. At a dollar a day, he could have made more if he'd stayed on the job back home.

"But they gave you clean underwear," Inez says helpfully.

"It could have been worse," Newman says.

The Germans were already a beaten bunch and on the run when he arrived in Belgium in October of 1944. "Obviously afraid of me," he says. There was no laughter his first day in the field, when he was sent out

His uncle gave young Newman Pratt some good advice. "Don't be too damn anxious. They shoot back."

Newman Pratt relaxing at a family gathering. There is always plenty of family around.

on a nighttime patrol. "I was shaking so bad, I couldn't get my boots on."

They were supposed to go out about 10 kilometres, until they met up with another patrol. Their password was 'Daisy.' The friends, in order to prove they weren't foes, we're supposed to answer 'May.'

"I don't know whether the fella was tongue-tied or he stuttered or he couldn't remember what he was supposed to say," Newman says . "There was silence for a long time, then he yelled, 'Li'l Abner, dammit.' Close enough. We laughed like hell." But it was a nervous laughter.

"The little kids I talk to in school all want to know if I killed anyone," he says seriously. But we don't want to go there. "They had a job to do and I had a job to do. I didn't hate the Germans. They were just like you and me."

Part of the occupying force because he hadn't been there long enough to warrant a discharge when the fighting in Europe ended, he even went hunting with former German soldiers while he waited for his discharge. "They were ordinary guys."

He tells a story about hitting a German during the last days of the war. Not shooting to kill, Newman's bullet caught him in the hip. As he approached the downed adversary, the fellow handed him his binoculars and sidearm, a 9 mm Luger. "I patched him up and sent him out," he says.

His route to victory took him through Belgium, the Netherlands and into Germany.

One night, sleeping in a barn in Holland, he woke up with a terrible pain in his chest. "I thought I was having a heart attack. It turns out a cow was standing on me," he says. It could have been worse. "The cow could have been taking a leak."

In one Dutch town, they came across a bank that had been blown to pieces. "There was money everywhere. We took as much as we could. We thought we were rich," he says. "Unfortunately, the stuff was useless." It could have been worse. "We used it for toilet paper."

They found a huge cask of wine one afternoon and couldn't resist the temptation, despite the fact the Germans were known to booby trap or poison what they left behind. A couple of hours later, after toasting their good fortune, the laughing stopped when one of their own fell over stone dead. "We thought he was poisoned. We thought we were all goners."

It turned out the guy had been hit with a sniper's bullet. "We started to laugh again," he admits sheepishly. It could have been worse. "At least it wasn't poison."

It was two days before the official end of the fighting when they came upon a locomotive all steamed up and ready to go. "One of our guys had trained as an engineer, so we decided to take her for a little spin"

 *"I had three choices. I could join the infantry, the infantry, or the infantry. So I joined the infantry."*

They got about 10 kilometres up the track and discovered there was no track. It had been blown up. It could have been worse. In fact, it was. They were also running out of steam. Since necessity is the mother of invention, they used a combination of their bladders and their helmets to get enough liquid for the return trip.

"We picked up a bunch of Germans who had dropped their weapons and were walking home," he laughs. "I guess that made us good Samaritans."

There was precious little to laugh about in Holland. The Germans had left a trail of ruin in their wake as they retreated home. Newman Pratt remembers one funny incident from that time.

"This old guy came running up and the interpreter said he was asking for chocolate and cigarettes. It was his anniversary and he had to take them back to his wife," he laughs. "We gave it to him and he ran like hell."

The next day, he was back again, repeating the same mournful plea. "Another anniversary," Newman laughs. "I wonder how many wives he had."

Newman was wounded in action, although it might not be in the official records. And action might not be the right word.

"We were on leave and there was a little inebriation going on," he says. "I was being a good guy, carrying this fellow who had passed out, when he bolted and kicked me right in the face. Broke my nose. The damn thing is still crooked."

Newman Pratt returned to Canada in 1946, rekindled his love affair with Inez and went back into the well drilling business with his dad. They bought their 35-acre property for $4,000 and lived happily ever after.

"It couldn't have turned out any better," he says.

# Friends For Life

The Canadian soldier
and the little Dutch boy

Roy Armstrong

**W**ar isn't all about foes. In Roy Armstrong's case, it is more about friends. The tears of anguish and horror were many during the Second World War. The tears of joy and happiness were a treasured few.

There was just something about the little boy that touched the heart of the young soldier in early 1945.

"He was such a polite little guy," says the old dispatch rider. " And I can't stand to see a child suffer …"

The suffering was all around them when the Canadians reached the Netherlands. The Germans had done their worst, leaving a ravaged country and a starving people in their wake as they retreated toward defeat. It was another cold, bitter April morning near the city of Utrecht when 10-year-old Bill Slinger showed up in the camp of the liberating Canadians.

"I didn't come to eat," he said. His English was broken, but his spirit was intact.

But he did eat. Roy Armstrong saw to that. "I gave him my mess tin. He had the biggest smile on his face."

Bill was there to offer an invitation. His mom played the violin and she wanted to play for the men who had come to her country's rescue. For Roy, it was almost too good to be true. After all, music was his first love. He could play almost anything, but the trumpet was his specialty. They set a time and picked a place – an old school that had been turned into a makeshift hospital.

"I expected his mom and her violin," Roy says. "She showed up with an entire

Roy Armstrong at the grave of his best friend, Harold Norwood. How unfair. He was a victim of an accident just days before the end of the war.

string quartet. It was beautiful stuff for a bunch of soldiers so far from home."

With something in common, Roy and the family became instant friends. Bill would come by often. Ironically, or perhaps not, it was usually around lunchtime. Roy would give him tea, coffee and sugar to take home to his mom. They traded pictures and hugs when the Canadians left for the march into Germany. Later, they traded letters.

Separated by an ocean and decades, the soldier and the boy thought of each other often. For 50 years, Bill Slinger carried a ratty picture of Roy Armstrong in his wallet.

"I always wondered what became of him," Roy says.

In 1995, nearing the 50th anniversary of the liberation of Holland, Bill Slinger reached out. He knew Roy had been born in Regina. He sent a letter to the *Regina Leader-Post*, asking if anyone knew the whereabouts of a Roy Franklin Armstrong. Roy never saw the letter, but his phone rang off the hook with calls from friends who did. He called the phone number.

The young dispatch rider on his trusty bike.

Bill answered. A friendship was renewed. "It was out of this world," Roy says.

Shortly after the call, Roy and his son Tom made the trip back to Holland for a long-overdue reunion. Together again, the two old friends visited Juno Beach, where Roy had come ashore on D-Day with the Regina Rifles. The trip gave him the opportunity to visit the grave of his best friend, Harold Norwood, who was killed by friendly fire on April 16, 1945, at the age of 27. So close to the end.

"A guy came into the barracks, threw his sten gun on the bed and the damn thing started firing," he says. "When I die, I know I will go to heaven. I have already been to hell."

He has been back two other times since 1995 and he plans to go again. The little boy is now 73 years old. The old soldier is 86. They talk at least once a month on the phone.

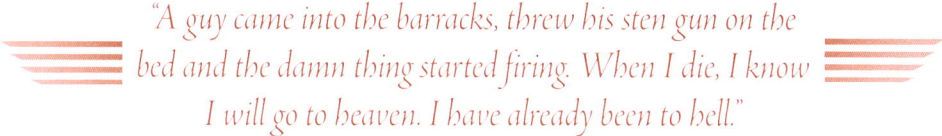

*"A guy came into the barracks, threw his sten gun on the bed and the damn thing started firing. When I die, I know I will go to heaven. I have already been to hell."*

Bill is shocked when a writer from Canada reaches him at home. "We had no food. It was a terrible time," he says. "Roy made it so much better. He is such a nice guy. He and the rest of the Canadians did so much for us. I had to try to find him." There is no end to the sad stories, he says. "This is a happy story."

There is a special bond between the Dutch and Canadians in general, but this one is personal. "I guess we love them and they love us," Roy says.

Music has always played an integral part in his life. Today, he is a proud member of the Saskatoon Jammers, a group of 70 and 80 year olds who play music from the '20s and '30s "at wakes and weddings." Their motto: "We play the music we like for the people who like our music."

It is for love, not money. Roy plays the trumpet and the harmonica. "We limit ourselves to one gig a week," he laughs. "We don't need anybody keeling over."

Music even led him into the military. In 1935, at the age of 15, he joined the militia in order to play in the band. "Marching with a trumpet was easier than marching with a rifle," he says. "And I got 75 cents a week. It was good money for a hungry kid. A hamburger was 10 cents and a Coke was a nickel."

He is a man who smiles often and laughs loudly. Keeping with the love story theme, he was even able to find happiness out of heartbreak. He lost his beloved wife Zoie after 52 years, three children, more grandchildren than he can count and one great grandson. Eight months earlier, Irene Scherger lost her husband and Roy's best friend, Harry.

"The four of us were always together," he says. And, in a sense, they still are. Roy and Irene married. "It's funny how fate works."

He is proud of his accomplishments during the war, but he didn't get into it to be a hero. "I didn't join to kill," he says. "I just wanted to come home with two arms and two legs. I just did my job."

He was tailor-made to be a dispatch rider. His size made him a hard target. "I never got hit, but I did get lost," he laughs.

Roy wanted to follow his dad into a career with the railroad. "I was hired on Sept. 1, 1939 by Canadian National," he laughs. "Bad timing. War broke out on 10$^{th}$."

D-Day was an awesome spectacle. "The largest armada in the history of the world," he says. "There were thousands of ships. I was so sick when we hit the beach, I didn't care if I got shot. We hit the beach running – you didn't dare stop for any reason – and kept going. I didn't sleep for four days."

The war took him through France, Belgium, Holland and into Germany. He drove every vehicle imaginable, but his favourite was the motorcycle.

"Funny story," he says. "I was driving for a Colonel Tanzman and he made me stop when we got to the German border. "I couldn't understand why. Then he unzipped his pants. 'Piss on Germany,' he said. Then he got back in the car and we carried on."

He remembers the day the bird did its business in his cup of tea. He remembers the ridiculous sight of the man roller skating on the flat deck of the aircraft carrier. He remembers seeing the changing of the guard at Buckingham Palace in London. And, yes, there are some nights he can't remember at all.

After the war, Roy Armstrong returned the railroad and worked as a conductor for 45 years, never leaving Saskatchewan. He wondered often about the fate of the little Dutch boy.

# Taking A Swing At It

'It doesn't look like you're going
to be much of a sailor.'

NORM McIVER

Norm McIver had no great aspirations when he joined the Royal Canadian Navy in the fall of 1941, with the Second World War already well underway.

He had no plans to be a hero. Especially a dead hero. He just wanted to come home in one piece … or not at all.

"Not many cripples came back from the navy," he says. "You either came back whole or you didn't come back at all. The infantry just wasn't for me."

He also knew what he was getting into. Like so many others growing up in the little towns that dot the Great Lakes, he went to school only until he was old enough to go to sea. In tiny Lion's Head, Ont., it was the thing to do. At that time, it was the only thing to do.

He was 23 when he joined the navy and headed off to basic training in Toronto. He had been seasick a couple of times during wild storms on the Great Lakes, but it wasn't cause for concern. And, it had been way back when he first boarded a ship.

"It was the second or third day in Toronto, in the old automotive building," he says. "They put me in this swing and I had to go back and forth for 30 minutes. I made it about 25 minutes before I got sick."

He was given a couple of pills and told to come back the next day. Same drill. "This time," he says, "I lasted about 20 minutes."

His instructor was not impressed. "It doesn't look like you're going to be much of a sailor," he said.

As usual, Norm had a ready retort. "I haven't been seasick in years," he said.

"But I've never been on a boat where I had to sit on a swing and go back and forth, either."

His explanation must have done the trick, because he found himself on convoy and anti-submarine patrols on the destroyer *HMCS Assiniboine* after completing his gunnery course. "I never got sick once in the navy," he says.

The best part of basic was when he was issued gators and an arm band and sent to Maple Leaf Gardens to make sure none of Canada's finest got out of line. "I was fairly big, about six feet," he says. "They figured that would make me a pretty good cop, but it didn't. I just took off my arm band, found a seat and watched the hockey game. I wasn't going to arrest anybody."

During his time on board, the *Assiniboine* was credit with sinking three German U-boats. He'll never forget the body parts floating in the water. "I don't want to give a big spiel on that," he says.

Some things are better left unsaid. Like so many others, Norm McIver didn't talk about his experiences until the last few years. He is 88. Time has healed most of the wounds, but there is still pain.

Like the time a Hedgehog anti-submarine weapon misfired and the shells rained down on their own deck. Fifteen sailors died that day.

Norm McIver didn't join the navy hoping to be a hero. He just wanted to come home in one piece.

"One guy was pouring coffee and it killed the two men on either side of him," Norm says. He was on his way down from watch when he met a friend on his way up to relieve him. They stopped and talked for a few minutes. "Ten minutes later, he was dead. He got a piece of shrapnel through the jugular. He was planning to go to work for his father in the trucking business when the war was over."

Norm had been saving his daily ration of rum. This was the time to put it to good use. There's a time for rules and regulations and this wasn't it. The men could use a drink, he thought. When the gunnery officer found out, instead of throwing the book at him, he went off and returned with another bottle.

"He was one of the better officers," Norm says. "It rallied the men a bit. They needed it. A good officer had to be blind sometimes."

He developed a little bit of a taste for rum. "I've been known to have some since I got out of the navy," he winks.

There was a lot of poker and a lot of cribbage on the ship. "But nobody expected to collect," he says. "It was just for fun. You had to have some fun." Even if it wasn't fun at the time.

"We came across an unidentified ship one night and raced up to it. Every gun was trained on her," he laughs. "It was a Newfoundland fishing boat. We must have scared them half to death."

It's good to have selective memory. Especially if the wife is in the same room. "I enjoyed the times up town on leave," he says. But enough about that.

At one point, he had to take a train from Toronto to B.C. to hook up with a new frigate that had been built in Esquimalt. "First class all the way," he says. "When we stopped in Parry Sound, an army girl got on board. She had been issued a ticket for the same berth as a sailor who had gotten on the train in Toronto.

"She had just come from a party and was drunk," he recalls. "She made a helluva scene trying to get into bed with the sailor and he wouldn't let her in." He shakes his head sadly. Opportunity knocked and he locked the door. "Stupid fella."

One of his best friends was a cook named Patty O'Neil. If you had to eat his biscuits, he was also considered the enemy. "We used them for ammunition," Norm says.

Patty's excuse is that he didn't want to be a cook. He wanted to be a stoker. He certainly a didn't aim high.

They had to wait six weeks for the new ship to be ready. There was an officers training school just up the road and that meant there were a lot of people around who thought they were more important than they were.

"A young officer wants

For Norm McIver and everyone else, it was good to have something to smile about.

you to salute him," Norm says. "An old officer would just as soon you didn't bother. They had to salute everybody and all they got out of it was a sore arm."

The two of them were in Vancouver one night when they met a young Lieutenant on the street. They were talking at the time and didn't notice him. He wheeled around, clearly offended. "Hey, you," he said. "You're supposed to salute me. I'm an officer."

Patty, Norm says, "was quick with the gab. He said, 'Then what the hell are you complaining about? I'm just a cook.' There was no shore patrol around. There was nothing he could do. We just kept walking."

Then, of course, they ducked into the nearest pub.

Norm McIver survived the war unscathed. But he knows first-hand that others didn't have his run of good luck. He saw many oil tankers on fire, lighting up the night. He saw friends die in the name of freedom. He did it for love of country, not money. "I spent every nickel," he says. "There was a lot of pride in being a returning veteran."

He came back to Lion's Head after the war. He knew Marj growing up. They met again at a dance. "He had two left feet, but I liked him anyway," she says.

He returned to the Great Lakes for a few months, but decided on a life of farming. It has been a good life. He is still razor sharp. "Nine times out of 10 I can remember my own name in an emergency," he laughs. "The difference between now and then is that I've gotten a little shorter and a lot wider."

They have four children, six grandchildren and four great grandchildren. "And I still have the odd shot of rum," he says.

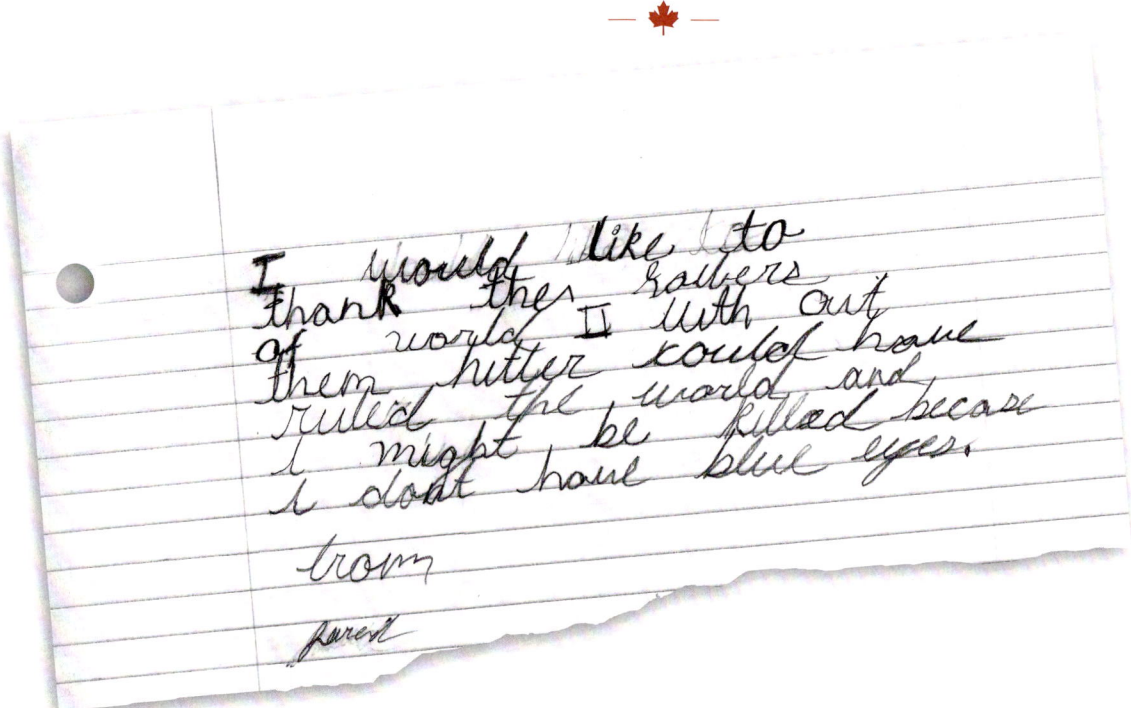

# Look Before You Leap

There was no way he was going to take the easy way out.

GORDON BREGOLISS

Gordon Bregoliss has been a lot of things. A fine baseball pitcher, for starters. And a 14-year member of city council in Kamloops, B.C.

He will grudgingly accept the fact that he may have made a difference during what has been an illustrious lifetime, but you're in for an argument if you dare to call him a war hero.

"Naw," he scoffs. "I was a nobody. I was a foot slogger, just a buck Private." Of his own making, as it turns out.

It's not false modesty. There is nothing false about this man. But don't for a second think the only thing he did was what he was told.

He joined the army straight out of high school. "I guess I was a patriotic Canadian," he says, echoing the words of so many others. "I was physically fit. I wasn't going to sit around waiting to be called. There was a job to be done."

He took his basic training in Victoria, joining the Royal Canadian Horse artillery. Since he had finished school and had his senior matriculation, it was just a matter of weeks before he was promoted to Corporal and made an instructor. He could have taken the easy road, staying in B.C. and paving the way to combat for others, preparing to defend the home front against an enemy that would never arrive, the Japanese. He would have none of that.

"They gave us a test," Gordon says. "The average score was 110 out of 210." He scored 165. "I was given a choice. I could join the Officers' Training Corps or I could drop down in rank and go to Europe."

Six men were given the choice. And six men chose the battlefield over the cushy posting at home. "I guess we must have gotten drunk one night," he jokes.

While war isn't always fair, it can sometimes seem brutally unfair. He spent 178 days in England. "I needed 180 days for the Battle of Britain medal," he says. But he wasn't in it for the medals.

Gordon Bregoliss' war began in Salerno, Italy, in 1943. "Right off the ship and on the line," he says of his baptism by fire. "There wasn't time to be scared."

He fought up the Adriatic side of the country. It was malaria, not the Germans, that felled him. "I lost 40 pounds," he says. But it didn't keep him down. War can also be ironic. His father was of Italian heritage. Although he didn't know it at the time, he came within 20 miles of his cousins. "We've been back four time since the war," he says.

The men who fought in Italy were sometimes called the D-Day Dodgers. Those are fightin' words. Gordon Bregoliss did a lot of things, but he didn't dodge anything.

"When we were pulled out of Italy and landed at Marseilles, the guys wanted to know if we had brought mail from home," he laughs. "We had already been at it for more than a year."

They certainly didn't get the respect they deserved. Knowing what they had done was enough for the men, regardless of what others thought. The battle through Italy, France, Belgium and Holland was hellish – good work was done by great men – but it did have its lighter moments.

"We were in a stationary position for a few days and that meant digging a number of latrines," he says. A big number. "We'd fill up one hole, then just dig another one." There were, obviously, also a number of slit trenches dug. A big number.

A young Gordon Bregoliss, facing page. Although he refers to himself as a buck Private, he was so much more than that.

One morning, the Germans hit them with an artillery barrage. As the Moaning Minnies rained down on them, the men bolted for the nearest hole in the ground. This was one time you didn't want to keep your head up.

"We had this one French Canadian," Gordon says, breaking into hysterics as his mind's eye recaptures the vision. "He dove for a trench."

But it was the wrong trench and he went into the sewage head first, with a splash and a splat.

It has been said many times, but it bears repeating. "War stinks," Gordon laughs. "He didn't dare get out until the shelling stopped and he was quite a sight when he finally did. What a stench."

Talk about a man with no friends. "We killed ourselves laughing," Gordon says. "We didn't want him anywhere near us for a while and we ended up burning his uniform."

Mostly, he says, fighting a war is all business. You find humour when you can, but you have to look for it. If there was a personal highlight, it was the liberation of Rotterdam, in the Netherlands.

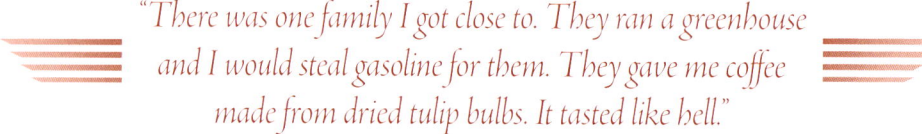

*"There was one family I got close to. They ran a greenhouse and I would steal gasoline for them. They gave me coffee made from dried tulip bulbs. It tasted like hell."*

"The people threw flowers at us. They were 10 or 12 deep, cheering us as we went past. It was something I'll never forget," he says. "It made us feel good. Those poor people had it so tough during the war.

"There was one family I got close to. They ran a greenhouse and I would steal gasoline for them," he says. "They gave me coffee made from dried tulip bulbs. It tasted like hell."

He was just outside the city of Oldenburg, Germany, when the war came to an end. He had no quarrel with the citizens. "The people were fine," he says. "They were all beat up."

The fight had gone out of the German soldier by the end. "I remember sitting on a fence, sunning myself," he says. "One of our guys walked past. He must have had 750 prisoners all by himself. They were singing songs, happy as hell to be done with it."

It was late 1945 when Gordon Bregoliss made it home to Kamloops. "I had a girlfriend when I left, but not when I got back." He planned to resume his budding baseball career, but a bout of tuberculosis put an end to that. He ended up with the B.C. Forestry Service for 33 years, getting into politics along the way.

He and wife Bridget raised three sons and three daughters. Today, he is kept busy with 13 grandchildren, including nine grandsons. "I have my own ball team," he laughs. His best days are when the entire family gets together.

"We're having a dinner tonight, just a small gathering. I think there will be 26 of us," he says. "We did what had to be done."

Life has been full and rewarding, but the haunting images of war have stayed with him and even intensified over the years. "It wasn't really until 1995 and the 50th anniversary that it started to hit me. I guess I had more time on my hands. I still wake up in a cold sweat sometimes."

But he'd do it all over again if asked. "I'm proud that I was a part of it. I don't have any regrets. I'm proud that I'm a veteran. I think my family is proud of me."

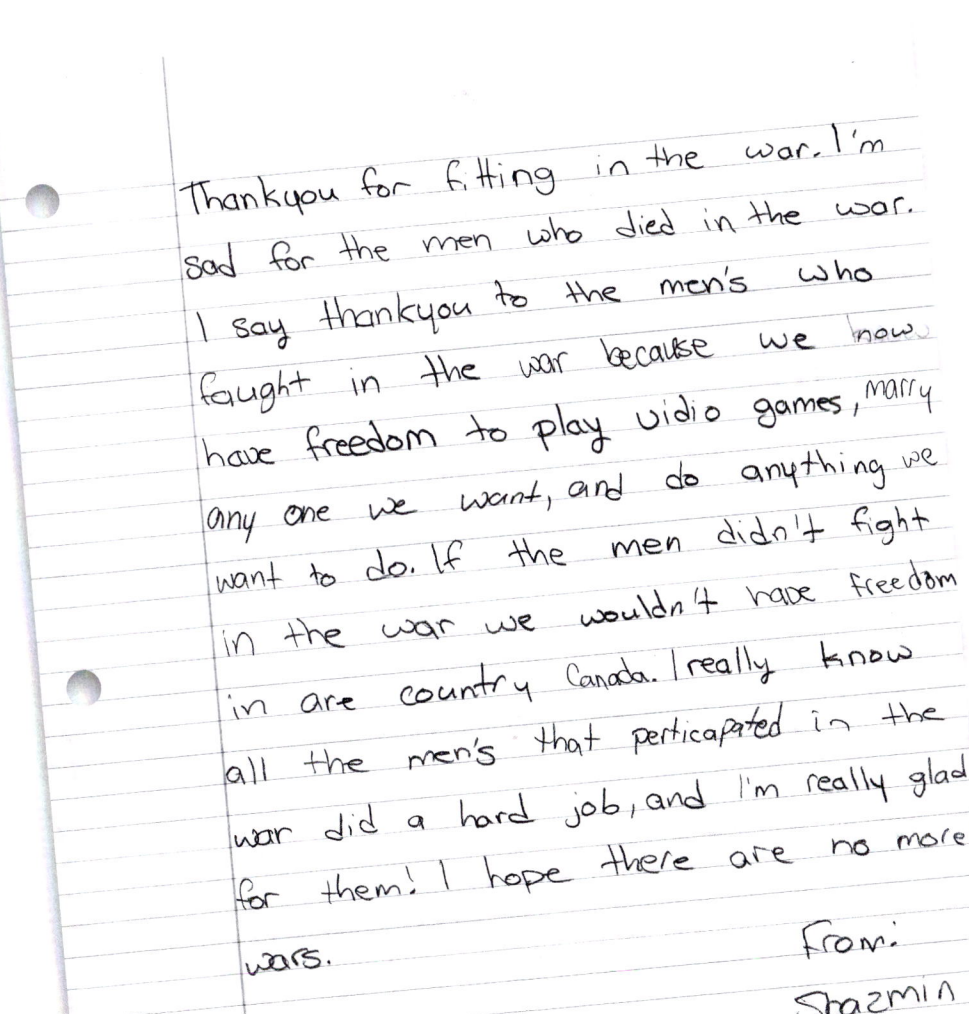

Thankyou for fitting in the war. I'm sad for the men who died in the war. I say thankyou to the men's who faught in the war because we now have freedom to play vidio games, marry any one we want, and do anything we want to do. If the men didn't fight in the war we wouldn't have freedom in are country Canada. I really know all the men's that perticapated in the war did a hard job, and I'm really glad for them! I hope there are no more wars.

From: Shazmin (Shaz)

# Of Friends And Enemies

Four of Canada's finest
go from hell to paradise

BANFF
BOYS

**I**n one sense, they represent four of a kind – brave men who answered Canada's call to arms.

But they're probably best described as a bunch of jokers.

Heroes? "I don't know if the experience turned me into a man," says Bill Waterworth, an 83-year-old lifelong resident of Banff, Alberta. "I just wanted to come home to my mommy."

He was just 19 when he joined the Royal Canadian Air Force. "I wanted to see if I could fly without getting sick." His serial number was R92606. "But the number I used most was J96U121." That was his prisoner-of-war number.

It is a most enjoyable day at Legion Branch 26 in the Alberta mountain resort, talking to four friends who found the best in life after surviving the worst of times. It is both inspirational and hilarious.

George Mandryk, 82, was a 20-year-old in tiny Hairy Hills, Alberta, when he enlisted in the army, eventually commanding a tank with the South Alberta Regiment, 4$^{th}$ Division. "I wanted to see the world and a free trip sounded good," he says.

A cigarette in one hand, a scotch and soda in the other, he tells the story of one harrowing night when a commanding officer had what can best be described as a bit of a brain cramp. George and his gunner were handed sten guns and sent out into the night, on foot, on a scouting mission. Putting it mildly, he was a little out of his element.

"We did what we were told," he says. "But was scary as hell." He calls it the dead of night and that's almost what he was. Or so he thought.

"We saw shadows and movement in the trees up ahead and called in that the Germans were advancing," he says.

He was told to come back to camp. "And don't hestitate." An intense artillery barrage followed, directed at the location on the map he had pinpointed.

"The next morning, we were told that the old man wanted to see us," he says. At first light, another party had been sent forward to check on the damage that had been inflicted on the enemy. What they found were 14 dead cows.

"That was our last recognizance mission," George laughs. "They put me back in my tank where I belonged."

Horace (Hank) Baker was born and raised in Calgary, a strange place for a boy with a great love of the sea. Then again, war never makes sense. He was 18 when he signed up and spent most of his time on a landing craft assault carrier. He was there on D-Day, ferrying troops ashore, trying not to think about what might happen if he stuck his head up an inch too high.

"You did your job," he says. "You did what you were trained to do." It was a hazardous job, but he didn't have to run ashore on Juno Beach.

From left, George Mandryk, Bill Waterworth, Hank Baker and Bob Edwards. The pals for life pose on the main street in Banff, Alberta.

George Mandryk, then and now. Tanks for the memories.

He also took part in landings in southern France and in Greece.

"The boys that went in," he says, shaking his head in admiration. The respect is clear in his 85-year-old voice. "Unbelievable." Looking back, he says, he had it pretty good.

"There was this one time, just off the coast of Naples (Italy)," he says. "The lookout spotted an officer and a local girl "having a go" on the beach. There was an entire flotilla of ships. And, after word leaked out – via loudspeaker – that the view was, well … worthy of viewership, every eye was trained on the couple.

"It was quite a sight," he says. "They didn't know they were entertaining 2,000 men." He pauses. "Or maybe they did."

Between the three of them, George, Bill and Hank have seven children and 10 grandchildren. George and Bill have lost the loves of their lives, but Hank still has his high school sweetheart, Marjorie. They also have four great grandchildren.

"Sharky is the smart one," George says.

That would be gunnery private Bob Edwards, 80, also a lifelong resident of Banff. Never got married. He is also the silent partner in this foursome. "That's because he never had a woman to tell him what to say," one of his buddies explains.

\* \* \*

If there is a comedian in the group, it has to be George Mandryk. Even today, there is no mistaking the mischief. It's a little scary to think what he might have been like as a young man. "I really should have been awarded the Victoria Cross for behaviour," he chuckles.

He'll never forget the parts he can remember from a 48-hour leave spent in Brussels, Belgium. It had been months since his last leave and he didn't want to waste the opportunity.

"I went to the paymaster and told him to give me everything I had," he says, sipping at his scotch. "My first stop was a place they sold liquor so I could load up. It's not like I was short of money."

There were 12 buddies. Today, they might call it a gang. They had one thing in common the next morning. "We were all broke," George laughs. "I had this .38 revolver I always carried. I woke up in a police station with no money and no gun. I'm told I gave it to one of the girls."

This was not the time to head back to camp. He found a buddy and borrowed more money. After all, he was thirsty. "I went through $1,500 in 48 hours. It must have been a record.

"A lot of booze. A lot of girls," George says. "You had to have some fun times."

He was badly injured in 1944 while in Holland. It was just before Christmas.

"We were waiting to cross a river, in the middle of the night. An idiot fell asleep and stepped on the firing switch in our tank." The recoil struck George on the leg. While being transported to a field hospital, the ambulance collided head on with a truck carrying a load of bricks. "Not a good thing," he says. The British doctors wanted to amputate his right leg, but he ended up being shipped to a Canadian hospital, where doctors saved it. He was in hospital 16 months, but he managed to escape on V-E Day.

It takes more than a wobbly limb to keep a good man down. He still had a cast on, but he borrowed a jeep and drove into town. "Was I ever popular. I was the transportation department," he says. "Everything was free in the pubs."

Bill Waterworth: Young and gung-ho.

\* \* \*

Bill Waterworth's story is decidedly different. He was a Flying Officer with the RCAF, assigned as a tail gunner on a Wellington bomber. Most of the missions were over the Ruhr Valley, usually as a Pathfinder, marking targets for those who followed.

"Scared stiff," he says. "The flak was so thick." On his 30th mission, on Sept. 19, 1942, his luck ran out. "We had to jump. The only thing you worry about is landing in the water because you're going to drown."

He spent the next two weeks travelling by night and hiding in barns and haystacks during the day. "I was going in circles," he says. He eventually ran into a priest who took him to a brothel in France. "He said he was going to get me to the Underground, but there were two million

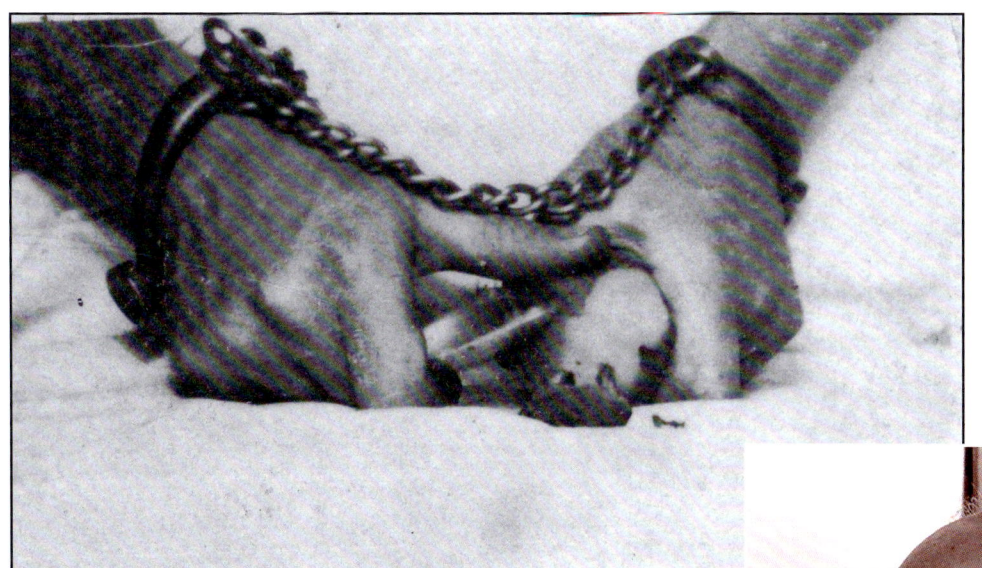

Bill Waterworth peeled more potatoes than he ate during his stay in a POW camp.

Germans searching for the people involved with the Underground."

Ushered out the back door when the enemy walked in the front door, he ran right into a trap. A German soldier was waiting. "For you," he said in broken English, "the war is over." Those are words he will never forget.

Bill spent the rest of the war in a prison camp. It was a horrible life, but it was better than death. It can be tough to find humour and even tougher to count your blessings when it seems like there aren't any. It was hell on earth. He lost more than 50 pounds over the next 30 months.

He lost his left eye when struck by the butt end of a German rifle. There wasn't much to see anyway. "We just walked the perimeter hour after hour, day after day."

The following story must sound much like the one about a man who thought he had it tough because he had no shoes. Then he met a man who had no feet …

"There were two camps, one for the air force and one right next door for the Dieppe and Dunkirk boys," Bill says. "There was this one guy who was really depressed and we had this other fella who was always up. It didn't matter what was happening. I'll never forget him leading the depressed guy over to the wire and pointing out a man on the porch. He had no arms and no legs, but he had the biggest smile on his face."

In a prison camp, it's all about perspective. The food wasn't good, but there

103

A young Hank Baker, left. It wasn't all blood and guts.

was food. There was crap, but also a lot of crap games. And poker games. There was always friendship. Soldiers, sailors and airmen are a tight bunch. Especially on leave. Most took up smoking. Almost all took up drinking.

"Booze and broads," Bill says. "We had this one guy in our crew. Every time Scotty landed at a new camp or went out on the town, he found a new woman. The night we were shot down, he met a girl and she hid him away in her apartment. Not a bad way to spend the war. You gotta admire ingenuity like that."

Even today, when Bill Waterworth flies commercially, he asks for a seat at the back of the plane. "It's the best position," he says. "If you're going down, it's the last thing to hit the ground."

\* \* \*

You don't have to spend much time with Hank Baker to learn you're dealing with a fine gentleman. Most of the time.

He did steal a jeep from the Brits, bring it on board his ship, paint it blue and stick a red maple leaf on the side. Finders-keepers. The lads kept it for all their late-night sojourns until the end of the war, then dumped it in the Thames River.

He recalls an inspection parade when the men were brought to attention. One of them had two condoms pinned to the top of his hat. (Note to kids: Do not use pins to keep condoms in place. Nothing takes the fun out of sex quite like the sound of a baby crying at 3 a.m.)

"The inspection officer didn't say a word to him, but when they got to me, he noticed that my hair was too long. He said it was like seaweed. I was told to explain myself and I said I kept it that way so someone could reach down and grab me if I fell into the water. He was pretty impressed by my answer so he let me keep it."

\* \* \*

Hank Baker today. A gentleman, but that wasn't always the case.

These are impressive men. All four have taken the time to talk to today's youth about their experiences. All four would do it again. "But I probably wouldn't be much use today," says George. "I've probably lost a step or two, but I'm proud of what we did.."

The town of Banff sent 480 men off to war. Twenty-nine never came home. The reunions aren't what they used to be. Most of their comrades are gone now. Every Nov. 11, men like these don their uniforms and march with great pride. Their sacrifices, their commitment and heroism shouldn't be forgotten, but it often is. There are fewer and fewer reunions for old soldiers now, because there are fewer and fewer old soldiers.

"We came back alive, but we lost too many buddies," Bill Waterworth says sadly. "A lot of young people don't have a clue what war is all about. Humans have short memories."

# Where There's Smoke

Tobacco saved David Dickson's life but he doesn't recommend it

David Dickson

David Dickson is a former Major in the Canadian army. He is a former lawyer. He sat on the New Brunswick Court of Queen's Bench and ended his sterling judicial career by spending 30 years on the province's Supreme Court.

Not bad.

This is a man who bought a $1 how-to book and then built his own home from the ground up. Because that's how the book told him to build it. You don't start with a roof, but you do start with a desire to put one over your family's head.

"It was 1951 and I had $1,000 to my name," he says. "I spent $900 on the lot. With the other $100, I bought a power saw, a hammer and a handsaw. I didn't have enough money for a level … so I just eyeballed it."

The home on Alicia Court in Fredericton still looks surprisingly good 55 years later. The walls are straight and true. Like the man himself.

There's little doubt we're dealing with a smart guy. Except for the time he got tossed off a galloping camel in the middle of the Indian desert. (More on that later.)

So it's shocking when he says that smoking saves lives. It's more than a nicotine-stained rule of thumb, according to the experts, that tobacco kills. Not as quickly as a well-placed bullet, of course, but twice as painfully.

David is a rare exception. Smoking probably saved his life that horrible day near Biemen, Germany, where 40 Canadians lost their lives and another 70 were wounded. It was March 25, 1945, a Sunday.

"Wars don't stop on Sunday," he says.

Life can be a game of millimetres. That made all the difference when a German bullet ripped into his stomach and tore out the middle of his back while he was crossing a dike. Doctors believe it struck something that altered its course of destruction.

The bullet went through a tin of tobacco his wife Lorna had sent him. "I didn't like carrying a pouch, so I carried a tin about the size of a can of soup," he says. "When they took my battle dress off, the tin rolled out. It had a hole right through the middle of it. The bullet barely missed my spine. If I hadn't been a smoker … I always felt that it saved me from being a paraplegic or dead."

He thought of both possibilities as he lay there in the mud and his own blood. David Dickson pulled a picture of his family out of a pocket and said goodbye before Bob Muir arrived to pull him off the dike.

"They trimmed up my liver and my lung, and repaired a couple of broken ribs," he says. His war was over.

Details are sketchy, but he does remember being loaded into the field ambulance. At six-foot-four, he was too long for the stretcher. "They banged my head on the steel bulkhead putting me in," he laughs. "Then, my legs were still sticking out when they tried to close the door. They closed the door on my feet."

The field hospital used to be an insane asylum. "Fitting," he says.

He was in a ward with 25 others, including a German Corporal who didn't understand the fuss being made over this newcomer.

"I remember he had to be on his stomach because bullets had ripped down his back," David says. "Because I was the senior officer, the

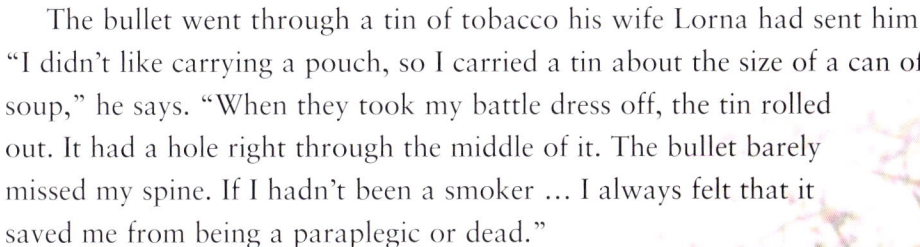

A young David Dickson with his trusty pipe that just might have saved his life.

brass was always coming by to have a picture taken with me. When it was explained to the German who I was, he was flabbergasted. We winked back and forth at each other."

His initial plan was to join the Royal Canadian Air Force. "A bunch of us went down to Moncton. I had read all the magazines and books about the First World War," David says. "I could see myself in a Spitfire, chasing M-109s."

Trouble is, he didn't fit into the cockpit. "They told me they'd call me back. I'm still waiting."

A few months later, while attending university, he opted for the army. "My professors thought I was being very valiant," he laughs. "Actually, it was because I was going to fail all my exams."

He landed in England with the Carlton and York Regiment before being transferred to the North Nova Scotia Highlanders. It would be three years until D-Day, but David Dickson didn't sit around. He got busy.

There just happened to be a photograher around when David Dickson was transported off the battlefield.

"We were in southern England near the tail end of the Battle of Britain, preparing for what we were sure was the German invasion," he says. "A group of officers were in a restaurant having lunch when I noticed an attractive girl sitting nearby. When she left, I followed her outside and asked if she'd like to see a movie that evening."

It was smooth sailing right up until they were to leave on their honeymoon a year later.

David and Lorna were married in Brighton. "The hall cost me a month's pay," he says. And that's not the worst part. "Bill Smith, a fellow officer, was in charge of the luggage. I remember him yelling from the platform as the train started to pull away. 'Don't do anything I wouldn't do, Davey' Lorna poked me in the shoulder. She said, 'Isn't that our luggage beside him?'"

> *A few months later, while attending university, he opted for the army. "My professors thought I was being very valiant. Actually, it was because I was going to fail all my exams."*

It was. But this was their honeymoon. They didn't have much use for clothes. The army's wedding present to the groom was a five-month officers' training course back in Canada. The bride was not happy.

David Dickson landed in France on June 6, 1944 and was one of the first into Caen. He very nearly didn't make it off the ship. The seas were rough that morning. When he went to leap into the landing craft, a wave propelled it away from the ship. Far away. "I think I met the Olympic standard for the standing long jump," he says. "If I had fallen between the ship and the landing craft …"

There is no need to finish that sentence.

His route took him through northern France, across Belgium and Holland and into Germany before his luck ran out in Biemen. There was constant, nerve-wracking pressure, but there were a few laughs along the way.

"I think it was February of 1945. We were on the west bank of the Rhine, occupying a position along a flooded-out dike," he recalls. "We had liberated a distillery a couple days earlier and two guys, a Corporal and a cook, got into the cognac and wandered off. I suspect they were looking for chickens or eggs." Perhaps trying to find out which came first. "But they wound up on the German side. You could see their heads bobbing up and down behind a wall as they walked along. It was like they didn't have a care in the world."

This was not a good time for a visit from Brig. Gen. John Rockingham. "He wanted to know what two men were doing over there, but one of the officers came to their rescue. He said they were on a daylight patrol. The General was some impressed by the courage of his men that day, but they didn't have a clue where they were or what they were doing."

After the war, David Dickson returned to Canada on a hospital ship. Lorna followed a few months later on a ship loaded with war brides. Unlike some of the others, she got off.

"Our first house in St. John had mice," he says. But he made it up to her.

He attended a number, a very large number, of learning institutions. Eventually it was time to go to work. When a friend of his father suggested management with the New Brunswick Liquor Control Board, he went off to St. John Business College to learn shorthand.

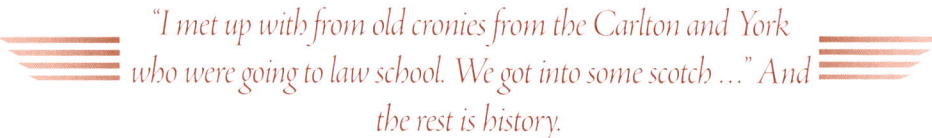

*"I met up with from old cronies from the Carlton and York who were going to law school. We got into some scotch ..." And the rest is history.*

"They gave me 20 books the first day and everybody else in the class was 16 or 17 years old," he laughs. When he arrived late the second day, the teacher demanded that he produce an excuse note. It would have been funny if it wasn't so stupid. He had been old enough to fight for his country. Now he needed an excuse note for being late to shorthand class?

"I met up with from old cronies from the Carlton and York who were going to law school. We got into some scotch ..." And the rest is history. Alcohol, apparently, can be good for you, too. "I turned in my shorthand books and went to law school."

From secretarial studies to the Supreme Court. Impressive.

Along the way, Lorna and David's life together was one long joyride until he lost her in 1993. They had two children. He now has two grandchildren in the area. "I've never taken life too seriously," he says.

Except when it comes to lawn bowling, where he still competes at the highest levels. He has been a licensed fishing guide and a member of the Canadian tuna fishing team. Which is shocking because it's hard to believe there is such a thing. At the age of 77, he climbed Mt. Everest, reaching a height of 18,000 feet.

Then there was that notorious camel incident in India.

"My stirrups were too big and I couldn't control her. I fell off and tore my wrist open," he laughs. "Our guide kept calling me Awrence. It was explained to me that he thought I was Lawrence of Arabia, charging ahead to the next oasis, but I was just trying to hold on.

"I've been carried away many times."

When he got to the hospital, "if you can call it that," they operated on his leg.

He is still running along, going strong at the age of 85.

"It has been a good life," he says. "Every day is a new adventure and every year gets better and better. My only problem these days is premature rigor mortis."

David Dickson has returned to Biemen twice since the war. He has no quarrel with the German people. "I don't think of them as enemies," he says. "That's really what led to the plaque …"

Yes, the plaque. Six years ago, he was instrumental in having it placed at the scene of the battle as a tribute to the men on both sides who fell that day. It was, at least at the time, the only plaque of its kind placed on German soil by that country's Second World War enemy.

He looks back at his wartime experience fondly. He found a wonderful wife. And, in a sense, he found himself. "Those were formative years for a lot of young men," he says.

It is suggested that there were heroes on both sides. He shrugs his shoulders. "Not me," he says.

By the way, he doesn't smoke anymore.

Miraculously, David Dickson has lived a full life. "I've been carried away many times," he says.

# A Bit Of Mischief

'If it was your turn,
it was your turn.'

Tom Ford admits there might be a person – or 27 – who would suggest the inside of his head is an awful waste of space. Anyone who has tried to keep him in line, for example.

As a Sherman tank gunner during the brutal Italian Campaign, he had good aim. But he didn't always aim to please.

He was an officer. And then he wasn't. He was an officer. And then he wasn't. Sergeant one night, Private the next morning. "After a while," laughs the 82-year-old, "I didn't bother sewing my stripes on. I just pinned them on."

It was an empty wallet, not an empty head, that led to a full, rich life in Yorkton, Sask.

After the Second World War, he ran into his brother in Vancouver. The two of them bought train tickets and headed East, but they didn't get very far. "We ran out of money in Yorkton and had to stop and find work on a farm." It was the spring of 1947. By the fall, he was in love. Tom and Kathleen Ford have been married 58 years. Together, they raised four sons and a daughter. They have 10 grandchildren and four great grandchildren.

His superior officers would not believe the difference a good woman can make. "I got into a bit of mischief," he winks.

Born and raised in Humbolt, Sask., he was one of 10 children. "My parents wanted me out of the house as quickly as possible when I turned 18. There was no work and I had to find a way to live. Joining up was the thing to do. I guess staying home would have been more sensible, so that must mean there were a lot of stupid people." He takes pride in being one of them.

Small in stature, he was the perfect fit for a tank. After training in Regina and Camp Borden in Ontario, he boarded the *Queen Mary*, bound for England and eventually Italy.

"Sick as a dog," he says. "I was too sick to be scared. I haven't been on a boat since I got home from the war and I have no intention of ever getting on one again."

The first things he learned at the holding unit in Aldershot is that men have to stick together. "We were called out one day and the commanding officer informed us – in no uncertain terms – that a mother and father were bringing their daughter in." She was pregnant and one of us, a fellow who had been wearing a patch over his right eye, was responsible.

When the troops assembled the next morning, every man wore a patch over his right eye. "Brothers stick together."

The second thing he learned is that you have to protect your helmet at all times. Even when you're sleeping. Especially when you're sleeping.

"Guys would come back from the pub," he says, not really making it clear whether he was one of those guys. And, well … it was dark. Either that or there was a plan and a purpose. "Guys would wake up the next morning, put their helmet on, and it was full of (pee)."

The memory cracks him up. "Poor bastards."

Italy and Sicily were hell on earth. In 20 months of fighting, 25,264 Canadians were injured and 5,900 died. Every Allied advance was met with fierce resistance.

"We were just a bunch of kids," Tom says. "You didn't give a damn. You didn't think about dying. If you made it to tomorrow, fine. That's just the way it was. If it was your turn, it was your turn." The ordeal was easier on him than it was on most. "I can find humour at a funeral," he says.

But not necessarily in a chicken coop.

Tom Ford: A small man made a big contribution.

113

"We made camp in an orchard and camouflaged the tank for the night," he says. "Somebody noticed a barnyard and we knew from past experience that meant chickens." Tom and two other guys were selected for this important mission.

"It was pitch dark, but we could tell there were some other guys in there with the same idea," he says. "All hell broke loose, but we didn't want to shoot anybody because we had no idea who we were shooting. We just got the hell out of there." No chickens.

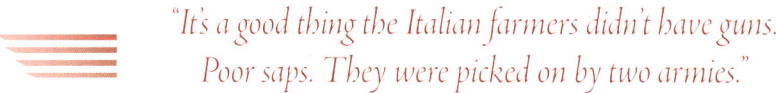

*"It's a good thing the Italian farmers didn't have guns. Poor saps. They were picked on by two armies."*

"We did a lot of stupid things," he admits.

Like using diesel fuel to burn the hair off a pig they ... borrowed. "Not a good idea," he says. "It ruined the pig. The damn thing was rotten. It's a good thing the Italian farmers didn't have guns. Poor saps. They were picked on by two armies."

They had to rob from the poor to give to the poorer, because the other option was mutton. Always mutton. "The food was horrible. To this day," he says, "I cannot look a sheep in face."

It's one thing to ruin a man's dinner. It's something else, something much worse, to ruin a man's drink. Italy meant there was always wine. That doesn't mean it was always drinkable. Like the man said, "We did a lot of stupid things."

"We traded gasoline for wine a lot of times, but we only put it in jerry cans once," Tom laughs. "When we poured it out it was black and probably poision. It actually started to eat the can."

The fighting was fierce, but there were good times. "You could get almost anything with cigarettes and chocolate," he says. "When it came to wine, we'd say, 'Oh, this is really good. It has been aged for two days.'"

There was a crew of five in Tom Ford's tank. And there was always a bottle of whiskey. "Just in case," he says. In the army, the most important thing is preparation.

It was in the fall of 1944, when German forces withdrew to what was known as the Gothic Line, a string of heavily-fortified positions north of Florence, that Tom Ford became a casualty of war. His tank was knocked out in battle and he sustained injuries to both arms during a nighttime counter attack.

Don't let the stern look on his face fool you. Tom Ford is no meanie.

He was sent back to Canada in December. "I wanted to stay," he says. "I wanted to be with the boys when they got to Holland." It is a regret that gnaws at him to this day.

The regrets, however, are few. "I'd do it all again," he says, "in a minute. I wouldn't hesitate."

Tom Ford, like most men who put their country first, is a proud man. He knows what was fighting for. He sees her almost every day, when his great granddaughter Erica marches, literally, around the house.

"She stops and salutes the flag," he says proudly. She is too young to realize she is actually saluting great grandpa.

Ready for action: Fred Burton dreamed of taking flight.
Going up was fun, but coming down could be hell.

# 'A Tin Can On Wheels'

'You made the most of your time on the ground.'

Fred Burton

Like a lot of young boys growing up in Lethbridge, Alberta, Fred Burton used to look to the sky and dream of taking flight. What could be better than that?

As an adult, if you can call a 20-year-old an adult, there were times when he wondered what could possibly be worse. The going up was the fun part, but the coming down could be hell. Your throat is no place for your heart.

"A tin can on wheels," he says of the Lancaster bomber he flew 20 missions in, most of them over the heartland of German industry, the Ruhr Valley. "We called it Happy Valley," he says with a chuckle. Their plane had no armour and only eight .303-calibre machine guns. Even on the move, it was a sitting duck for enemy fighters and anti-aircraft fire.

At 82, sitting in the comfort of his living room, he can laugh now.

He was 19 when he joined the Royal Canadian Air Force in 1942. "I wanted to be a pilot, like everybody else, but I buggered the exam," he admits sheepishly.

He wound up as a wireless operator, putting his life literally in someone else's hands.

But they were good hands. Bob Wall was the pilot for the seven-man crew. "A great man," Fred says. "We would have followed him anywhere." Not that they had any choice.

Every time they went up, there was a good chance they wouldn't return. On almost every sortie, one or more crews didn't. On average, five per cent of the bombers sent out each night failed to return. Service in bombers was

Fred Burton today. For him, he says, the war actually ended too soon.

considered the most dangerous job in the military.

The Lanc was the Bomber Command workhorse, carrying 64% of the total tonnage dropped by RAF and RCAF crews during the Second World War. There were 3,932 Lancasters lost and 55,000 aircrew, including 10,000 Canadians.

In the air, luck was your only ally. There were many close calls. He remembers nights when the flak was so thick it was like tinsel. "You bastards can't hit us," he said during one mission. Seconds later, shrapnel tore through the plane. "Oh, I guess you can."

Another time, they returned with 16 holes in the old girl, including one just behind Fred Burton's head. "There were anxious times, but I was never really scared," he says. "Too stupid to be scared. Besides, there wasn't time for that."

Not that there weren't good times in the air.

"One of the guys had the switch the wrong way when we were over England," he says, "and we dropped thousands of 'surrender' leaflets."

Another time, during a recon mission when the war was over, they buzzed an old outhouse. "You had to have a few laughs," he says. "This old girl came running out with her pants down."

When the war in Europe ended, the first thing the crewmembers did was re-up to fight the Japanese, but that war in the Pacific ended before they could get into it. Breaking up and heading their separate ways was one of the hardest things they had to do.

Looking back, it's the camaraderie he remembers. The crew members were more than best friends. In fact, he says, "We were closer than brothers." Five of the seven are still alive. "We still keep in contact. There is a special bond," he says.

Stationed near Leeming, in Yorkshire, there were plenty of pubs and lots of poker.

"You made the most of your time on the ground, because you never knew if you were going to be here the next day. We hated the Polish crews because they were good dancers," he says. "They got all the girls."

Well, not all of them. One night

changed his life. "I met Mollie at a dance," he says, smiling over at his war bride. They were married Sept, 29, 1945. Last year marked their 60th wedding anniversary.

"I thought he was in his right mind," she says. "It turns out I was sadly mistaken"

Then he had to go and invite her to live in Canada and ruin her good first impression. "She arrived in Calgary on April 1, 1946," he laughs. "April Fool's Day."

It was a tough transition for Mollie, but the fact she got pregnant almost immediately made running back to England impossible. They had four daughters. They now have eight grandchildren and eight great grandchildren.

Fred Burton came out a Warrant Officer and is a life member of Royal Canadian Legion Branch 4 in Lethbridge. After the war, he farmed for 25 years, worked for the post office and became a respected auctioneer. He still does various charity events in southern Alberta.

Regrets? "Only one. We needed 10 more missions for our tour operations badge. The war ended too soon."

Fitting. Like so many others, he wanted to do more.

Members of the air and ground crews pose with the Allied workhorse, a Lancaster bomber.

# Of Dogs And Craps

'I've never been one to elaborate on the grim side of war. It serves no purpose.'

Albert Threatful

Albert Threatful was just 18 when he hitched a ride on a westbound freight train, from his home in Revelstoke, B.C. to Vancouver. It was the spring of 1940. The world was at war and he wasn't about to miss all the excitement.

"There's no fun in that," he says.

It is early in the morning and the bar's not open in his hometown Royal Canadian Legion branch. Too bad. "I could use a little memory juice," laughs the 84-year-old former communications officer with the 5$^{th}$ Armoured Division. "That's when the BS really starts to flow."

He was sent overseas in 1943 and fought up through Italy, France and the Netherlands, after beginning his trek to victory in Algiers, North Africa.

"It was," he says, "a hellva time, a depressing time. I've never been one to elaborate on the grim side of war. It serves no purpose. I put it out of my mind."

The lighter side is another story. Which is good, because that's what we're after.

"Personally," he says with a wry grin, "I was pretty well behaved for a guy known for his misbehavior. Except for that time I overstayed my leave by about 36 hours. I guess I got lost."

It has been said there are no atheists in a foxhole. Albert laughs and shakes his head as a memory pops into it. "We had this padre," he begins. "We were going into a battle for a bridge in a particularly stubborn spot and many of the men where reinforcements who had never seen any real action. He gave us all quite a lecture, saying, 'You must have faith that you can overcome any obstacle.'

Albert Threatful was without his trusty "memory juice," but the memories of his time at war are something he will never forget.

"We hadn't made much headway by morning, so the men were sent back to the rear in twos and threes to eat. It was a scary trip because you were totally exposed both ways. We knew that if you could hear a shell, you didn't have to worry about it, but the padre didn't know that. One came over and up went his soup, down went his coffee, and he made a dive for the nearest haystack. One of the guys said, 'There goes Old Faithful himself.' The human element creeps in."

At one point, Albert came down with yellow jaundice and was sent to hospital. Upon his release, he was sent to a reinforcement depot, but that was not the place he wanted to be. "I wanted to be back with my buddies," he says.

 *"The courage they showed was inspiring. I'll never forget that. It made me proud to be a Canadian."*

As luck would have it, a Lieutenant from his old unit happened by and spotted him.

"Get in," he said "You're coming with me."

On the way back, they passed an officers' club. The Lieutenant tossed him one of his coats with the appropriate insignia. "Consider yourself promoted," he said.

"We had a grand old time," Albert chuckles. "There was plenty to drink." Unfortunately, the promotion only lasted a short time and was a one-time thing.

Albert Threatful began the war as a Private and ended the war as a Private. "I was a little too rang-tang. I guess I just wasn't suitable to be in charge," he says. "Besides, I didn't want the responsibility." It was harrowing enough worrying about his own hide without having the fate of others resting on his sometimes-questionable decisions. Those who were in charge impressed him greatly.

While the British brass would conduct their war from the safety of the rear, the Canadian commanders, he says, were right there on the front lines, side by side with their men. "The courage they showed was inspiring. I'll never forget that," he says. "It made me proud to be a Canadian."

The constant as the tanks rolled up through Italy was wine. "We always had gallons of the vino," he says.

The other constant was craps. And it had nothing to do with a latrine.

It didn't matter where they were. Even a brief lull in the shelling meant the bones came out and the groundsheet went down. "Even in the mud. The game was the most important thing." When the shelling started, the men grabbed their money and dove for the nearest hole in the ground. When it stopped, they scrambled back into the open and the game continued. The guy who was down wasn't always wounded or killed.

"The game slowed down, but it never stopped." When you talk about luck and gambling, winning didn't mean nearly as much as living.

War turns boys into men very quickly, but a soft side remained for even the most hardened vet. "We had this little mascot dog, Sparky. We'd lose him from time to time. Sometimes he'd be gone two or three days, but he always showed up. The artillery shells might be exploding around us. No matter what the danger, I can still hear the guys: 'Is Sparky all right?' It was a sad day when we finally lost him."

Bitterness? Yes, with a touch of irony and humour. "When we met up with the guys who landed in France, they called us the D-Day Dodgers," Albert says. "We were there before they were. We did our part."

He suggests much of the everyday humour is lost on those who never experienced the war. But not all of it.

"There was this (place) where there were seven or eight ladies," he laughs. "It was an old factory and the boys would have to take their coats off and line up. The only thing the girls knew how to say was, 'OK, next.'" Love and war. Even if it wasn't true love.

It was possible to get almost anything by trading a bar of soap. Especially wine. "I remember the old Italian peasants were so friendly. Christmas Eve of 1944, an elderly couple invited us in for dinner. They had no shoes, but they shared what they had. Momma made spaghetti and we all ate out of the same bowl. It's the hospitality of the people that sticks with me. It was a different Christmas and I remember it every year on Dec. 24."

War is not an exact science, but some mistakes are bigger than others. As the Allies overran German positions and the front line became blurred, the Germans would flee their tanks and hightail it out of there. Left in perfect working order, it wasn't uncommon to find six or eight with the enemy insignia being used against them. Then one day they ran into a genius.

The German commander showed up, pulled into formation at the back of the line and came along for the ride for a couple of hours. Then he peeled off into the forest and was gone.

Albert Threatful shakes his head in amazement and grudging admiration. "It was pretty impressive. It would have been a shame to shoot that guy."

Then he wonders out loud when the bar opens.

# 'Six Square Meals A Day'

The Lifer and the Laugher somehow managed to stay afloat

BREWSTER & WILSON

Rollie Phillips tells the story. It just wasn't meant to be for a groom-to-be. Too much of a good thing can be a very bad thing. A fella ending up passed out on a train in Vancouver. Which wouldn't have been so bad if it wasn't headed for Regina.

"Of course we put him there," he chuckles. "It seemed like a good idea at the time."

Even your most basic of training should teach you to keep your eyes open at all time. Friends can be every bit as dangerous as foes.

"Never saw him again," Rollie says. "We just propped him up on a seat and left him there. I have serious doubts that he made it to the wedding."

Fate doesn't always smile on you and karma has a way of evening out. "I coughed my teeth into the toilet once," he points out.

John Aulin smiles knowingly. "We were at Camp Borden," he says. "I threw a bucket of cold water on this guy who was taking a shower and I made tracks with him right behind me. I laughed like a damn fool, but not as much as the three nurses who happened to be standing outside. They got an eyeful."

Every town has a war hero, because anyone who has ever fought for their country is a war hero. Some made a career out of it. Some didn't last a week. The picturesque B.C. interior town of Chase is no different. The old warriors meet every morning, 10:30 sharp, at Royal Canadian Legion Branch 107. It's more about the camaraderie than the coffee.

Harry Brewster is on his second cup when Joe Wilson walks in with a bad limp and a friendly wave. Even in old age, kidding each other is the

Harry Brewster, left, and Joe Wilson pose together at the Legion branch in Chase, B.C.

first order of business. "Here comes a real hero," Harry says. "This guy is looking for funny stuff that happened in the war, Joe. Did you do any laughing in the lifeboat?"

No, he did not.

Harry wanted to be a gunner but wound up in the stoke hole. It was a dangerous place to be, but you learn to look on the bright side. "At least we were warm," he says.

Why would a kid from tiny Dadsland, Sask., choose the navy? "The uniform," he says. And his lot in life at the bow of the ship, under the water line? "I wanted to shoot somebody, but it would have been dangerous to give me a gun. I was colour blind."

There was an obligation and a duty that almost every young man felt during the Second World War. "You couldn't sit at home," he says.

Harry saw six ships become victims of U-boat torpedoes during his North Atlantic runs between Halifax, New York and Newfoundland.

He's not sure how close his ship came to being hit. "That's the thing," he says. "You never knew."

Joe Wilson knew. It was April 16, 1945, just 22 days before the end of the war. "It was 6:30 in the morning. I had just come on watch when I heard a bang and everything went silent," he says. His ship, the Bangor-class minesweeper HMCS *Esquimalt*, was hit and almost immediately began its journey to the bottom of the ocean.

The *Esquimalt* was just outside Halifax harbour, on anti-submarine patrol. Joe was at the stern, manning the detection equipment, when the torpedo from U-190 struck its intended target. "I guess I didn't detect that one," he says.

He's not sure how he made it into the water, but staying alive that long was the easy part. At 4 C, the ocean was often referred to as liquid death.

It was a cruel twist of fate that people on shore saw the Carley floats in the water and thought they were little recreational fishing boats. Even crueler, HMCS *Esquimalt* was the final Canadian warship to be sunk during the war. Of the 71 men on board, only 27 were alive 6½ hours later when sister ship HMCS *Sarnia* arrived to lend assistance.

"Hypothermia got them," Joe says sadly. "A lot more than 27 got into the water." The years have not dulled the pain. It's OK for a grown man to cry. "I had a hard time for a while, but I came to the conclusion that I couldn't do anything about it." He says. "For a long time, every time I talked about it, I cried."

The minesweeper HMCS Esquimalt on patrol before it became the final Canadian warship to be torpedoed and sunk by a German submarine, on April 16, 1945.

There is an uncomfortable silence before Harry rescues the situation.

"Good eatin' in the navy, eh, Joe," he says lightly, a big smirk on his face. "When it came to food, you had two choices – take it or leave it. You could eat or you could starve."

"Six square meals a day," Joe says.

Harry nods. "Three going down," he says.

"And three coming up," Joe says.

They are old, weathered and worn, but still not worn out. That's one of the things that makes them so delightful. Harry is 83. "The old man," Joe says. And Joe is 82. "The young punk," Harry says.

They carry on like school kids. While they never served together, the fact that they did serve constitutes an unbreakable bond. There is no shortage of pride. And rightfully so.

While Harry served his country, including volunteering to go to Japan when the war in Europe ended, he was happy to get out when the fighting stopped. "The first thing I did was try to drink the brewery dry," he says. "I did my best, but they made more beer than I could drink."

He went on to work mostly in construction. Fifteen years ago, on a vacation trip from Vancouver to Edmonton, he and his wife stopped overnight in Chase to visit friends. They fell instantly in love with the place and wound up buying a house. They've been here ever since. He has two daughters and four granddaughters. "I specialize in girls," he says.

Harry Brewster finds himself thinking back to those days more and more as the years go by. "I have a stomach full of ulcers," he says.

There were some fun times, but it was certainly more work than play. "There were a lot of arguments but very few fistfights. Scores were going to be settled after the war, but we never saw each other again when it was over."

Navy life, he says, stinks. "The ship was your home, but it was close quarters all of the time and it got a little ripe." To make matters worse, he says, "the last place you wanted to be if a torpedo hit was in the shower. We didn't spend a lot of time in there."

Joe Wilson was a five-year-old boy when his parents emigrated to

Joe Wilson, in a bar, with a drink in his hand. Imagine that.

Canada and settled in Prince Albert, Sask. He always knew he would serve his new country one day. As for which branch of the service, it didn't really matter to him. "Whoever would have me," he says.

As a teenager, he joined the local militia. "I was gung-ho to go when war broke out, but the militia wasn't being mobilized," he says. He tried to convince a recruiter that he was 21. "No you're not," the recruiter said. So he went back to school. "I dropped by every once in a while to see if they would have me."

He counted the days until becoming old enough to fight for his country, this time opting for the navy. But he should have spent more time at that school. He failed to read the fine print. He had no idea he was signing on for seven years with the permanent force. "That was my first mistake," he laughs.

But he soon discovered that it wasn't a mistake, at all. He fell in love with the sea. "I just sort of took to it," he says. "I loved every damn day of it. Every ship I sailed on was different, but every ship was a good ship. The comradeship was something special."

So was Canada's contribution to the Battle of the Atlantic. Thanks to people like Harry Brewster and Joe Wilson, this country became a naval superpower. In 1939, Canada could muster only six destroyers and five small minesweepers. The permanent force numbered a paltry 1,800. By 1945, Canada boasted a fleet of 373 fighting ships and a force of 113,000 men and women. At the height of the war, Canada supplied nearly half of the escort ships for convoys between North America and Britain.

There is a quiet dignity about Joe Wilson. His Legion jacket is covered with 17 medals. "Seven on the right side and 10 on the left," he says. It is not a boastful statement. Harry is proud to know this fellow. "Joe is one of the special ones," he says.

When Joe closes his eyes, he still sees friends slipping off the Carley floats and disappearing beneath the waves. When he opens them, he is standing beside Werner Hirschmann at the 60th anniversary of the sinking of *HMCS Esquimalt* on April 16, 2005, in Esquimalt, B.C.

Hirschmann was an engineer on the U-boat that sunk the ship that day.

He has been a fixture at the ceremony marking the event for the past 10 years. Anger and bitterness? There is none of that.

"Sailors have one common enemy and that is the sea," Hirschmann told the *Victoria Times Colonist* newspaper in 2005. He is not an unwelcome man, having emigrated to the country he fought against after the war. He is an honorary life member of the HMCS Equimalt Association. Instead of awkward silence, he is met with hugs.

"He was doing his job and I was doing mine," Joe Wilson says. "He's a good guy and I'm glad he comes."

After his seven-year tour, Joe signed on for seven more. Then seven more. He retired from the Royal Canadian Navy after 25 years and 29 days, after also serving in the Korean War. He eventually became an anti-submarine instructor stationed in Dartmouth, Nova Scotia.

"Time of my life," he says. In all those years, he spent only 24 hours in the brig. "What can I say, I was a good boy."

Apparently he learned to do what he was told. He went into farming. Why? "Because my wife said so," he laughs. "I didn't know the first thing about it, but I learned the ropes." They had a good life together even when his job forced them to be apart so much, adopting two children.

He lost her in 1994, but now has a new companion, and five new adopted children. He moved to Chase 10 years ago.

Both Harry Brewster and Joe Wilson have been zone commanders and Legion branch presidents.

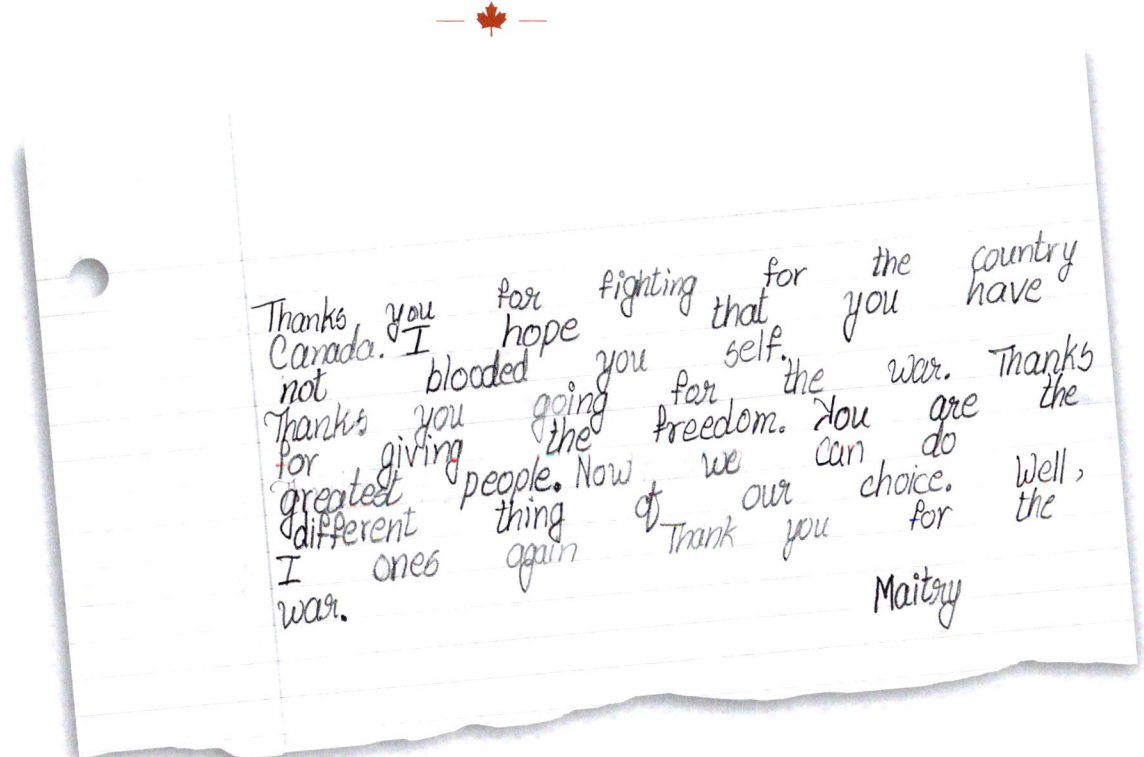

Muriel Kochanski, left, and Peter Guthrie. The same, only different.
Two great friends and one laugh after another.

# Two For The Show

## Legionnaires for a hundred years and a million laughs

GUTHRIE & KOCHANSKI

To look at them, you can't see how Peter Guthrie and Muriel Kochanski could be any more different.

One is a man born in Scotland, the other a woman born in Saskatoon. One was with the Royal Navy, the other with the Canadian Women's Army Corps.

Listen to them, however, and it's obvious the two longtime friends are the proverbial two peas in a pod. To say they're characters does not do their personalities justice. Because they are so close, they wanted to be interviewed together at the Royal Canadian Legion in Regina.

Muriel was a driver for all the "big-wigs." It was a good gig that took her to virtually all corners of the country. "There were only three females in the garage," she giggles. "I had 2,300 men under me." Nudge-nudge, wink-wink. Talk about having your pick of the litter.

Peter remembers the night the canteen caught on fire when he was stationed in Sri Lanka. As catastrophes go, they don't come much worse than this. It was a real, honest-to-goodness rescue mission.

"THE BEER WAS IN THERE," he shouts. "You never saw so many brave sailors in your life. They literally ran right into the flames."

Muriel is 81 and Peter is 80, both going on 12.

She describes herself as a railroad brat. "I was a street kid. I raised hell a little bit," she says. The army gave her discipline and a sense of purpose. She weighed all of 98 pounds when she joined in 1942, but she was no 98-pound weakling. Muriel never left Canada, but that doesn't mean her life wasn't in jeopardy. She knows many of the officers' wives wanted to kill her.

"We were in Ottawa. The officers partied with their wives, but the women never cleaned up," she says. "I was sick and tired of cleaning up after the wives." So she told them so. It was a little icy for a while.

A lot of the women who joined the service couldn't exactly be described as worldly.

"We were in Prince Albert (Sask.)," she says. "One of the girls went to use the washroom and came back to the barracks very impressed that there was a place to wash your feet. It was the trough in the men's washroom."

Her husband of 59 years, Edward, was with the Manitoba Dragoons. He drove a tank in the war, she says, "but he won't drive a car. He doesn't even have a licence." She calls their wedding day a day of infamy, "like Pearl Harbour."

 *"They sent me to cooking school. No matter how hard I didn't try, I still passed."*

She is kidding, of course. She is always kidding. Her husband is of Polish decent. "I've had a lot of Pole in 59 years," she says. And there's that mischievous wink again.

Muriel and Edward have been heavily involved in the Regina branch for years. They give to the Children's Hospital every year. They make a difference. And they continue to live happily ever after.

On the day of our visit, Edward is hard at it peeling potatoes for a special Year-Of-The-Veteran dinner. "Business as usual," he says.

"We've had our ups and downs," she says. Edward, the strong, silent type, has learned to just shake his head and continue on. He has heard it all before.

After the war, she drove a taxi, worked for the Royal Canadian Mounted Police in the office and was a Girl Guide leader.

Peter Guthrie was only 17 when he volunteered for the navy in 1942. "I tried the army and the air force, but I couldn't report right away and I wanted to get started," he says.

He wouldn't have been in such a hurry if he'd known what was in store for him. "You're this, you're that," he says. "In my case, I was a cook. They sent me to cooking school. No matter how hard I didn't try, I still passed. I can still cook.

"But he doesn't," says his wife Thomasina. Peter smiles and winks. "You don't survive a war by being an idiot," he explains.

He spent the war years on minesweepers and gun boats and came to Canada in 1951, because his sister married a Canadian and moved across the pond. Four children, eight grandchildren and two great grandchildren later, their love endures.

"This is home," he says. "I'm proud to be a Canadian. This is the greatest country in the world."

And, thanks to his experiences in the '40s, he has seen the world. "I visited the Taj Mahal," he says. "I went wild elephant hunting and tiger hunting near Calcutta, India. I had great experiences, things that will stay with me forever." And he cooks some mean scrambled eggs.

His 19th birthday was memorable. If he could only remember more than little bits and pieces.

"I was only allowed to have two beers, but I think I had more than that," he says. "We captured an Italian ship that was loaded with beer and a fight ensued. I remember standing on a table, cheering everybody on. And that's the last thing I remember. I woke up back on board the ship, but I don't remember how I got there."

He also doesn't remember how his tattoos got there. "They just showed up one morning," he says.

Peter fondly remembers the Burmese people. "Great people. They would give you their last piece of bread," he says.

Between the two of them, they have been Legion members for almost 100 years. Between the two of them, they have had a million laughs.

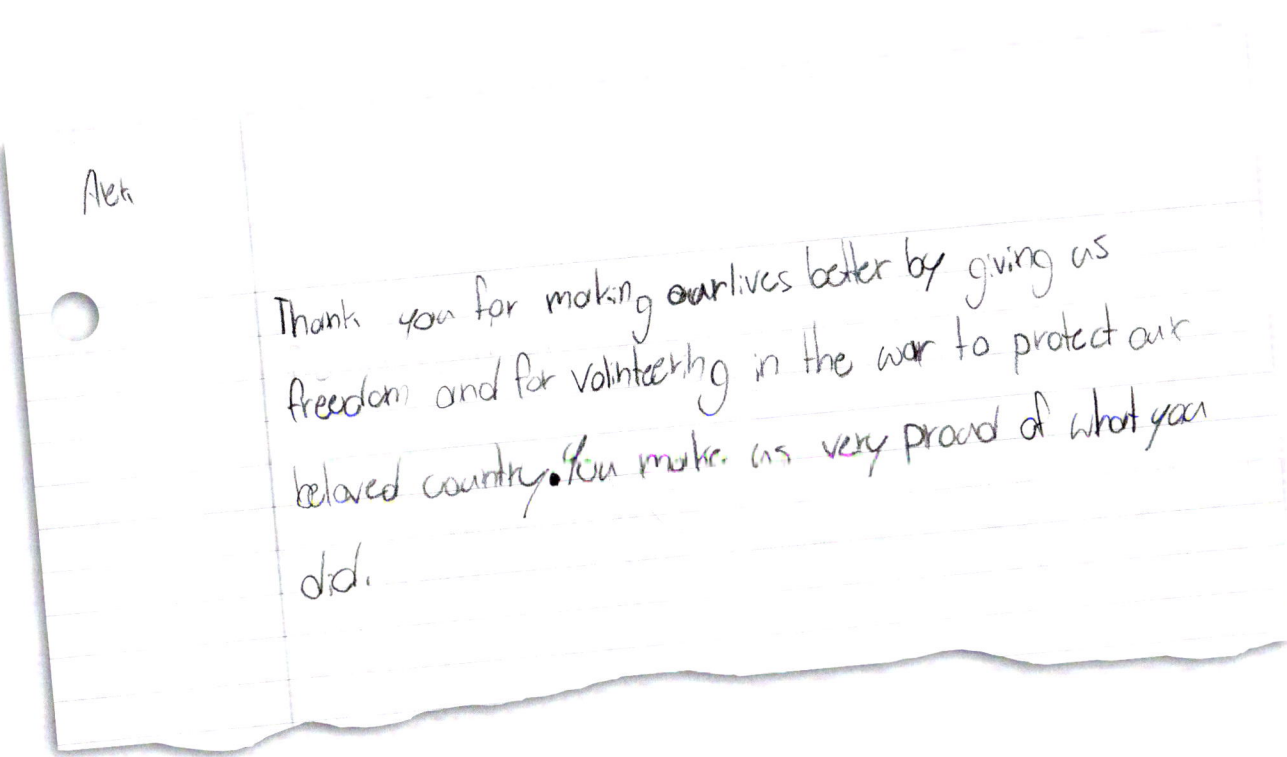

Alex

Thank you for making our lives better by giving us freedom and for volunteering in the war to protect our beloved country. You make us very proud of what you did.

# 'Anybody Want A Roll?'

### Two of the very best kind at their absolute worst

Lunchtime at Royal Canadian Legion Branch 6 in Moncton must be much like lunchtime in a reform school cafeteria – totally unpredictable. And usually unacceptable.

Truth be told, which isn't very often the case, there is precious little reforming going on. You almost expect a food fight to break out at any moment. That's the level of maturity we're dealing with.

"Of all the stories you've heard, how many do you believe?" Gerald Murphy wonders.

"I'm up to three now."

"You'll still be at three when you leave here," he chuckles. "This is no place to come if you're looking for facts. There's enough fertilizer around here to grow a good lawn, I'll tell you that."

The way the shots are flying, it's almost like a war zone. Introductions are made.

"Don't get up."

"I can't."

Ken Duke makes his grand arrival. "Here comes the Duke of Hazard," somebody says.

It's the friendship and the camaraderie that matter most to these people. If you're coming, leave your feelings at home. "Did you see Bill? He doesn't look too good. Then again, he never did."

Bear in mind, you only insult your friends.

A female server comes by the table with an offer than cannot be ignored.

"Anybody want a roll?" she asks. It is an innocent question, but the boys snicker like a bunch of seven year olds. She shakes her head, smiles in defeat and moves on to the next table. "Why do I bother?"

M & M, Gerald Murphy and Henry McGlynn, are at the centre of much of the nonsense. Both are 87 years young and overflowing with life. Henry was born in England and joined the Royal Air Force. Gerald was born in West Bathurst, New Brunswick, and joined the army.

Why the army? "He needed a new pair of shoes," Henry says. Actually, it was because he had two brothers in the navy and his mother didn't really want the whole family going down with the ship.

Bill LeBlanc happens by the table. "I'm looking for information," he says, but it's hard to believe he can see anything out of those Coke-bottle glasses. He is quite clearly a ringleader in this little gang, but nobody seems very willing to follow along.

This is a special occasion because residents of the nearby veterans' home are in attendance. But that doesn't exactly mean the regulars are on their best behaviour. There is a special bond between these men and women. Even if they were in different parts of the service or different parts of the world during the Second World War, they were all in it together during their glory days.

You can probably tell who the troublemaker is. Henry McGlynn, left, and Gerald Murphy up to no good, as usual, at the Legion in Moncton.

Gerald was at Dunkirk in the spring of 1940. He describes it as "organized confusion." The newsreels at the time didn't begin to tell the story. "You didn't hear the noise, the screeching and the screaming," he says. "It was all cleaned up."

Humour had a way of sneaking into tragedy. "You laughed when you could and maybe even when you shouldn't," Henry says.

"The Battle of Britain was the worst," he says. "We were literally fighting for our lives. I remember this one German raid. They hit us pretty good. When it was over, one of the guys called me up on a roof and we looked down at two hangers that had been destroyed. Right between them

Duck and cover. Gerald Murphy prepares to take a good-natured swing at his buddy Henry McGlynn. Cooler heads prevailed.

was this guy sitting on chair like nothing happened. It turns out the concussion from the bombs had killed him."

They laughed. "Some of the things you did then, you wouldn't be caught dead doing now," he says. "There was always somebody up to no good."

And it wasn't always the men. There was blood and guts, but there was also fun and games. Anne Arsenault was a member of the Canadian Women's Army Corps. She balks at first, but she can't help herself when she learns we're on a quest for humour.

"This is a true story," she begins …

"We were in Peterborough, Ont., and a group of girls were sitting around debating which course they were going to take," Anne says. She stops in mid sentence to point out once again that this is true. "Every last word of it. One of the little girls was sitting there and she said, 'I'd like to take intercourse.' That's not even the punch line. Then one of the other girls said, 'Oh, that sounds real good. I think I'll take intercourse, too.' Neither one of them knew what the hell they were talking about."

The gun is loaded at this point. "You know something," one of the men says, "I think I met her."

The laughter eventually subsides to a dull roar. "We had a good time," Anne says. "Some of the girls were right off the farm."

War always stinks, but there are times when it stinks to high heavens. Henry was the one up to no good once when a shipment of rotten eggs arrived at the base from Ireland.

"You could smell them from the other end of the building," he says. "Our torpedo bombers had flare tubes. We filled the tubes with those rotten eggs and dropped them in a town in France the Germans had taken over. I guess you could call it germ warfare. I don't think we were very popular after that."

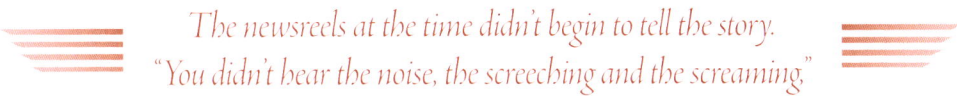

*The newsreels at the time didn't begin to tell the story. "You didn't hear the noise, the screeching and the screaming."*

Then again, war is hardly a popularity contest. Good manners have nothing to do with it.

Henry had an engineering scholarship, but he didn't wait to be called. "If they called you, they could send you anywhere. If you stepped up, you had your pick," he explains. "I was with Fighter Command and Transport Command."

Another time, they had taken refuge in shelters and the men could hear this strange commotion on the roof they were hiding under. "One of the boys had cracked. He was just gone, his nerves were shot and he was dancing around on top of the shelter. The Germans were just pouring the coal to it and they didn't hit him. A charmed life.

"The same fella was out one day on a bicycle. He was going to a nearby village when a German came over very low. He stood at the end of the runway, in the open, and fired away with his .45-calibre. What he expected to hit, I don't know."

The boys from the army, navy and air force got along pretty well at the pub. Everybody got along. "Until the Yanks finally showed up," Henry says. "The Yanks had lots of money. They were hated." Because lots of money meant lots of girls.

Henry was a war groom, meeting and marrying a Canadian girl when he came to Canada on an 18-month assignment. It was not love at first sight, at least when it came to the weather. He arrived in a snowstorm, quickly realizing that life in Canada consisted of six months of winter and six months of bad skiing.

Mary and Henry met at a dance in Charlottetown and had three children.

Gerald arrived in France five days after D-Day. His tour lasted 3½ years. "As the years go by, you kind of forget things," he says. "You remember the better times, but you don't remember the bad times.

"One thing was quite humourous. The Germans had broken the dikes in a little town in Holland and one of our Lieutenants stepped into it." For lack of a better word, let's call it a bathroom. "We wanted to get rid of him after that," Gerald laughs.

"We had some fun." Many of Gerald's memories are his own as he bursts out into hysterics from time to time, but won't get into details.

"Another thing that made me laugh. We were going along in a field or a ditch, I can't remember, and apparently one of the Germans had to have a bowl movement. We didn't know what to do with him when we found him. One of the guys tapped him on the shoulder and he keeled over. He had been shot right through the forehead.

"Just a young fella. It was humourous at the time but, come to think of it, he was about the same age as me. He just wanted to enjoy life."

The trick was to find humour when at all possible. "Especially in Paris," Gerald winks. "There are some things I can't tell you."

"One time on leave …" he says. Then he catches himself. Sixty-one years later, discretion is the better part of valour. It has something to do with a padre and a house where you might find a woman. Or six. Needless to say, the padre took his collar off.

"We were just south of Oldenburg, Germany. There was no fraternization, but the boys overcame that by borrowing civilian clothes," he laughs. Whether it was approved or not, there was going to be fraternization. The girls would go by on their bicycles and they would wave. 'Canada! Canada!' "

And the boys would wave back.

It's the camaraderie Gerald Murphy cherishes. "I'll never forget it," he says. "To this day, I keep in touch with a lot of the guys."

# Love And War

'We were civilized.
We had running water.'

Ethyl Julseth

Ethel Wood was a young girl, all alone in a world gone mad. She was her own rock. Or her own anchor. It was up to her.

Only 17, she had lost her mother when she was six. Many kids would have quit right then. Her father, although he would stop by long enough to sign the papers that would change her life, played no real part in her life.

Walter Julseth was five years her senior, someone she couldn't have imagined even existed. He didn't come from the end of the earth, exactly, but it was just up a dusty, dirt road from the middle of nowhere.

She had heard of Canada, but that's about it. The province of Saskatchewan? The tiny town of Laverna? Most of the people who have spent their entire lives in Saskatchewan couldn't pinpoint tiny Laverna on a map. Because it isn't there anymore.

She was from Sunderland, on the northeast coast of England. "We were civilized," she says. "We had running water."

He was born on a farm that straddled the Alberta-Saskatchewan border, almost as far away from civilization as you can get by horse and buggy. When war broke out,

Young and beautiful. Ethel Wood before she fell for "a bit of a jerk" from Canada.

joining up was the right thing to do. What else was he going to do?

She was a driver in the Women's Auxiliary Air Force. Everything from ambulances to officers. "Sometimes we would drive 50 miles by lunch," she says, making it sound like a long way. In 1942, it was a long way.

And he was an air frame mechanic in the Royal Canadian Air Force.

As fate would have it, they were both stationed at a base near Leeds. As good fortune would have it, on one cold, miserable, rainy night, they found themselves together in a truck searching the area for a Lancaster bomber that had not returned from its mission. They visited every dispersal point before eventually finding it.

It wasn't exactly love at first sight.

"Later on, he would say I was just dying for him to ask me for a date, but that's not true," Ethel Julseth says. "You wouldn't know it today, but I had bright red hair and he called me Red. I hated it. I thought he was a bit of a jerk."

He did eventually talk her into going to a dance with him. Desperate times called for desperate measures, she figured.

"He warned me that he had two left feet. He was right," Ethel laughs. "He never did learn how to dance." But he must have done something right. They were married within 10 months after their chance meeting, on July 27, 1944.

Explain yourself, young lady. "This was wartime," she laughs. "You didn't wait around."

Five months later, nearing the end of the war, Walter was discharged and sent back to Canada to await his bride's arrival. She followed four months later, in April of 1945. Ethel remembers standing on the wharf, about to board a ship that would take her to a strange land and a new life. "I was tempted not to get on."

She had plenty of time to contemplate what awaited her. The voyage took 28 days. She docked in Halifax and immediately boarded a westbound train along with dozens of other war brides. Many of them never reached their destination.

"One by one, the girls got off and boarded another train back to Halifax," she laughs. But not Ethel. How bad could it be? "I was determined to make it work." Marital bliss was not immediate. You could say they got off to a roaring start.

Bill was late getting to the train, you see. He ran into some buddies en route, you see. And, well … it's not the one thing. It's the one thing that leads to another. And then everything stops making sense.

"I guess they talked him into stopping for a drink," Ethel says.

It was about this time that she probably started thinking about the jerk she first met. "I expected to see my husband. I thought he'd be there waiting for me. He told me he would." But Walter's friends were persistent. Either that or his arm was easily twisted.

It had taken a week to travel from Halifax to Regina. When Ethel found herself alone, she gave her husband 15 minutes. "I was going to get back on the train," she says. And the tone of her voice indicates she isn't

Smooth talker. Walter Julseth offered his new bride everything but a toilet.

Walter and Ethel Julseth on their 50th wedding anniversary. The post-war population explosion was their fault.

kidding. Walter, proving once again that timing is everything, arrived with a minute to spare.

"He wasn't a drinker, you know." No, of course not. Men are just such misunderstood creatures. Especially when friends are involved.

There was a little ice in the honeymoon cottage for a few minutes, but Ethel was true to her word. She would make this work. This was home, even if home is where you keep your rolling pin.

Walter had told her everything about Canada. OK, maybe not everything. He may have left out a couple of small details. When the young couple arrived at the home of Walter's parents, Ethel was perplexed when she couldn't seem to find the washroom.

"Where is it?" she asked Walter.

Realizing discretion was the better part of stupidity, he took her hand and quietly led her outside. "I had no idea where he was taking me," Ethel says. "There was this little wooden thing and he opened the door." Inside was another wooden thing – a bench with a hole in it. Welcome to Canada.

"We had running water and indoor toilets in England," she says. "I was a little provoked about that."

She had every right to wonder what she had gotten herself into, but Ethel Julseth was no quitter. She made her throne speech loud and clear, but her commitment never wavered.

The late '40s were tough on everyone. But, help from the government for returning servicemen allowed the couple to purchase half a section near Plenty, Sask. Apparently there was a lot of love on the farm. It was a land near Plenty, but it was not exactly a land of plenty.

Together, they grew wheat and raised six children – Gary, Jean, Glen, Linda, Janice and Dave. Today, there are also 11 grandchildren and nine great grandchildren. They populated the province pretty much by themselves. Only Dave lives outside Saskatchewan.

"Walter was a regular kind of guy, but we had a classic romance," says Ethel.

"I didn't know that bad things happened to other people," says daughter Janice. "Our home was close to perfect. My dad was a wonderful husband and father."

They lost him in the fall of 1995, just four months after Edith and Walter celebrated their 50th wedding anniversary. Walter went in to have a heart valve replaced and doctors discovered a hole in his heart. It was not considered a major problem, but he never recovered after the surgery.

"People are always saying it'll get better, that the pain of losing him will go away," Ethel says. "It doesn't."

Her knees give her fits, but Ethel is still going strong at 80. She is warmed by her family's love during those cold, Prairie winters. Her apartment in Saskatoon is like a drop-in centre. "Especially my granddaughter Kady," she says. "She's always there to help me, no matter what."

Ethel eventually got her indoor toilet, of course. And her new home grew on her. "I miss England from time to time, but this is a wonderful place," she says. "I'm glad Walter showed up at the station and I never got back on that train."

And they lived happily ever after.

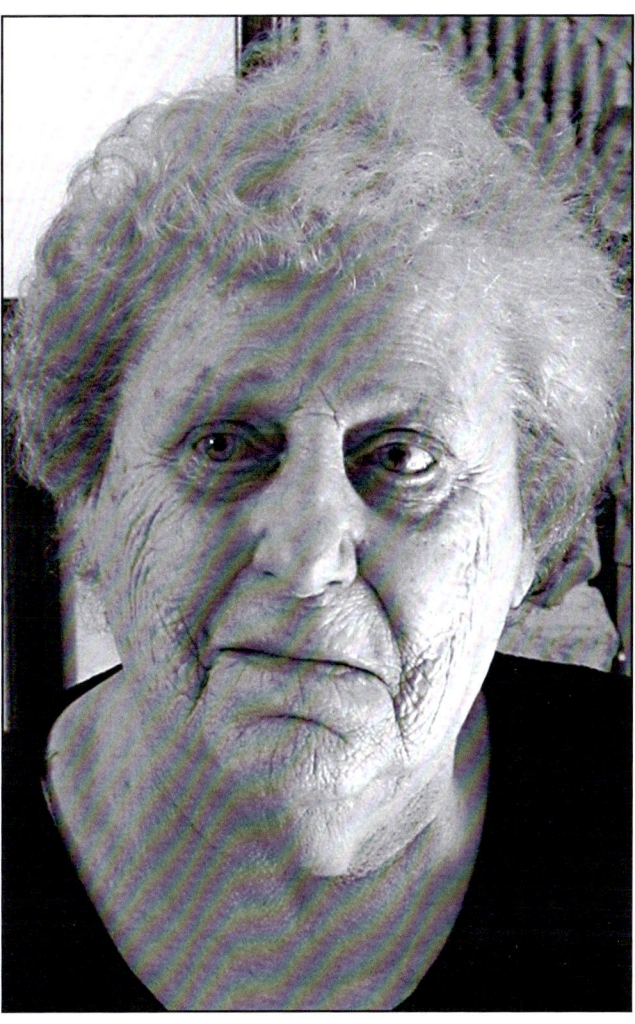

Ethel today. The pain of losing her husband has not subsided, but her family gives her strength and great joy.

# Tanks For The Memories

'It was Christmas of 1943…
and we borrowed a barrel of beer.'

Sal Polito

Don't blame Sal Polito for his wicked ways. As explanations and excuses go, they don't come much better than this …

"My dad was Italian," he says. "And my mom was Irish."

He shrugs his shoulders. Enough said. Talk about being resigned to your fate. Life isn't meant to be smooth sailing from start to finish.

"I've always found time for fun," he says. "I've always been a bit of a joker. You have to look hard sometimes, but there's always something to laugh about."

Even during war. Especially during war.

"There were going to be bad times, so you had to have some good times along the way or you'd go nuts." Not that he wasn't scared. "Damn scared," he admits. "We were just a bunch of kids who didn't know what the hell we were doing."

Born in Toronto, the family moved to the town of Lindsay, just north of the city, when Sal was eight. You grew up fast in the '30s. Joining the military, in some respect, was taking the easy way out.

"I remember the summer when I was 17. Five of us had rented a cottage at the lake and one of the moms came by and cooked the ass end of a bear. True story. It was still sitting on the table the next morning when we left."

Toronto, to enlist, was the destination. The way the boys figured it, things couldn't get a whole lot worse. Although he liked the navy and air force uniforms better, he chose the army. You might say he was loaded for bear.

He planned on becoming an engineer, but the inside of an M-10 Sherman tank became his home.

"It was our best," he says proudly.

He took his basic training in Brantford. Not without incident.

"I was on leave one time when I came across a wedding dance," he laughs at the memory even though it's a bit foggy. "In I went." The next morning, when it was time to return to camp, he did so without his boots. "I have no idea what happened to them, so I must have had a helluva time. I was AWOL for a few hours. I got in a little bit of trouble."

Sal made the trip overseas on the *Queen Mary*, his heart stuck in the back of his throat the entire way. There were good times when they finally got to England. Preparing to save the world was thirsty work.

"It was Christmas of 1943," he says. "We were stationed south of London and we borrowed a barrel of beer. The only way to get it back to camp was to roll it the whole way with our feet. The beer filled a bathtub, but it got a little flat by New Year's Eve."

The fear of crossing the Atlantic was nothing compared to the fear of crossing the English Channel. He arrived at Juno Beach in France on June 10, 1944, four days after the D-Day invasion. His commanders and his

Sal Polito takes a seat during basic training. "We were just a bunch of kids who didn't know what the hell we were doing."

head told him the Germans had been pushed back by then, but the rest of his body wasn't easily convinced. When it was time to drive the tank up on shore, he couldn't do it.

"My leg was shaking so much, I couldn't step on the gas," he says.

Sal Polito was in Europe for the duration, right through the end of the war and beyond. He lost good friends, but never his sense of humour or his spirit. There is justifiable pride in his voice. He did so much, "but I wish I had done more.

The young, the proud, the brave. Sal at attention. He wasn't always this well behaved.

"I don't know how to explain it, but the experience changed my life," he says. "I think about it every morning when I wake up. Not a day goes by that I don't think of the guys who didn't come home."

It could have been him. It should have been him. "We were hit by an armour-piercing shell," he says. "It came through the side of our tank, right under my feet, and it never exploded."

You can have the biggest guns and the best intentions, but survival often comes down to luck.

Regardless of the situation or the circumstances, the enemy was never the fellow wearing the same uniform. "If I didn't like someone, I figured I had to get to know him better," he says.

Imagine a world where we all lived by those words.

There was gambling, of course. "Poker was good to me," he says. "I was never short of money … but some guys were." Wink-wink. And there was drinking. "We did a lot of liberating and a lot of celebrating."

The best assignment of his war is easily pinpointed. "Some fool ordered me to guard the distillery in Meppen, Germany," he says. "It was the best job I ever had."

Like so many others, he also discovered that jerry cans, especially the ones that hadn't been used to carry gasoline, were good for carrying something a little more tasty.

"I don't talk about the bad things that happened," he says.

It's the friendship and the camaraderie Sal Polito recalls fondly. The men all looked different, but they were all the same scared out of their mind. Even those who put on a brave face.

"We needed each other," he says. "There is a lot of character when it comes to war, but there were also a lot of characters. You had to laugh or you'd be a mess. The pressure got to a lot of guys."

There was more a grudging respect than outright hatred for the enemy. "We were going by a slit trench and I heard a German yelling for help. Like a fool, I helped him. It's just something I thought I should do. He could have shot me."

When the war ended, he got to know some of his former adversaries. "They were good guys," he says.

One adventure still makes him shake his head. "I don't know how I did some of the things I did. I guess I was young and naive," he says. "It was after the war. I took a truck full of cookies and headed for what was then Czechoslovakia. People were starving and we had to help, but I was all by myself. I stopped at every dance hall along the way."

When he returned to Canada in 1946, he got into the family fruit and vegetable wholesale business in Lindsay. He and wife Betty had five children – four boys and a girl. Grandchildren? "I'm not sure," he laughs. "Forty, I think. I have had an excellent life."

Sal Polito is proud that he answered his country's call. He'd do it all again. "But I wouldn't be much use now," he says.

He is a proud member of Royal Canadian Legion Branch 67 and is quick to say yes when asked to speak with area school children. They don't need all of the details, but it's important that they understand what happened and honour the sacrifices and courage of old men who were once young boys.

"I don't have a problem doing that," he says. "The kids are so clever. They ask all sorts of questions."

What does he talk about? "Gun safety," he says.

Amen to that.

Sal's trusty Sherman. Inset, when he talks to school children about his time in the war, he talks about gun safety.

# 'It Was Like… Hallelujah'

They were heroes before they even got off the ship.

Ed Hayes

Edward Livaria John Hayes knows all about practical jokes. They have played a part in his life since he was 45 minutes old.

And not necessarily a good part, either. It's not the John, it's the Livaria that has posed a bit of a problem.

"A hot water bottle burst and burned my feet pretty badly the day I was born. I guess it was a Sister Livaria who saved me," he explains. There is a look of resignation on his face that indicates she didn't do him any favours.

"That's where I got whacked with my middle name." He is, by this point, resigned to the fact. But it's not the kind of thing you want getting around in the Royal Canadian Air Force. Friends can be worse than enemies.

Corporal Hayes guarded his name it like a case of scotch. There was no upside to letting the truth be told.

Born in Guelph, Ont., "on Aug. 17, the same day as Julius Caesar," he joined the RCAF on Jan. 2, 1942, attending the Galt Aircraft School before going overseas to join the 405 Pathfinder Squadron as a Lancaster bomber mechanic.

Engine work was his specialty. That and foolishness. He could take it apart and put it back together. The engine, I mean. The results of the foolishness weren't always easily fixed. "I choose to remember the good times," he says.

Not that fear wasn't a factor.

"A friend of mine, Wally Schneider, and I decided that we were going to bring a couple of bottles of whiskey when we boarded the ship. We placed them in the middle of our kit bags, but we had to be careful that we were the only ones handling them. We didn't need somebody throwing them into a corner. We guarded them with our lives. This was precious cargo. When we got to England, it was like … hallelujah."

They were war heroes before they even got off the ship. Needless to say, the lads were happy to see them.

It was fun and it was often games, but their mission was nothing to laugh about. It was the job of the Pathfinders to mark the targets for the main bomber Force that followed.

Lives were at stake every day. Your friends depended on you. There is no more pressure than that.

"It's easy to laugh now," Ed says.

They played hard, but they worked even harder. "We were fighting for freedom. That was the only thing that mattered. There was a lot of boozing, but we were always sober when it came time to do our job."

The first thing you have to do upon arrival is stake your claim as a worthy adversary. Ed describes himself as an "independent thinker." When it comes to the measure of a man, heart is much more important than height.

"I hate bullies," he says. "It was shortly after I arrived. This big guy was mouthing off, so I poured a can of corn syrup on top of his head. I had to pay for the uniform, but he never bothered anyone again." It turned out to be a small price to pay.

Tanks and troop carriers. Planes, trains and automobiles. And then there were the rickety old bicycles. Some of them actually had tires. But not very many. You could get just about anywhere on a bicycle. The problem was getting back.

"I've often said that more Canadians were wounded or hurt badly on bicycles

Bright eyed and bushy tailed. A young Ed Hayes doesn't exactly look like a fierce fighting machine.

A proud man. "We were the first to go and the last to leave," Ed Hayes says.

coming back from pubs than were hurt during the war," he says. "And that's a fact."

There was a friendly rivalry between the Canadians and Americans. "They'd walk into a dance and steal our women," Ed says. Then it wasn't quite so friendly.

He travelled all over England and Scotland on various leaves, having his share of fun and getting into more than his share of trouble. "But I always came out smelling like a rose."

Some things happened that Ed Hayes isn't overly proud of, but the overall experience? "There's a lot of pride," he says. "We were the first to go and the last to leave."

# 'I Came Back With Two Prisoners'

'We were so in love,
it hurt to be apart.'

Les
Garnham

Les Garnham knows all about hard times. He was an old hand – actually a young farmhand – by the time he was 10 years old.

Before the war, it was often a battle just to survive what circumstances and fate combined to throw at a family of 14 – yes, 14 – in Portage La Prairie, Man. Seven brothers, four sisters and more difficult times than he could count. And this was *before* the Great Depression.

"My father came to Canada from England on a cattle ship," he says. "He had no education, but he was a hard worker who refused to accept help from anyone. He didn't get married until he was 37."

Les laughs. "My parents obviously got along very well, because they got busy." No kidding.

There was no time, and certainly no money, for education. "I went to work when I was 10." His father couldn't pay him, so he toiled for a neighbour. All day, every day. For $15 a month. In the wintertime, still just a young boy, he chopped wood and fished Lake Manitoba. Life was so hard, fighting the Germans almost seemed like taking the easy way out.

He wanted to follow two of his brothers and enlist in the fall of 1939, but the army didn't want him. "They said I had bronchitis," he says. "I smoked like a chimney." They would get less picky as the war wore on.

Instead, he married his dear Irene. "I paid the minister $5," he says. "I had five cents in my pocket. I didn't have the proverbial pot or the window."

He's not sure how they made it through the next two years, but apparently you can live on love. Irene became pregnant with a son almost immediately.

Les worked the farms in the summer. When there was no work, he picked roots. When winter hit, and it always hit hard, it was back to Lake Manitoba. "I got two cents a pound for jackfish."

In the spring of 1943, the inevitable call to arms came. It was both a blessing and a curse. By now, there were two young sons at home. He was sent to Winnipeg and joined the legendary Royal Rifles. His back, undoubtedly from carrying the weight of the world, wasn't in the best of shape. His left eye hadn't worked properly since the time a shell went off in the chamber of his rifle while hunting and filled it with gun powder when he was 14. They took him anyway.

Les Garnham is 89 years old now, but the memory of returning home on leave for the first time in his uniform is crystal clear.

"I was there for five days," he says, "and Irene cried for three of them. We were so in love, it hurt to be apart."

Les Garnham only looks mean. A good wife meant a good life. Leaving Irene was the hardest part of going to war.

When he was transferred to North Bay, Ont., and told he'd be there for five or six months, he sent for her. It was a wonderful time, but very short-lived. Soon, he was back in Manitoba, at Shilo, for advanced training on the six-pound, anti-tank gun.

Irene, pregnant again, returned home to Portage. "I was supposed to have leave, but this jerk of a Sergeant made me check my gas mask before leaving." He missed the train home and the next day found himself headed to Halifax on a troop train.

"It was a month after Irene gave birth before I found out it was a little girl," he says. Sardines had more room than he had on the voyage to England in November of 1943. He remembers standing on the deck of the ship, tears rolling down his cheeks. He missed Irene so much. "At that point," he says, "I realized I was a soldier. And soldiers don't cry."

Moved to the holding station in Aldershot, he was appalled when he was sent to the Algonquians because they were short an anti-tank gunner. "A bunch of lumberjacks and miners. Huge men," he says. His commanding officer didn't exactly offer a warm welcome.

"What's a little sh— like you doing here?" his CO said.

"I'm so small because I had to work so hard in order to feed you easterners," Les said. And a friendship was instantly forged.

He was to have been a part of D-Day on June 6, 1944, but a bout of pleurisy forced him to stay behind. He got to France in late July, just in time to be a part of the epic Falaise Gap battle near Caen.

"We had a Captain for two hours. Then he turned chicken and went and hid," he says. Les Garnham's war would take him through France, Belgium, Holland and, finally, into Germany. "In one stretch, I went 23 days without taking my boots off."

War turns a boy into a man in a hurry. Like most, whether they admit it or not, he had great apprehension on the eve of battle. How will you hold up and stack up? How will you do what duty forces you to do?

"I didn't think I could handle it. I didn't know if I could patch up a wounded guy," he says. Then he thought about what would happen if he was injured. Wouldn't he want someone to tend to him? "I had to do it and I did it. I got good at it. After a while, it didn't bother me. I guess you could say I got hard boiled."

Except when it came to the kids. He had three at home, remember. In Holland, during the liberation of Nijmegen, Les encountered a young girl who changed his life and made him realize the absurdity and callousness of war. It is a brutal business. It is the children who suffer most.

"She had suffered an injury to her leg, but that wasn't why she was

Les Garnham in his Legion dress clothes. When the time came, he did what had to be done.

crying," he says. "Our translator talked to her. He told me she was crying because she had lost her mother and father. All I could do was give her chocolate. I often wonder what became of her."

But there are also the times he laughs about now.

Like the time he was on leave in Paris for three days. The bands, the beer, the luxury hotel. And the hooker.

"She came over to talk to me, but I wasn't interested. I had Irene at home with our children," he says. Then he really wasn't interested. "She said, 'Business is business and love is bullshit.' Just then, a louse scurried out from under her hair and was sitting on her forehead." Then it ran back under cover. He did the gentlemanly thing. He excused himself and went to the washroom. Then he high-tailed it out the back door.

 *"I'm not saying I'd do it all again, but I'm proud to say I did my part."*

He remembers the night in London during another well-deserved leave, when an English Bobby took exception with his haphazard dress. Two dozen beers will do that to you. " 'Straighten that tunic,' " he said. "Like he knew what war was all about. I said to him, ' Hey, son. Go home and tell your mother you saw a soldier.' He was going to put me in jail. I wish he had. I wouldn't have had to go back to the front lines."

It was near the end of the war, during a lull in the action, when nature called and he headed for a nearby wheat field to do his business. When he stood up, he noticed two young German soldiers who obviously had the same idea.

"I came back with two prisoners. They were just kids, Hitler Youth," he says. "We laughed about that for the rest of the war. That's the kind of soldier I was." They kept them for weeks, too. The CO needed somebody to polish his boots. "They did our dishes and did a damn fine job until we had to give them up."

He never suffered as much as a scratch. It was luck, of course, but you make your own luck.

"It was like I had a sixth sense," he says. "It's like there was always something telling me what to do and where to go. I remember four of my buddies clamouring into an old building and I chose to dive into a shell hole instead. A mortar came in and killed all four of them."

After the war, Les Garnham returned to Portage La Prairie and his family.

He returned to Lake Manitoba as a commercial fisherman. He guided American hunters in the fall and worked as a carpenter.

"Jack of all trades, master of none," he says.

He lost Irene to cancer in August of 2005 after 65 years of marriage. The tears indicate there will be no getting over it. "We had a good life," he says. "I couldn't have married a better woman.

"I think about it every day. I'm not saying I'd do it all again, but I'm proud to say I did my part."

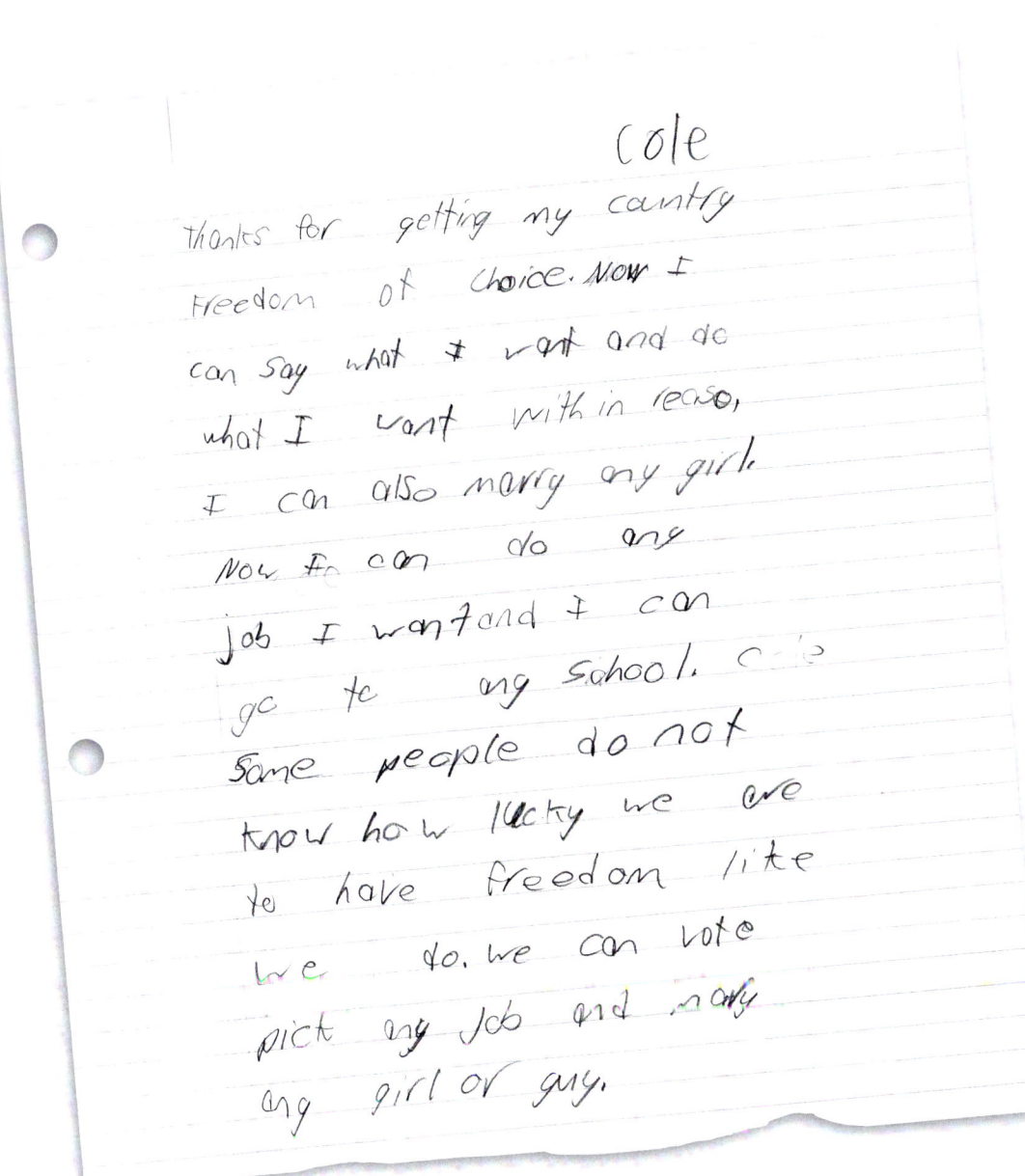

Cole

Thanks for getting my country freedom of choice. Now I can say what I want and do what I want within reason. I can also marry any girl. Now I can do any job I want and I can go to any school. Some people do not know how lucky we are to have freedom like we do. We can vote, pick any job and marry any girl or guy.

# To Sea The World

A neat guy, except for the house.

Harry Urwin

*"Courage: Do not follow where the path may lead. Go instead where there is no path and leave a trail."*

The sign hangs on a wall inside the modest home of John Henry (Harry) Urwin in Fort MacLeod, Alberta. It is more than a collection of words.

For the native of Moose Jaw, Sask., they have been words to live by.

When the end comes, and it must for all of us, he will leave this world a better place than when he came into it. He has left a trail of goodness and caring, whether it's a fellow senior in need of a ride to the doctor or the little boy across the street in need of a bicycle. He is not a bitter old man. You will not find a better old man.

Age doesn't have to mean a state of ruin or decline. "It's a state of mind," says the 84-year-old.

So what if he has suffered three strokes. He may have slowed considerably, but there is still a wonderful life to be lived. The body balks occasionally, but the mind is sharp. Even if the house isn't exactly pristine. "I'm allergic to housekeeping," he explains.

As a little boy, while his father fought overseas in the First World War, Harry sold war bonds. He is a 60-year member of Royal Canadian Legion Branch 46. He has driven the Legion van. For 10 years, he donated his time to Meals On Wheels. "I like looking after old people," he says, blissfully unaware that he might be considered one himself. It's not rocket science. "If you can help, help. Do something useful with yourself."

Signing his John Henry. Literally. Fortunately, Harry Urwin didn't sign his life away when he joined the Royal Canadian Navy.

He has lost his wife Audrey and his only son, Bob, failed to give him any grandchildren. So he went out and found one right across the street – little Kesho. "I became attached to the kid," he says. "I guess you could say I adopted him."

The family has since moved to Edmonton, but they remain close. "They were just so friendly. When I met them, it was like I had known them for 50 years. When I had surgery recently, the mom came down to stay with me. I try to go to some of Kesho's hockey tournaments. It's just a super relationship for everybody."

Perhaps it's because of the little boy he met during the Second World

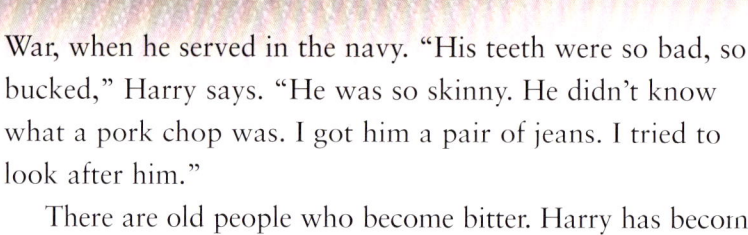

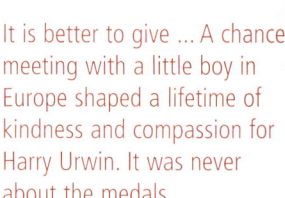

It is better to give ... A chance meeting with a little boy in Europe shaped a lifetime of kindness and compassion for Harry Urwin. It was never about the medals.

War, when he served in the navy. "His teeth were so bad, so bucked," Harry says. "He was so skinny. He didn't know what a pork chop was. I got him a pair of jeans. I tried to look after him."

There are old people who become bitter. Harry has become better. He genuinely likes the younger generation. "The most important part of what you earn is what you save," he says. Make a difference in the world, he says. Don't make a spectacle or a nuisance of yourself. "Be the best you can be."

If that sounds like a recruitment speech, it is. Partly. "The world is what you make of it. Get a job, buy a house, work hard." And don't forget to play hard.

"You had to have fun when you could, because any day could be your last," he says of his naval days aboard the minesweeper *HMCS Noranda*, most of them patrolling for U-boats in the waters around the East coast. He spent 32 months running at sea.

There are worse places to sleep, especially during wartime, than the opulent Waldorf Astoria Hotel in New York City. "Twenty-five cents a night," he laughs.

The sailors were highly thought of by the residents. "Beer was five cents, but I never had to buy one."

He remembers vividly the day the lads accidentally on purpose set the depth charges at the wrong depth and obliterated a school of fish.

"We missed the sub, but we had a damn fine meal," he laughs.

Harry was only 19 when he joined the navy. "I wanted to do something to help my country. I felt it was my duty. I was very proud," he explains. But a sailor from the landlocked Prairies? Why? "I don't know. I guess I wanted to see the world. I had a million-dollar experience for $1.50 a day. I was only seasick one time in my life."

He followed brother Tom into the service. Tom had joined the army a few months earlier by memorizing the eye chart. How blind was he? "When we were kids, we used to use his glasses as a magnifying glass to light cigarettes."

He had never been on a ship, had never even seen a ship, until he boarded one for the trip from Vancouver to Victoria for training. It was love at first sight. "Or maybe it was just the fact that we got a shot of rum every morning at 11:30," Harry says. The smart thing to do was save it up till you had what might be called a useful amount. "And I was pretty smart. At 19, you think you know everything."

 *"I remember the night we stole a taxi in New York. We went from pub to pub and parked it outside with the motor running."*

Was he ever scared during the war? Dumb question. "I was scared stiff, but I tried not to think about what could happen," he admits. "If you weren't scared, you were crazy. You never took your clothes off at sea in case something happened."

Like most, he saved his craziness for shore leave. "I remember the night we stole a taxi in New York. We went from pub to pub and parked it outside with the motor running. We could have gone to jail, this was somebody's bread and butter, but you don't think about things like that."

Guilty, Your Honor, with an explanation. "Young and stupid," he says. It is a defence many of his comrades use.

Last year, he made the trip to Europe to commemorate the 60th anniversary of the V-E Day. "I went to Juno Beach," he says. "It was a great trip. We had special seating and were treated like kings."

Because, in a sense, they are kings. All of them. Harry Urwin considers himself fortunate. "I've been blessed with pretty good health," he says. "I've had a great life, a lot of fun."

After the war, he took a job with Canada Packers for 60 cents an hour. And he renewed his love affair with the automobile. "I bought my first car when I was 14. I paid $50 for a 1926 Chevy touring car. As a kid in the '30s, I used to race Model-T's. "First prize was $1."

Out of the service, with money in his pocket because he was a bit of a gambling whiz at sea, he purchased a 1947 Club Coupe. "It cost me $2,495. I put $5 down and I put 57,000 miles on it the first year. I went through three sets of tires."

His jobs after that were many and varied. He has lived in Fort MacLeod for 40 years and once served on town council. He is a member of the Lethbridge Car Club and still owns 10 old relics. You can't say he retired to a life of leisure at 65, because Harry Urwin believes we are put on this earth to help others.

"I played golf until I lost my ball," he quips. "That was the end of golf." His life remains rich and full. He made himself useful as a teenager and he hasn't stopped yet.

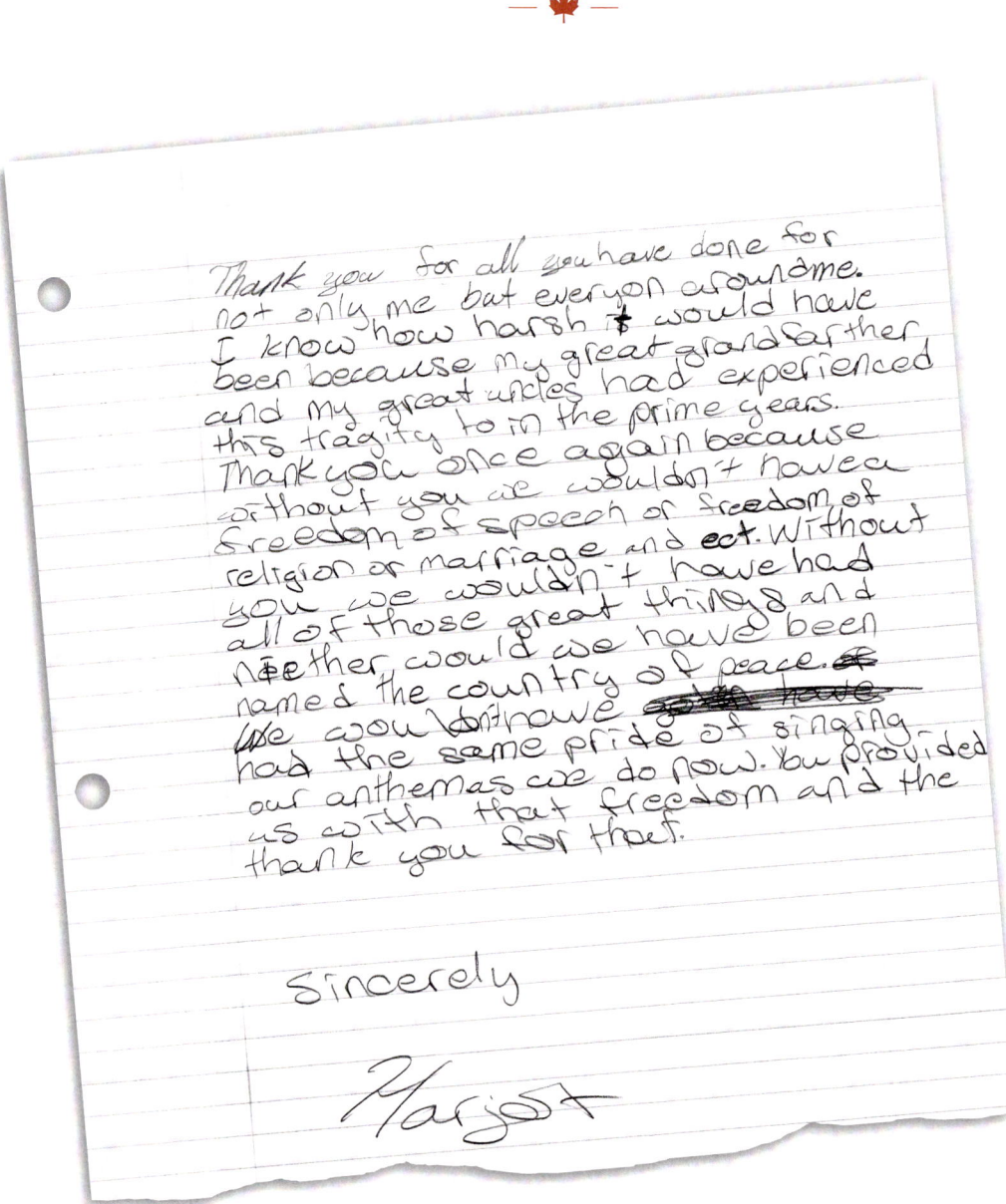

# Whine But No Whining

'If you can help out, why wouldn't you?'

ROBERT WESKETT

Even the place, the tiny speck on the map where Robert Weskett grew up, sounds funny. Calabogie.

It sounds like a word you might make up if you you're playing Scrabble. And you're desparate.

Bordering the Ottawa Valley, it was a little piece of heaven for a young boy who had experienced his share of hell by the time he was eight months old. It made perfect sense to him, but some things didn't.

"My father died of tuberculosis," he says. "He was in his late '20s."

So he knows unfair. He knows anger and pain.

His parents had met in Ottawa, but Bob was born in Flint, Michigan. When his dad died, his mother returned home to Canada and remarried. His stepfather died 16 months later.

It's not surprising that he would one day grow up to be a courageous soldier. He learned about courage and perseverance at a young age, shuttling between his mother, his aunts and his grandparents. He learned that you are what you make of yourself.

Despite it all, he says, "I grew up happy." His yard in Armstrong, B.C., is somewhere between immaculate and perfect. He pulls up a lawn chair. "I couldn't have been any happier."

He is a man of great dignity now, all grown up to the point where he is starting to shrink. At 82, he is hobbled physically but still sharp as a tack mentally. All anyone with a good cause has to do is ask for help. He'll be right there. He is the president of the local Royal Canadian Legion,

It's your lucky day. Bob Weskett and his wife Georgina on their wedding day in 1946.

Branch, No. 35, in Armstrong.

"I've always been that way," he says of his penchant for volunteerism. It is not a chest-beating boast. "If you can help out, why wouldn't you? It's just the right thing to do."

So, when war broke out, it was only natural that he would want to help. Bob initially wanted to join the Royal Canadian Air Force. "They didn't want me," he says.

So joined the Canadian Armoured Corps and was eventually assigned to the Royal Canadian Dragoons with the $5^{th}$ Armoured Division.

His war was almost over before it started. In November of 1941, en route to England, he slipped under a cable on deck and was about to be pulled overboard when he was grabbed from behind by a passing shipmate. "They didn't stop for anyone," he says. "I would have been lost at sea for sure."

Imagine bobbing in the water in the middle of the Atlantic Ocean, a ship, your ship, disappearing into the distance. Many men faced such a fate.

The fear of U-boats was something you learned to live with. "It was a great day when we saw the Hurricane fighter overhead that had been sent out to meet us," he says. In Aldergrove, England, there was training. And then there was more training. "We marched so much, I thought I was in the infantry."

Bob Weskett landed in Sicily in the spring of 1943, before crossing over into Italy. "Anybody who says they weren't scared is slightly demented," he says. Recon and dispatch work with the $1^{st}$ Canadian Armoured Car Regiment was a harrowing experience. "Especially when you got lost as often as I did." It's not like there were road signs.

But there were good times. "Those are the things I choose to remember," he says.

Like the time he was sent into a town with two empty jerry cans and a few bars of soap. "Money was never a factor. We used the barter system." He returned a hero, with plenty of wine. And, since they had been accused a

It wasn't all smiles in the army. "When you were told to jump, you had to ask to come back down," Bob Weskett says.

day earlier of raiding an Italian farmer's corn field and had done no such thing, they figured there was nothing to lose. If you're going to be presumed guilty, well … you may as well be guilty.

"We drank the wine, boiled up the corn and had a helluva time," he laughs. "Then we buried the evidence. There were a lot of lies told that night."

It wasn't the only thing he buried. Since it never really bothered him, Bob was often assigned to burial duty. Friend or foe, ally or enemy, the task was performed with dignity. There was always grudging respect for the German soldier. "It was just one of those things that had to be done. It wasn't pleasant, but I did what I was asked to do."

Everyone had a nickname. "Mine was 'Hey You.'" He also had a favourite saying when dealing with the brass. Not that he dared scream it for all to hear. "Talk to my ass," he giggles, "my head's aching. When you were told to jump, you had to ask to come back down."

It was the little things that made life tolerable on the march to victory.

163

Socks or soap were always worth a good Italian meal. And there was wine everywhere. At least Italy was good for something.

There are highlights and lowlights to every soldier's story.

In Holland, with the help of the Dutch Underground and his wireless operator, he saved an officer's life. "A young Lieutenant went racing through our checkstop. Two Dutchmen in a ditch called us down and pointed out that there was a German machine gun in the tower up ahead. We found the proper frequency and got word to the Lieutenant just before the sniper opened up on them."

An artillery strike took care of the menace. "If the chicken hadn't crossed the road," he says. He doesn't relate the story because it's a big deal. It was his job. You did your job.

This man has experienced sad.

 *"Talk to my ass," he giggles, "my head's aching."*

One day they came across a huge supply of red wine – 800 litres of the sweet nectar stored in huge casks. But, since there was no way to be sure if the enemy had somehow poisoned it, they had to take axes to their windfall, watching it cascade to the ground. He shakes his head. "What a waste," he says. "It was a very sad day."

There are different kinds of sad during wartime. With the writing on the wall and V-E Day fast approaching, Bob was just inside the German border when a 48-hour stand down was ordered. This should have been the best of times, a celebration of a job well done, a victory lap.

"We set up a loudspeaker. We had the tunes going. We were having a ball," he says. "More than anything, it was as relief that it was over."

Guards were still posted, of course. The party was in full gear when a single shot rang out. "One of our guys got hit just below the helmet. I was the one who found him," Bob says. "We had to bury a chap, a new reinforcement, two days before the damn thing ended."

It is, horribly, the nature of the beast. Bob Weskett is one of the lucky ones. He didn't have nightmares upon his return. He stayed in the service with the ordinance Corps for the next 28 years, before leaving in 1974 to work with the RCMP as a coroner and guard. He lost wife Georgina in 1996, after 50 years of marriage, and has suffered a couple of minor strokes himself. But his spirit is always willing.

He is a father, grandfather and great grandfather. "It has been a great life," he says. "I've been a very lucky boy."

Along the way, he has enriched many of the lives he touched through the Legion, the Knights of Columbus, the Air Cadets and the Boy Scouts of Canada. A proud resume by anyone's standards.

A man never stands taller than when he stoops to help someone else. That, in essence, is the story of Bob Weskett's life.

A proud soldier. Bob Weskett offers a crisp salute to his comrades from the Second World War. He did his part and the good fight continued when he came home.

# Lady Chatterley's Lover

What's that sheepish expression on your face?

FRED GILBERT

Fred Gilbert was too good for his own good. But it all turned out for the best.

You'd think somebody who had grown up on the Great Lakes and went to sea at a young age would be just what the navy was looking for. It didn't work that way. Experience was a disadvantage. They wanted to create their own problems.

He had shuttled freight between Nova Scotia and Newfoundland as a teenager, but Fred had that sinking feeling when he tried to enlist. "I was told they wanted to train their guys their way. They were afraid I might have picked up some bad habits," he says.

The army wasn't an option. "No thanks," he says. Which left the air force. It was 1942. He was 19. "They took me in a heartbeat. I walked in the door and they wouldn't let me walk out."

Life and death is often the difference between good luck and bad. Especially in wartime. "The merchant ship I had been on was sunk by a German submarine shortly after I got off her," he says. "I had been in the stoke hole. The guy who took my place went down with the ship."

His goal was Bomber Command. "I wanted to be a navigator," he says. But a stuttering problem made that impossible. "Too bad I couldn't sing what I wanted to say. I never stuttered when I sang."

He went over on the *Queen Mary*, zigzagging his way through the U-boats, going as far south as Bermuda to avoid them. "They could never catch her, but I slept up on the main deck just in case."

He did make it to Bomber Command, but as an electrician with the ground crew. It wasn't for him. "You're assigned to one plane and you become attached to it and the crew," he says. "It's tough on you, waiting to see if it would return from a mission. It bothered my nerves. I lost some friends."

He asked for and was granted a transfer to a Sunderland flying boat squadron in Northern Ireland. You could say it was partly the navy. The best part is that he worked on all planes.

The experience changed his life. One of his best friends became Jim Chatterley from Toronto, who was also an electrician. "He had the top bunk and I had the bottom." So it was impossible to miss the photo of the lovely young lady he had taped to the wall. It was his sister, Jean. Jim had a girlfriend over there and Jean would send her nylons and chocolate.

After the war, the two friends met again in Toronto. Jean and Fred were introduced and the magic was instant. "It was like we were supposed to meet and be together," says Lady Chatterley's lover. "I had a girlfriend at home when I went overseas, but this was something special." It was July of 1945, while the two friends were home on leave, waiting orders to ship out for the war against Japan. Jean and Fred were married seven months later. They celebrated their 60$^{th}$ wedding anniversary this year.

Fred Gilbert doesn't wake up in a cold sweat when the memories come flooding back. Most of them are happy. The good times outnumbered the bad. He looks back at the war years with a smile on his face. There were plenty of laughs.

It's only natural that he would become airborne since he was in the air force. "We were on a run to the Shetland Islands to check out a new plane when we hit an air pocket. I was asleep below, in the galley, when the plane dropped about 600 feet. I can still remember myself floating in mid air. When I looked out the porthole, the wings were flopping like crazy. I don't know how we survived."

It was on the same run that the pilot came on the intercom with some instructions. Or orders. "There wasn't a tree to be seen, but there were

How did Fred Gilbert get into the air force in 1942? Simple. "I walked in the door and they wouldn't let me walk out," he says.

plenty of sheep," he says. "I wondered why we were all told to bring our rubber boots. 'But don't touch the sheep with the red X on its back,' the pilot said. 'That one's mine.' "

Talk about your strange bedfellows.

The best part about being stationed in Northern Ireland is that there were no Americans. "They had so much money." And the girls' interest was in director proportion to the amount of money you had in your pocket.

 *'But don't touch the sheep with the red X on its back,' the pilot said. 'That one's mine.'*

Fred Gilbert ended up a Leading Air Craftsman. The air force is where he learned discipline that stayed with him throughout his lifetime. "Even today, my towels and washcloths are hung perfectly," he says. "There's no telling what might have happened to me if I hadn't joined the air force. I look at young people today and I think it would be so good for them to be in the service for a year or two. They would learn so much."

Like he did.

He has trouble pinpointing his favourite memory, but not his favourite people. There was Corporal Scully. He was, Fred admits, the brains of the operation. He knew all the King's Rules and Regulations. When someone got into trouble, which was all the time, Corp. Scully was the man they sought out for advice.

"He knew more than the prosecutors," Fred says. It's a good thing, too. "He went down to Dublin one time, got drunk, and stole a car. Then he ran into a horse and buggy. He had to pay off the people he hit, but he still had lots of money coming in on the side."

The Brits were known for their pomp and circumstance, something the Canadians didn't put much stock in. Wing Commander Sumner was "one of the guys. He didn't care if you saluted him, but the Brits disciplined him because of his attitude by taking away his car." The boys built him another one.

"We found this burned-out old wreck and completely restored it," Fred says. "New upholstery, new engine, a fresh paint job, the works. She was a thing of beauty. Then we presented it to him. He had tears in his eyes."

And there was always gas in his tank the 100 octane they took out of the Sunderlands when they had to pull them out of the water to be worked on. "One of the guys found a 200-gallon tank that wasn't being used and buried it. We kept it full for Commander Sumner."

A lot to smile about. As the owner of Gilbert Shoes in Wiarton, Ont., seemingly forever, Fred Gilbert learned quickly that it's good for business to put on a happy face.

After V-E Day, Fred and his buddy Jim Chatterley flipped a coin to determine whether they would stay as part of the occupying force or put in for the war in the Pacific. It was heads – Japanese. They were home on leave when V-J Day brought the Second World War to and end.

Fred went to Toronto for his discharge. He saw Jim. More importantly, he saw Jean.

Jean loved the little town of Wiarton when Fred brought her home. He managed a furniture store for a couple of months, then followed his dad into the shoe business. Gilbert Shoes on the main street has been there ever since. It's still in the family.

Fred and Jean had three boys and girl. There has been hardship. "We lost our oldest son," he says. But it has been a long, happy life. They have eight grandchildren and nine great grandchildren.

"I'm glad I was a part of it," Fred Gilbert says.

# The Devils, You Say

Front and centre with the
First Special Service Force

RECTOR &
PEPPARD

**P**erhaps never before have two men who started out with so little in common ended up so much alike.

Millard Rector was well into his 20s when the Second World War began. He had a wife and baby girl at home, and a job at a hat factory in his hometown of Parrsboro, Nova Scotia.

One day, he just didn't come home for dinner.

"I had this old car. I was cruising around in the middle of the afternoon when I saw two of my buddies walking down the street," Millard says. "They said they were going down to enlist in the army. I said, 'Jump in.' We all went down and joined."

He was 24. And he was in big trouble. It was six months before he got around to telling Dorothy why he had disappeared. "She was some wild," he says. "It was an awful thing to do."

Herb Peppard was 19 when the war began. Unlike a lot of others who literally ran to enlist in his hometown of Truro, Nova Scotia, he was in no big hurry. The idea of being a dead hero did not appeal to him.

"I have no trouble admitting that I was afraid," he says. "I read so much about the First World War, what it was like in the trenches. I read *All Quiet On The Western Front*. I held out as long as I could."

One by one, his buddies joined up. "I felt an obligation, he says. The initial plan was to join the Royal Canadian Air Force, but you needed Grade 10 to be in the air crew. "I only had Grade 9." When he did join the army, it wasn't with the idea of charging up a hill.

"I opted for the artillery," he laughs. "The big guns were back from the front line. I figured it would be safer there."

Neither man knew that their paths would soon cross. They would find themselves in the teeth of the battle, front and centre with the First Special Service Force, a 50-50 mix of Canadian and Americans that would become known as The Black Devils.

\* \* \*

Millard Rector was assigned to the West Nova Scotia Regiment and soon found himself in England. "We didn't stay in one place very long," he says. Which was good, because they tended to wear out their welcome very quickly. "The girls were friendly," he winks. "And there were lots of them."

War is serious stuff, but it's when the shooting stops that it gets really dangerous. There's a fine line between borrowing and stealing. And most of the guys had no idea where it was.

"We took a Bren gun carrier into town one night. At least we tried to, but we didn't get far," Millard says. "We dropped into a big bomb crater and couldn't get it out again. We were lucky to get ourselves out. Many people had an idea who did it, but nobody said anything."

There were always things like that happening. And, almost always, alcohol was involved. It's a good thing mothers and wives weren't around. Anybody who had one or the other – or both – knows they would not have been proud of their young men or their old man.

"We borrowed the Colonel's station wagon one night. Me and another guy picked up some company." The plan was working perfectly until they hit the black ice … and then the guardrail. "We were lucky we weren't killed."

Their reception back at camp was decidedly rude. "It's a good thing I had a couple of stripes they could take away. They probably saved my life. I would have been in the jug a long time."

Regrets? Only that he can't recall the names of the old man and woman in Scotland who kept him fed and watered during one leave. "They ran the pub and, since I had no place to stay, they took me home every night with them." Whiskey for breakfast, beer for lunch and dinner. "And they wouldn't take a dime."

Millard Rector can laugh now, but it wasn't very funny when he had to face his wife Dorothy after the war. He went for a drive one day and didn't came home.

He eventually started his war in Italy. "The First Special Service Force had been shot up pretty good and they needed replacements," he says. "I volunteered."

There wasn't a lot of fun to be had after that.

"But I do remember the time we found cellars full of wine casks near Nice, France. We didn't open them. We used our Tommy guns to fill them full of holes, then we got down underneath and let it pour into our mouths," he says. "Good stuff. That was the good thing about Italy and France. There was always plenty to drink."

The officers didn't turn their heads and pretend they didn't know what was going on. "They were right there with us," he laughs. "I have a lot of good memories."

The First Special Service Force had one of the highest casualty rates of the war and Millard Rector did not escape unscathed.

"I had my right thumb shot off," he says. "They found it, put it in a bag, and sewed it back on." He was only out of action for five weeks. "I wanted to get back with the boys."

When the unit was disbanded on Dec. 5, 1944, Millard was transferred to the Cape Breton Highlanders. He was in the thick of it for two years, right through into Germany.

The only time he was really scared was when he got home. Dorothy didn't have a gun, but she did have a good memory and she could get her hands on a rolling pin.

Miraculously, his marriage did survive. She must have forgiven him eventually, because they had another daughter. They settled in Truro. He opened a bakery. When it went belly up, he sold insurance. When that didn't pan out, he became a carpenter.

"I've had a good life," Millard Rector says. He used to wonder if veterans received the respect they deserved, but that all changed in 2005.

The Remembrance Train trip from Halifax to Ottawa to mark the Year of The Veteran was something that still warms his heart. The little boys and girls were at every stop and along the track, waving their little flags, saluting these old men. It made them feel young again. It made them remember why they put their lives on the line. "The respect we were shown was really something," he says. "I'd go to war again."

But he might want to let his wife know where he's going this time.

* * *

Herb Peppard had gone through his basic training in Halifax and was stationed in Newfoundland when the First Canadian Parachute Battalion was being formed. They asked for volunteers and he stuck his hand up.

"I found the artillery a little boring," he says.

Boredom would not be a problem after that.

You had to weigh 180 pounds or less. He hit it right on the nose. His physical was done in Ottawa. "You had to take an IQ test," he says. "That never made sense to me. You have to be smart to get killed?"

It turns out he did indeed have an IQ. Of the 120 men who volunteered, Herb was one of only 15 selected. He was training at Fort Benning, Georgia, when an officer from Helena, Montana, arrived. He was looking for volunteers for the First Special Service Force. "There were 127 men on parade that day," he says. "Ninety-seven volunteered."

This is a man who wasn't even sure he wanted to fight. "I guess my plan went all to hell," he laughs.

 *"The girls were friendly. And there were lots of them."*

He soon found himself at Fort Harrison, Montana, with 1,999 others. The training was intense, but he handled himself well. "Except for the downhill skiing," he laughs. "I broke my leg." The Americans and Canadians who comprised the unit got along well. Unless it was payday. "Their Privates made more than our Sergeants."

Herb Peppard was good at everything. Except skiing and doing what he was told. He was absent without leave five times during his time in the service. Guilty with an explanation, sir. "I got sick of being on parade all the time," he says. "When I wanted to go somewhere, I went. I guess I had a mind of my own."

The first time was while training at Fort Harrison. A group of 15 Canadians decided to head home for a week. It's a long way from Montana to Nova Scotia. They didn't even get out of the state before being arrested and thrown in jail. "I lost a couple of stripes that time."

Their first mission was to the Aleutian Islands to ward off what was thought to be a Japanese invasion. "I was afraid to fight an enemy that wasn't afraid to die," Herb says. "What the hell kind of enemy is that?"

Fortunately, by the time The Devils arrived, the Japanese had departed. Scared the fight right out of them. They came back to a camp in Vermont in preparation to head overseas. Vermont is close to Nova Scotia. If discretion is the better part of valour, stupidity is the worse part of discretion. Herb Peppard headed for home. Bad move, but it's tough to argue with the result.

"I met my future wife," he says. "I was walking down the street in Truro

Herb Peppard didn't plan on becoming a war hero when he joined the army, but his plans changed. A Silver Star citation probably saved his hide.

when this beautiful, young thing came out of the telephone office and hollered at me. Her name was Greta. She noticed my uniform and wanted to know If I knew her brother. I got up the nerve to ask her to a movie, but to hell with the movie." It cost him 29 days in jail and 29 days of pay. "But it was worth it."

Their first overseas stop was Casablanca. The thing that stands out about that first night was the argument that ensued between George Tratt of Montreal and Jim O'Brien of Connecticut. The two were always going at each other, but they reached new heights of absurdity this night.

"I know this is hard to believe, but it's true." The question they debated was whether you read the black type in a newspaper, or the white around it. "They went at it all night long and they still hadn't come to an agreement when the sun came up."

Another night, the absurdity level off the scale again, someone made the mistake of putting them in the same foxhole, manning the same machine gun. "George wanted to move it forward. Jim wanted to stay where they had been told to stay. The bullets are flying all around them and they're sitting there arguing."

It wasn't an American-Canadian thing. It was just two men, or two children, who always had to have the upper hand. They met their match, but it was a match made in hell. Somehow, and it was more a case of good luck than good sense, they managed to survive.

The Black Devils were on the push to Rome when Herb Peppard got hit. They had taken a hill from the Germans, but the enemy mounted a fierce counter-attack. Herb moved down to a better firing position. "It was my own damn fault. I left myself exposed," he says. "I felt something smash into my leg."

He knew immediately that he had been hit, but he couldn't find the courage to look. The bullet entered high on his right leg, near the groin area. There are privates in the war … and you want to come home with them.

To make matters worse, the soldier who came to his aid, George White, also got hit. "The front of his uniform exploded," Herb says. George was the first to be rescued, because he was in worse shape. Herb waited two hours before he could be dragged back up the hill to safety. While the battle raged around him, he was quite content to sit it out. He had checked.

All the moving parts were present and accounted for.

"I was so happy," he says.

After being taken to a field hospital, he was sent back to Naples because of the fear of infection. After five months, he found himself at a rehabilitation facility 300 kilometres outside of Rome. And, since all roads lead to Rome ...

"I decided I wanted to go to Rome," he says. "I was so close, and I might never have a better opportunity." Of course he asked for a week's pass. Of course the powers that be said no. You know what happened next, of course. "I took off," he says. "They gave me an overnight pass and I was gone for a week."

He saw all the sights and even scratched Greta's initials on the stone walls of the Coliseum. "I had the most wonderful time," he says. But it was soon time to go home and he knew what that meant. "Jail."

When he returned to his unit, he knew it would not be a joyous reunion, but his commanding officer had a problem. On one hand, he should throw the book at this young man who seemed to follow his own rules and make them up as he went along. On the other, he was supposed to pin the Silver Star medal on his chest.

  *"All those people saying thank you, It brought tears to my eyes."*

Because of the makeup of the Black Devils, Canadians were eligible for U.S. citations. The Silver Star is the third highest decoration designated solely for heroism in combat. Herb Peppard had carried a wounded comrade to safety. "And a few other things," he says, unimpressed by himself. "Nothing very important."

He was happy to receive the medal, but mostly because it saved his sorry hide. "They couldn't put me in jail," he laughs. Herb got off with a severe reprimand ... and a pat on the back for a job well done.

When the First Special Service Force was disbanded, he returned to the First Canadian Parachute Battalion, but he never saw action again. After all of the jail time, he somehow managed to end up a Sergeant. He might have been Prime Minister if he'd behaved himself.

The man who readily admits he took his sweet time getting started, ended up with commendations, and memories that have lasted a lifetime. Fear struck out.

On his 80$^{th}$ birthday, on July 7, 2000, he parachuted out of an airplane to mark the occasion. He competes in bodybuilding contests and looks 15 years younger than he is.

If it's not funny, it's certainly ironic how things turned out. This is a guy who couldn't get into the air crew because he didn't have enough education. When he turned 40, he got Grades 10 through 12 and became a teacher in Bridgewater, Nova Scotia. "It's something I always wanted to do," he says.

If Herb wants something, he goes out and gets it. Greta didn't stand a chance when he returned to Truro. She had been seeing an English serviceman, but Herb marched down to the telephone office and recaptured her heart. He became an electrical contractor.

Herb and Greta had three kids. He lost her to polio 14 years ago, but they lived a happy life. He has seven grandchildren, but no great grandchildren. "I'm encouraging it," he says.

Like Millard Rector, Herb Peppard was on that train to Ottawa. It was also a life-changing experience for him. "All those people saying thank you," he says. "It brought tears to my eyes."

That first night in Halifax, when he arrived for basic training, still makes him laugh. He arrived with German measles. "I just got there and I was already in trouble with the enemy," he says.

He didn't know what barracks he was supposed to be in. He didn't know which unit he belonged to. The nurse was surprised he even knew his name. "Take this man to Ward 4," she said. "And see that he doesn't get lost."

Herb Peppard was his way out the door when he overheard the nurse talking to a colleague. "Thank God we still have our navy," she said."

He surprised her. And himself.

---

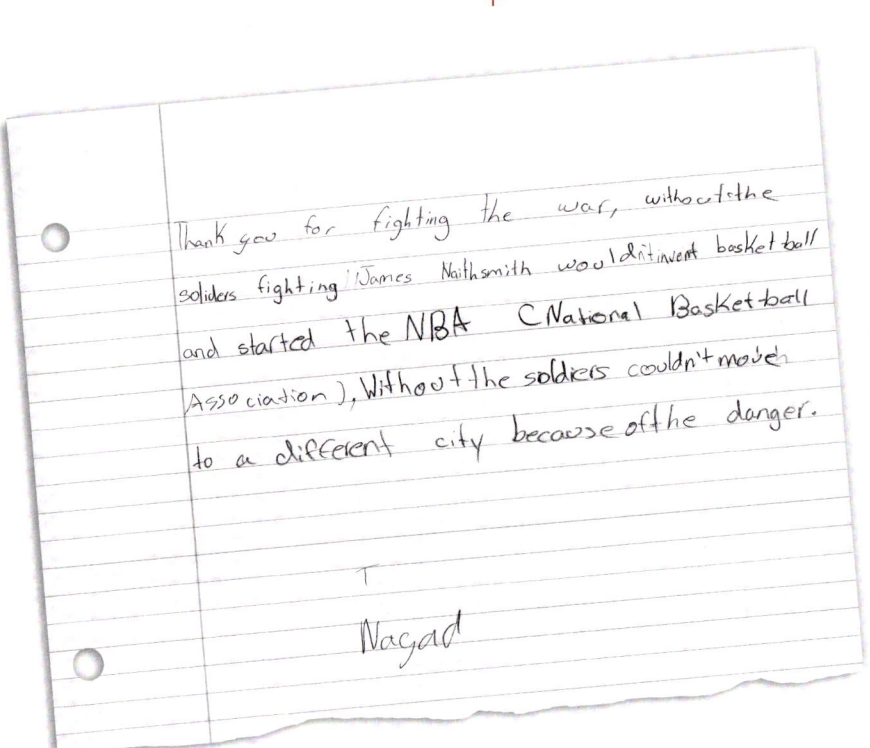

Thank you for fighting the war, without the soliders fighting James Naithsmith wouldn't invent basketball and started the NBA (National Basketball Association). Without the soldiers couldn't move to a different city because of the danger.

Nagad

# Not Exactly Ship Shape

It was just before Christmas
and they needed a Christmas tree

JACK TIERNAY

**J**ack Tiernay doesn't mind admitting he has always been a bit of a yo-yo. In fact, he takes it as a compliment.

"I was the Canadian yo-yo champion when I was 16," he says more sheepishly than proudly. "Pretty good deal, though. I got to spend six months in England demonstrating the toy. I was there for the coronation of King George VI. It was my first time on a ship."

But it would not be his last.

North Bay, Ont., is a long way from the ocean, but he opted for the navy when war broke out. It was partly the uniform and partly the daily ration of rum, but mostly it was a love of his country that made him enlist at the age of 18. "People pay big money for an ocean cruise," he says.

Forget the Germans. Jack was his own worst enemy. Starting almost immediately when he arrived at Toronto's old exhibition grounds, then HMCS York, for basic training as a wireless operator.

It's actually quite amazing that he is now in his 85th year, a father of nine, grandfather of 22 and great grandfather of three. Wife Lorette doesn't know how lucky she is. If lucky is the right word. If his name was Tom, his nickname would be Foolery.

"I think it was the first week I was in Toronto," he says. Someone who knew even less about what he should be doing than Jack did assigned him to guard the main gate and issued him a pair of canvas gators that covered the bottom of his pants and indicated he was someone of authority. "The gators allowed you to go almost anywhere."

It was a few days before the mistake was rectified and Jack was relieved of his duties. But not his gators. Instead of turning them in, he kept them. "I could just walk out the main gate and nobody asked questions," he laughs. "I had a two-day pass whenever I wanted one."

Pretty nervy. Especially during inspection before he was sent on to Ottawa for additional training. Jack hid the gators under a bag, but the jig was up when the officer discovered them. "What do we have here?" he asked. Jack Tiernay's life flashed before his eyes, but before he could answer, a leading seaman, a man he didn't even know, rescued him.

"That's OK, sir," he said. "This man was on guard duty. I'll take the gators back."

Close? Too close. "I could still be in jail," he says. "That fellow really must have hated the officer to come through like that for me. I never saw him again after that."

 *"If you're lucky, you have to stand at attention and hold a rifle straight out with one hand. If it starts to dip, you get a kick in the ass."*

After spending three months in Ottawa, he was drafted to Newfoundland and stationed in the little town of Harbour Grace. An incident on the train known as the Newfy Express still brings a chuckle.

"It was just before Christmas. One of the guys figured we needed a Christmas tree and the train was so slow going uphill, he was able to jump off, run into the bush, cut down a little tree and bring it back.

"We cut the tinfoil from cigarette packages into little strips and decorated it," he says. "It was beautiful. We sang Christmas carols and I supplied the music on an accordion I had with me."

While in Harbour Grace, he was billeted with the Stevenson family. "My mother sent me an Eaton's catalogue, but Mrs. Stevenson couldn't order anything because Newfoundland wasn't part of Canada at the time. I ordered lots of things for her. She was so grateful, just a wonderful woman."

Speaking of lots. "Girlfriends," he winks.

He doesn't know if it's true, but the thought of it still messes with his mind. "There were reports that German submariners were dressing in civilian clothes, coming ashore and going to our dances in the little town of Carbonear," he says. "The reports even had the names of the girls they had danced with.

"We were all issued revolvers, but it wouldn't have helped me. I couldn't hit a thing."

A young Jack Tierney had a good reason for joining the navy. "People pay big money for an ocean cruise," he explains. He got more than he bargained for.

After moving on to Gander, Jack figured it was high time he saw the bright lights of St. John's. "My first time ever in an airplane was in the back of a Liberator bomber that was on a test run. I thought I was going to freeze to death." A good time was had by all at the pub, but he missed the flight back and had to return in a tiny Harvard Trainer for his wireless shift. "The pilot had to show me how good he was. After all the dips, dives and rolls, we landed and I was so anxious to get out of the harness that I pulled the wrong cord and the parachute went flying out behind me.

"The pilot laughed like hell. He said, 'That'll cost you $10 to have it re-packed.' I guess it was a small price to pay."

Jack's first ship was the frigate *HMCS Dunver*. "She was a real beauty," he says. "We led the convoy to Ireland." By the time they arrived eight days later, he had an old whiskey bottle almost full of rum saved up for his shore leave. "It was better than money," he says. He had also volunteered to be a mailman.

Coming back, as usual, he was running late. Then he was sprinting. He missed the ship by about five feet. "I was running up and down the dock. The guys were all yelling for me to jump." To make matters worse, he had the ship's mail.

Now, after so many close calls, it seemed like his luck was about to run out. He had heard stories about what happens on a ship when you're guilty of an indefensible act of stupidity.

"Imagine a stack of 20-pound cannonballs in the shape of a pyramid. You have to take it apart and rebuild it 10 paces away." This goes on all day. "If you're lucky, you have to stand at attention and hold a rifle straight out with one hand. If it starts to dip, you get a kick in the ass."

This was the epitome of a no-win situation and, miraculously, he still managed to win. *HMCS North Bay*, the Corvette named after his home

The music man. Jack Tiernay has been a performer his entire life. He's still at, playing for whoever will listen, around Alliston, Ont.

town, no less, was pulling out of port a few minutes later. He related his predicament and was offered a lift. When the *Dunver* sent a launch over to deliver orders, he got a ride back.

"None of the officers even knew I was missing," he laughs.

On one of the return trips to Canada, the boys got into a little sauce. Actually, it was a lot of sauce. The result was an impromptu sing-along. "There were four or five of us," Jack says. "We were singing, *'Please don't burn our shithouse down, mother has promised to pay.'* This did not go over well."

His punishment was moving chairs at the YMCA in St. John's. Jack's not kidding when he says, "I led a charmed life."

His only problem was timing. He was home on leave when the *Dunver* was sent through the Panama Canal to Vancouver for a refit. He missed the boat and never saw it again.

"That hurt," he says. Instead, he was assigned to *HMCS Humberstone*. "It was basically a big tub."

Jack wasn't one to accept his fate without putting up a fight. He asked, begged actually, to be allowed to return to Harbour Grace. "I said I had gotten a girl pregnant. Beautiful, eh."

Upon his return, he was assigned to *HMCS Wentworth*, another state-of-the-art frigate. He made nine trips across the dangerous North Atlantic during the war. He saw ships sunk and a torpedo barely missed the *Wentworth* once, but his confidence never wavered.

"I never thought I wouldn't get home in one piece," he says.

Jack Tiernay returned to North Bay after the war. He met Lorette when his father came home from the bank and told him about this lovely, young teller who worked there. "The fire started," he says.

Growing up with seven brothers and two sisters, Jack wanted a big family. He got one. But nine children? He laughs. "The train would come by in the morning and wake us up. And it was too early to get out of bed."

He is all class. That much is obvious as soon as you meet the man at his home in Alliston, Ont. He is a former president of Royal Canadian Legion Branch 171. Painting is a hobby, but music is his passion.

He has been making beautiful music since the day his mom brought a piano home when he was a little boy. These days, he's happy to play almost anywhere. One of his great joys is when he packs up his keyboard and heads to the Legion for Sing Along With Jack or entertains at the local retirement homes.

It is a great joy for Lorette, too. "It means the damn thing is out of the house," she laughs.

# To Dieppe... And Back

"The guard couldn't speak any English. I wrote, 'Shoot this SOB on sight.'"

BILL ORSER

I t has been said countless times that 'military intelligence' is an oxymoron. Like jumbo shrimp. There was no better example, or worse debacle, than Operation Jubilee.

The Allied situation had gone from bad to worse in the summer of 1942. The Germans had fought deep into Russia, the British army in North Africa had retreated back into Egypt and mainland Europe was thought to be an impenetrable enemy stronghold.

There was only one way to find out for sure. The raid on the French port city of Dieppe would prove to be the mostly costly intelligence-gathering operation of the Second World War, and the bloodiest single day in Canadian history.

Of the 4,963 Canadians who left England on the morning of Aug. 19, 1942, only 2,210 returned. There were 3,367 casualties, including 907 dead. Prisoners of war totalled 1,946.

Bill Orser was one of them.

Born in the tiny railroad town of Capreol, north of Sudbury, Ont., there was no sitting on the sidelines for him. "I felt like I had to join," he says. In the fall of 1939, he walked into the navy recruitment office and offered his services.

"They told me to go home and wait for their call," he says. "I waited as long as I could." On Dec. 4, 1941, three days before the Japanese would attack Pearl Harbour, he joined the army instead. He was 21. When the navy finally did call back, it was 13 months later and he was already in England.

Bill Orser tried to join the navy but, when the call didn't come, he joined the army instead. His reward was spending almost three years as a prisoner of war.

"I guess it was meant to be," he says. "When your time comes, it comes. The guy behind me in the landing craft never knew what hit him."

Like D-Day 18 months later, the Allies were supposed to land under cover of darkness. Like D-Day, it was already daylight when the front of Bill's landing craft crashed down. He has no idea how he made it to the stone wall on the beach. "We carried a smoke canister," he says. "Mine had a bullet hole right through the middle of it. Anybody who raised their head above the wall got it. When we looked behind us, the tide was coming in and our wounded were drowning."

He remembers an officer giving them the news of the raid the night before. "Sorry, boys," he said, "we're going to Dieppe."

Bravery and courage were a given. Ridiculously, given the circumstances, there was also humour. "Jackie Woodhouse was beside me," Bill laughs. "He got hit in the shoulder and I said, 'I heard it going by my ear.' He said, 'You SOB. You never told me it was coming.' He said it with a straight face and then laughed like hell. What a character."

There was no shortage of character that day. But there would be no victory, either. Surrender was the only option and Bill Orser found himself a prisoner of war at a camp northeast of Berlin. "Hitler considered us gangsters," he says. "We had ropes and chains on us for 13 months."

After being marched to another camp, they were assigned to huts with Russian prisoners. "That's when we knew we were lousy," he says. "We smelled worse than they did."

A sense of humour was key to survival. "You had to have it," he says. "You couldn't keep it all in or you'd never make it to the end."

Bill Orser made it to the end. He had to search for humour sometimes, but he usually managed to find it. "Friends become so important. We picked each other up. We shared everything we had and we kept each other going."

He has a famous nephew, figure skater Brian Orser, but Bill is the hero of this family.

There wasn't always fun to be had with the guards. But sometimes …

"We had this really rotten bastard," he says. "So we planned an escape for when he was on duty. They sent him to the Russian Front. The guards were more scared than we were. One wrong move and they were facing the Russians." One favourite trick was to give the new guards a cigarette and then report them for stealing."

Another time, a young German guard who was about to be transferred came to them in tears. "We found one of our guys who could speak German and discovered he wanted us to write a nice letter for him, to explain how well he had treated us, in case he was captured. We were happy to oblige." Bill wrote the letter. "The guard couldn't speak any English. I wrote, 'Shoot this SOB on sight.'"

If all's fair in love, it is certainly fair in war. Bill Orser found himself a member of work parties. He worked as a carpenter's assistant for a while, but most of the time was spent in the fields.

"We had this one guy who liked to do crazy things. We were supposed to weed this beautiful garden full of radishes. He kept pulling them out, eating the radishes, and sticking the tops back in the ground."

One day, they managed to steal a chicken that was intended for the government. After burying the feathers in a field, they threw it into a big pot with the potatoes in the cattle stable where they were being billeted.

"When a German officer came by for inspection, one of the guys sat on the wooden lid. He burned his ass pretty good, but it was worth it. We had a really nice meal."

The farmers treated the prisoners well, better than their own soldiers treated them. "One Christmas, this old couple arranged for two of us to come for dinner," Bill says. "They had very little, but they gave us sandwiches and coffee. It was a really nice time. They just watched us eat."

Bill Orser's escape to freedom can't exactly be described as great or even hair-raising. They were marching from Hanover to Hamburg when liberated. Or, rather, they liberated themselves. It was April of 1945, with the Russians closing in on one side and the Allies closing in on the other. Instead of walking, Bill and some others ran.

He laughs at the mental picture of the German officer yelling at them. "Hey," he said, "where do you think you're going? You have to stay here as long as we're here."

The Germans were more concerned about saving themselves than killing anyone by this point. "There were Germans in trenches and they just let us go," he says. "We just walked right past them."

When Bill Orser left England, he weighed 163 pounds. When he returned 33 months later, he weighed 129 pounds. Others, he admits, had it much tougher than he did.

He saved much of his luck for when he came home. It was not a happy occasion as he wandered aimlessly down a dangerous road. "I went down to Toronto to see this girl and I got into the booze," he says. "I was plastered night after night."

Fortunately, he ran into an old pal who was going on a wilderness canoe trip up north. Letting himself be talked into it probably saved his life. "We had a great time and I got away from the drinking."

He got into the construction business. He remodeled kitchens, drove a streetcar in Toronto and worked for Ontario Hydro. The beautiful grandfather clock in the home of Margaret and Bill Orser in Lindsay, Ont., is a testament to his woodworking skills.

They have a daughter, three grandchildren, three great grandchildren and a wonderful life. They have a famous nephew, too – eight-time Canadian champion and world champion figure skater Brian Orser.

But Bill is the hero of this family.

# In The Swim Of Things

Welcome to the Bay of Bengal:
A true wartime story.

DAVID BOWMAN

*"To the brave eight who died: Sleep well in the deep, and at the going down of the sun … I will remember you."*

Not a day goes by that David Stanley James Bowman doesn't think of what might have been. And what was. "Why me?" he asks.

Like most youngsters who joined the Royal Canadian Air Force, he wanted to be a pilot. Like most, he had his dream dashed. "I didn't have the education," he says. "They made me a WAG (wireless air gunner)."

He was born in Brantford and grew up in Toronto, but he became a man in a far-off corner of the world he had never heard of – Burma. Stationed in India, his war was fought against the Japanese.

"I enjoyed my time over there," he says. Except for one day, one fateful day. As horrible as it was, it could have been much worse. Thanks to a mother's prayers and more good luck than any man deserves, he was left on this good earth to write his own book, *Welcome To The Bay Of Bengal: A true wartime story*

David is a big believer in humour. "I don't think I could have made it through without it," he says. Hence the title of one of his chapters: "Great takeoff, poor choice of landing."

It was the morning of April 23, 1945. Just another day, just another mission, when the crew of 10 took off in their Liberator (B24) bomber for a raid on a munitions factory near Rangoon, Burma (now Myanmar). Having dropped their bomb load, they were on their way home. "There was a little flak, but nothing serious," he says.

David thought nothing of it when the pilot sent the flight engineer to the rear of the plane to investigate a tail assembly that wasn't working properly. Five minutes later, 10 miles out over the bay, he heard the words that would change his life and end the life of the man who said them. Plus the lives of seven more of his friends: "Dinghy! Dinghy! Prepare for ditching."

"I had been looking forward to a beer," he says.

Instead, he found himself fighting for his life in the water. Somehow, he managed to free himself from the wires and cables of the downed aircraft. He remembers thinking of his mother. She prayed every day at 2 p.m. It was about 2 p.m. Then he remembered what he had been told about the Bay of Bengal. Sharks! He was bleeding. Was it true that sharks could track blood for miles? If it was a question of whether exposure or sharks would get him, he welcomed exposure.

Air gunner Dyck was the only other crewman to make it back to the surface. The two of them were alone with their thoughts.

He couldn't help but smile weakly when he thought about his buddy Colridge, the only other Canadian stationed at the Royal Air Force base. After 32 days at sea on the voyage from England to Bombay, India, there were six air gunners in line for two replacement positions that had become available. The only fair way to pick was to divide up into pairs and draw cards. The four with the lowest cards would likely be assigned to the post office. "The Colridge and Bowman families back home wanted air victories, not mail processing victories," he says.

The first pair pulled an eight. The second pair pulled a queen. "I was nearly ready to start sorting mail," he says. Colridge pulled an ace, the ace

One minute, airman David Bowman was looking forward to a beer. The next, he was looking for sharks in the Bay of Bengal.

A little prayer and a lot of good luck probably kept David Bowman alive after his bomber crashed. The ace of spades wasn't the death card, after all.

of spades. "I was ecstatic," David says. "Then he leaned over and whispered in my ear, 'The ace of spades is the death card.'"

Colridge hadn't been on this mission. Like a good friend, he picked up David's mail when he didn't return. Inside one care package from home was a box of Laura Secord chocolates. "My buddies waited two whole days before they ate the chocolates," he says."

Although they didn't know it at the time, the crew of a Royal Navy ship had seen the plane go down. Knowing they were about to be rescued was actually the toughest time. "It seemed to take forever for them to get there and I couldn't get the sharks out of my head."

Safely on board, one of the first orders of business was to get Bowman and Dyck a little medicinal brandy. Now he was really scared. It was almost like he had forgotten how to drink. "It seemed to drip off my chin, like they had given me one of those trick glasses," he says.

No, the problem was a huge gash in his chin. It was so pretty, the first mate wouldn't give him a mirror. He called it a "little gash." But it was more like a huge hole.

David Bowman remembers the mosquito netting the little beasts ate right through. He remembers the stifling heat. Mostly, he remembers fondly the times he and Colridge spent on leave. One time in particular, in Nainital, where he accomplished something it's safe to say no other man has ever done. He was charged with speeding. On a horse.

Because a local woman figured all Canadians were cowboys, and she had a horse named Miss Moody, the two just naturally were made for each other. Not exactly. David and his friend usually rented horses when they were in town, so he jumped at the chance to exercise Miss Moody.

She had a mind of her own. At first, she wouldn't go. Then, she wouldn't stop. The result was a terrifying ride of a lifetime that included a sprint through the marketplace, complete with an overturned vendor's cart. It's not like it was his fault, but David was blamed for it and told to report the next day at 0900 hours.

The charge was "speeding on a horse." He paid a 100 rupees fine and gave the vendor 10 rupees for tipping his cart over. The lady who owned the horse wasn't nearly as friendly after that. "She likely believed the horse's tale of the incident," he says.

When their services no longer required, Bowman and Colridge were sent to England where they spent more than a month wining and dining, and playing tennis. "War is hell," he says.

He got what he calls "that hole in my head" fixed when he got back to Canada. He spent 25 years working for General Motors and another 10 teaching at Centennial College. He and his wife had four children. He has four grandchildren and no great grandchildren "that I know of."

It was at the urging of son Robert that *Welcome To The Bay Of Bengal* was finally written. He took a computer course and wrote the entire book by himself over the course of a year.

David and his new partner Ruth live in Fenellon Falls, Ont. A sports nut as a kid, he still manages a little golf despite being in his 80s.

He uses a cane. "It's a real sympathy getter," he winks. "Women open doors for me."

# History In The Making

A great man and his great escape

Ivan Lockhart

Ivan Lockhart had no reason to suspect anything out of the ordinary. The ordinary was exciting enough.

It was just another bombing mission, No. 29 if you're counting. And he was. One more and he would reach the magic number that would mean a leave. After 30 missions, he could go home to Canada for a well-deserved rest.

"There was a slight change of plans," he says.

What he couldn't see was a future that would make him an unwitting but also very willing part of history, and history on film. It would be a 20-month test of courage and cunning that would change his life. Miraculously, it didn't end it.

You train yourself not to think in terms of worst-case scenarios. At 1815 hours, on the night of Sept. 29, 1943, 352 bombers took off from bases in England. Squadron 434 included seven Halifax bombers, including one dubbed L, for "Love." Old Faithful might have been a better name. She had never let them down.

Three hours later, over Holland, an ME-109 piloted by Hauptman Weisenfeld recorded a kill. His frontal attack ripped open the fuselage, igniting a cargo of phosphorus bombs. Ivan Lockhart didn't know where he was when he bailed out. It turned out to be hell.

He was 19, just a boy. It was a cruel fate, but nothing compared to that of flight engineer Scudder. He was 18. This was his first mission, and he was on board only because the regular flight engineer was ill. His charred body would be found in the wreckage.

The Dutch Resistance found Ivan first, but there would be no escaping the Gestapo. Within a couple of days he was being held and interrogated. "It cost me a tooth," he says. He was then sent to Dulag Luft, the reception camp for all Allied air force prisoners. It was a decidedly rude reception. More interrogations.

After eight days, Flight Lieutenant Lockhart and 60 other officers were herded into boxcars. "We had a nice bucket for a toilet," he laughs. It was a two-day trip to Sagan, southeast of Berlin, and Stalag Luft III.

If the name doesn't ring a bell, the circumstances and story probably do. This is the camp where *The Great Escape* took place. Steve McQueen, James Garner, Charles Bronson and James Coburg starred in the 1963 movie, but Ivan Lockhart was one of the true heroes.

There were English and Scots, Canadians and Norwegians, South Africans and Greeks, Lithuanians and Poles. Despite what the movie suggests, not a single American was involved in the planning or the escape. "They didn't join in anything the rest of us did," says Ivan. "They didn't play rugby or baseball, or anything else. They kept to themselves."

Ivan has no idea why he chose the air force. And he had no idea what he was doing here. He was selected by the lads in hut 110 as their new roomie. "Because I was Canadian. They told me what I should instruct my mother to send in food parcels – spices. You can make anything taste passable with spices."

The first order of business was to boil his clothes. "I was covered in bugs," he says. Oly Twist, an Englishman, scrubbed his back. Ivan didn't know that the trumpet sounding meant he was to go immediately outside for roll call and body count. A German "goon" dragged him outside and took him to face the

Even today, Ivan Lockhart is justifiably proud of the part he played in The Great Escape. "It was so inspiring," he says. "We pulled one over on them."

commandant. Picture 1,200 men, all of them cheering and laughing.

When the senior British officer came to fetch him, the others whistled and chanted, "Leave Junior alone." From that day on, he was Junior. He had just turned 20.

Not that he was necessarily Mr. Popularity. "I snore … loudly," he admits. A pulley system was devised. When Ivan got too noisy, a pile of books landed on his head and woke him up.

Wife Shirley is no fool. "We have separate bedrooms," she says.

For six weeks, he couldn't understand where the boys in his room were going at all hours of the day and night. He had to gain their trust before being taken to a meeting with bunkmate John Travis and the other members of what was known as X Committee, including project mastermind Major Roger Bushell.

His mind told him something was going on, but not even his wildest imagination could have prepared him for the size and scope, and ingenuity, of what he saw.

"It truly was out of this world," he says.

Not only was there a tunnel. There were three of them – Tom, Dick and Harry. Tom had been discovered earlier and Dick had been sealed for the time being. Harry would be used for the escape. It was a marvel of engineering, 30 feet underground and 350 feet long. To this day, it is the longest prisoner-of-war tunnel ever dug.

The entrance was hidden under a heating stove in one of the huts. Below was a workshop and an air pump fashioned out of tin cans. There was a fresh air pipe buried under the tunnel floor. A trolley was pulled manually by ropes in order to transport escapees. Sand that was collected during the excavation was hidden in trouser legs and discarded in the compound. The entire creation was ingenious and, as it turned out, ill-fated. Alas, it would come up 15 feet short of the woods. The escapees would become known as the Tunnel Martyrs.

"I was proud to be a part of something like this," Ivan says. Having gained the trust of the others, he was put to work as a messenger, delivering the British Broadcasting news to each hut. As the day of the escape drew near, he was put on cooking duty, preparing high-energy food from whatever had been scrounged and saved – mostly chocolates, sugar, rolled oats, raisins and prunes.

The conditions were horrible, but the camaraderie is what Ivan Lockhart remembers about those days, everyone pulling together in order to prove the Nazis were anything but the Master Race. "It was so inspiring," he says. "We pulled one over on them."

*"He had me put a pail in each hut hallway and instruct the men to spit into it. When I had a good amount in the pails, I would gather and pour it over potato and turnip peelings. It worked like yeast, starting the fermentation process."*

The night of March 24, 1944 was selected for the escape. It was Ivan's job to keep everyone quiet and in numerical order. "I was lower in rank than a lot of them," he says, "but they respected my authority."

Seventy-six men escaped to freedom, but the thrill of victory was short-lived. Thirteen were captured almost immediately and returned to various prison and concentration camps. They turned out to be the lucky ones. Only three made it back to England.

"We feared the worst for the others," Ivan says.

And their worst fears were realized. The other 50 escapees were re-captured by the Gestapo in the ensuing days. Hitler ordered them shot.

The courage of men like Ivan Lockhart cannot be overstated. "They couldn't stop us," he says. Within two months, a new X Committee had been formed and a new tunnel, George, was taking shape.

Ivan manned the air pump. He was also the ration officer for his hut. And, most importantly, he was in charge of the still. "It was my greatest pleasure," he says, "but the entire experience was so rewarding, the way we were all there to help each other."

A man will go to great lengths when he's thirsty. But you also need a little luck. It turns out one of the camp residents just happened to be Frank Rath. And he turned out to be a chemist who had worked for Seagrams before the war. "Bonus," Ivan laughs.

"He had me put a pail in each hut hallway and instruct the men to spit into it. When I had a good amount in the pails, I would gather and pour it over potato and turnip peelings. It worked like yeast, starting the fermentation process," he says. "When it was ready, I would commence distilling during the night on the central cook stove in the barracks kitchen. I had to stand on cold cement for four to six hours, then hide the bottles, dismantle the still and hide it until the next batch was made."

So how was the finished product. "Drinkable," he says. "And very potent."

It was an impressive accomplishment, but not nearly as impressive as the fact Ivan also baked cakes. The men were given bread rations. As the rations officer, he went from hut to hut dividing up the bread. He kept every last crumb.

"I'd combine them with raisins or prunes. Margarine or butter would be mixed into the pulp of raw potatoes and I'd bake it for Christmas or birthdays. The icing was prepared from potato starch mixed with chocolate and sugar."

 *"The pubs were open and everybody was drinking. I was too tired. I just wanted to sleep."*

By early January, 1945, the Russians were closing in on one side and meeting up with them was not a fate the Germans wanted. The prisoners knew a forced march to the west was in their future and made preparations. Ivan fashioned two crude backpacks, for himself and best pal John Travis. They rounded up blankets and food, and anything else they could carry. Neither smoked, but they had cartons of cigarettes to barter with along the way.

The announcement came on Jan. 27 that the men would be leaving the next morning. The next three months would be an unrelenting hell. But at least this time there would be a happy ending.

"It was so cold the morning we marched out. I don't think I've ever been that cold," Ivan says. But he had it better than most. "I had a long wool scarf and boxing glove mitts. Before leaving, I found a can of syrup that had been punctured and I stuck it in my pocket. That syrup kept me going."

To keep warm at night, Ivan and his pal Travis slept head to toe, holding on to each other's feet. "We slept the sleep of the dead," he says.

The men marched from Sagan to Spremburg, then went by train through Leipsig, Halle, Hanover and Bremen, to Tarmsted. From there, they walked again to Hamburg and finally Lubeck.

At the time, the men had no idea where they were or where they were going.

But each step was a step closer to freedom. There was no sleep in the crowded boxcars, and no water. It was a journey of attrition that hundreds of men would not complete.

"I remember walking in a heavy rain for hours. Guys were laying in the mud from complete exhaustion," Ivan says. "This was the first time my mind switched to the First World War and I understood why my father never spoke about his experiences. He wiped it from his mind, just as I did. I was well into my 70s before I could talk about it."

They reached Lubeck on Feb. 6. In exchange for cigarettes and soap, they were able to obtain eggs and bread from the locals at the wire. "Our daily pastime was watching V2 rockets zoom overhead."

With each day, the Allied armies drew closer. On April 9, the prisoners were marched to Bremen, but there were fewer and fewer German guards as they deserted in droves.

On April 27, the prisoners awoke to discover they were no longer prisoners. The "goons" were all gone.

Ivan and some others walked into Lubeck. It proved worthwhile in the sense that they came across an American forcing a young girl into his truck. "Six of us went over and freed the girl," he says. "We took care of the Yank with a few whacks and reported him to headquarters." On the way back, they met a British convoy and hitched a ride.

On May 6, Ivan Lockhart boarded a Lancaster bomber for the short flight to England. He remembers being driven through London the next morning. "The pubs were open and everybody was drinking," he says. "I was too tired. I just wanted to sleep."

Born in Toronto, Ivan Lockhart, 85, worked 39 years for Bata Shoes. He met Shirley during a business trip to Winnipeg and they lived happily ever after. They have three children and five grandchildren.

The rest, and the part before that, is history.

# Robbery Victim Would Be Proud

Her son answered the call
and found his calling

ELMER PHILLIPS

He'd be the first to admit not all of them are good, but Elmer Phillips is a creature of habit.

"Every morning, 10 a.m. sharp," he says. That's when he arrives at Royal Canadian Legion Branch 5 in Summerside, P.E.I. "There are only two exceptions when I don't go there for my first cup of coffee – Good Friday and Christmas day."

With good reason. "The Legion is closed."

Sharp is probably the best word to describe this 82-year-old gentleman. He has a memory like a steel trap. "Sometimes it's too good," he says. "I can't forget some of the things I'd like to forget."

Growing up on the Island, in Souris, his three older brothers – Everett, Ralph and Herb – all joined the service as soon as they became eligible. Elmer, just 15 in 1939, wasn't going to wait on the sidelines. The navy wouldn't take him, but he was pretty sure somebody would. His childhood wasn't something he wanted to escape, but it was his life and he was determined to get on with it.

"I stole a five-dollar bill out of my mother's purse and bought a one-way ticket to Halifax," he laughs. "I had a friend in the Merchant Navy who said he'd help me. I slept at the Salvation Army. A cot cost 25 cents a night."

Just a few days later, he found himself on board the *Novasli*, a Norwegian freighter, bound for Scotland. There was a crew of 32 men and one boy. "They were good to me," he says. Elmer made 100 kroner a month. Seven kroner equalled one dollar, so it's hardly worth doing the math.

"We got a air raid bonus when we were in London," he points out.

He did eventually tell his mother what had become of him. You can imagine how pleased she was.

His second ship was a Texaco oil tanker. He made four trips across the Atlantic Ocean. It was the good life. In New York for a refit, he saw his first television and visited his first bar. "I had a great time. The entire experience was something I'll never forget."

In January of 1943, having finally reached the necessary age, he came home and joined the navy as a gunner.

His first ship was the Corvette *HMCS Alberni*, patrolling Canadian waters as far inland as Quebec City. The mind goes into overdrive again. "There were 24 ships sunk in the Gulf of St. Lawrence in 1942," he points out. So it wasn't worry-free work despite being so close to home. There were perks. "I had a girl in Quebec City." There is a brief pause while his thoughts are collected. "HMCS stands for Her Majesty's Canadian Ship but it could stand for Hitler, Mussolini, Churchill and Stalin."

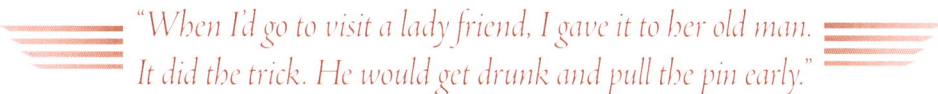

*"When I'd go to visit a lady friend, I gave it to her old man. It did the trick. He would get drunk and pull the pin early."*

His second ship was the brand spanking new Frigate HMCS *Port Colborne*. And since they spent a lot of time in St. John's, Newfoundland, "I had a girl there, too."

The trip across the Atlantic in April of 1944 for the D-Day buildup was something he still sees in his mind. "We left in the fog," he says. When it lifted, the convoy stretched out 12 miles wide and included 164 ships. "It was unbelievable."

While he didn't storm a beach on June 6, his ship did play a part. The *Port Colborne* was one of 165 warships stretched out across the top and bottom of the English Channel in order to keep the German U-boats away from the armada.

They got one U-boat. "The first thing I saw was a soccer ball pop to the surface," Elmer says. "Then blueprints, a wooden box with the address Hamburg, Germany, on it. Then part of a body."

In July, they spent four weeks in Belfast, Ireland, for a refit.

"I met a girl at a pancake place. We must have walked two miles in a blackout. I gave he my money and off she went to find us a room for the night," he laughs. It was the last time he saw her.

Elmer Phillips made good use of his rum ration. It went to the fathers of his dates.

Elmer was a little bit of a businessman. The cigarettes he was issued he sold for 10 cents a pack and used the money to buy beer. The daily ration of rum was saved and kept in a quart bottle hidden in his locker. "When I'd go to visit a lady friend, I gave it to her old man. It did the trick. He'd get drunk and pull the pin early."

War is all about fighting. "We were at port in Gibraltar and we got into it pretty good with the Brits one night. There were about 1,000 of us from six ships and they were mad because the Canadians wouldn't sing with them. I went in by the door and out by the window. I ran like hell back to that ship, I'll tell ya."

There is always fear. Especially on convoy support during a trip to Murmansk, Russia, in November of '44. "You never knew when you were going to get it," he says. "But there was always fun, too. You made the best of every situation."

Which reminds him of a certain rendezvous during one stopover in Belfast. "Flaming red hair," he says …

In February of 1945, Elmer returned home to the Island for a four-month leave. He volunteered to go to the Pacific, but the war was over before he could get there. He was discharged in October, becoming an engineer and a surveyor.

The war years and the years since have been mostly good to him. He still has his health and his spirit. There is certainly no questioning the size of the man's heart.

"I've travelled a lot," he says. And not just to lay on a beach or take in the sights. He wasn't about to sit around doing nothing when retirement came. His hobby is photography and he has used it to bring peace and closure to other families that weren't as fortunate as his own.

"I guess I started it in 1986 when I went back to Europe for the first time." He started taking pictures of the graves of Islanders who fell in the wars and returning them to family back home. Is there a better feeling in the world than knocking on a door and handing a photograph of a father's grave to a son?

"It's an unreal feeling," Elmer says. "I got into it a little bit and the idea just kind of took off." He returned another time in 1986 and has been back six more times. Every nickel spent has been his own.

"I slept in my car at Vimy Ridge," he says of the First World War memorial. "I guess it became my labour of love."

He gets the names, regimental number, date killed, age and parents' names from the War Graves Commission in Ottawa. He has been all through, France, Belgium, Italy and Holland.

He has been to 60 cemeteries and discovered Islanders in 42 of them. "Of the 360 who died, 330 are buried in Europe. There are Islanders buried in 19 different cemeteries in Italy alone. "There are 34 Islanders at Beny-sur-Mer, another 34 at Ortona, in Italy …"

Copies of the fruits of his labour are available at the Provincial Archives in Charlottetown.

Elmer Phillips is planning another trip. "I'm determined to find all of them," he says. The mother he robbed, the one who wanted to hunt him down and drag him home by the ear when he ran off to sea, would be very proud today.

# The Luck Of The Draw

Doing what he was told paid off in the long run

Jim Miller

Jim Miller will tell you that life is a game of chance. You win some and you lose some. As long as you don't lose your head. Good timing is something you can't have too much of.

"The Lord has been good to me," he says. "I guess I've been a little lucky." A little?

"Come on over," the 84-year-old air force veteran says over the phone. "We'll chin the wag." He apologizes for the length of time it takes to make it from the living room into his office. "I don't run the four-minute mile," he laughs. "I don't run at all."

But he did run to enlist on June 30, 1942, 13 days after he turned 18. He had been an army cadet, something that would come back to haunt him, but he chose the air force, following in his brother Lloyd's footsteps.

Lloyd was a fighter pilot in Burma, but Jim had no grandiose aspirations. "I didn't want to be a pilot," he says. "I was more comfortable at the back of the thing." They made him a wireless air gunner. It was a perfect fit. Jim was pretty good at hitting things thanks to a youth spent duck hunting in his hometown of Grande Prairie, Alberta.

He could have found himself at the back of a Lancaster bomber, flying the unfriendly skies of Europe. Instead, when 42 men graduated from wireless school in Winnipeg, he was one of six WAGs lucky enough to be shipped to British Columbia and Coastal Command.

"I've been asked how I managed to stay clear of the bombers," he says. "I did what I was told." Flying boats became his calling. It was a good gig that lasted 18 months before his crew was sent overseas. Most of the time was spent flying army freight around Alaska, the islands and the mainland. "We visited every nook and cranny." They were always on the lookout for enemy submarines, but they never saw any.

His friend Jack Banks did, though.

"True story," he says. "I asked him about a picture on his office wall one day and he told me about the time they were sent out at 4 a.m. and his skipper, Charlie, had been out all night. They had to dig him out of bed and pour him on to the plane. The other pilot told him to go back and lay down and it wasn't long before they spotted a sub.

"They dropped two depth charges, but they came down too fast, and at the wrong angle, and missed him. The skipper was summoned from the back, but he still wasn't flying when they came around and dropped two more.

Jim Miller, left, poses with his two brothers during the war. He has been a lot of things, but mostly he has been lucky. "The Lord has been good to me," he says.

Blew it out of the water," he chuckles. "Guess who got the Distinguished Flying Cross? Charlie."

Good fortune smiled on Jim in the form of a great fortune during one trip into Prince Rupert. With just a single dollar in his pocket, they showed up at the mess as a crap game was in full swing. "What the hell," he says. "It's not like I had anything to lose."

In a run of uncanny luck, without even touching the dice, he turned his one dollar into $1,400. "I was a pretty happy boy when the pilot came over and said it was time to go … right now. I used the money to buy a car." Needless to say, he was a pretty popular guy.

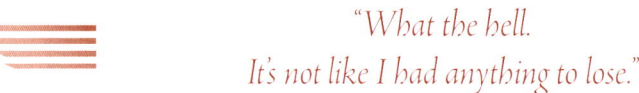

*"What the hell. It's not like I had anything to lose."*

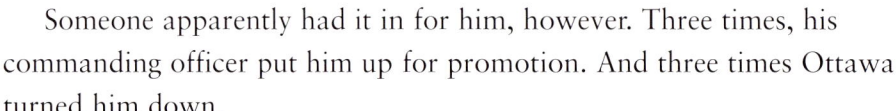

Someone apparently had it in for him, however. Three times, his commanding officer put him up for promotion. And three times Ottawa turned him down.

The problem, he learned, was that he failed to turn in all of his army cadet gear. At least that's what the paperwork said. "They said I didn't turn in my boots," he laughs. "What would I need with those dirty old things? They said I was a thief."

Because someone forgot to put a check mark indicating his boots had been returned, Jim Miller lost out on a lot of money, but the promotion to Flight Officer did eventually come.

In the fall of 1944, the entire 10-man crew was sent to Scotland and given a Sunderland Flying Boat. "Right out of the factory," Jim says. "It was absolutely beautiful."

You'd think May 20, 1945, would have been a very good day. It was a Sunday. Hostilities had ceased, but German subs were rising to the surface and, says Jim, "we had to keep an eye on them."

On this day, two U-boats had surrendered in the Bay of Biscay, but they were menacingly close to an American tanker ship. So Jim Miller's Sunderland was dispatched. At first, his good fortune held. Or so he thought.

Since there were three WAGs on the flight, and manning the mid-upper turret wasn't necessary until they were on scene, they flipped a coin. Jim won and headed downstairs for a nap with a smile on his face.

He was asleep on his bunk when a terrible crunching noise woke him up. The plane, travelling in thick fog, struck the top of a hill. A section of the bottom was ripped out and Jim's right leg was ripped apart. Somehow, he managed not to fall out by straddling the hole in the fuselage as he made his way to a ladder.

The others were sure they had lost him. "Well, well," Flight Lieutenant Ollie Olson said when he looked down and saw Jim. "Look who's here."

They couldn't land on water, of course. When they broke out of the fog, as luck would have it, they spotted an airport below. "Do not land," the control tower instructed. "Your wheels are not down."

Jim laughs at the absurdity. "We had no wheels," he says. They came, literally, to a grinding halt. "Lucky, lucky. The boys barely got out. I was on my way to the hospital when I looked back and the whole thing exploded."

He returned to Canada in August and met Eula. They had five children – four boys and a girl. One of the boys, Murray, is a beer salesman. Another, Mark, is a priest. That must make for some interesting family gatherings.

Eula is gone now, a victim of breast cancer, but the family remains close. Jim Miller has eight grandchildren and one great grandchild. He worked 35 years for Cadbury, the chocolate company.

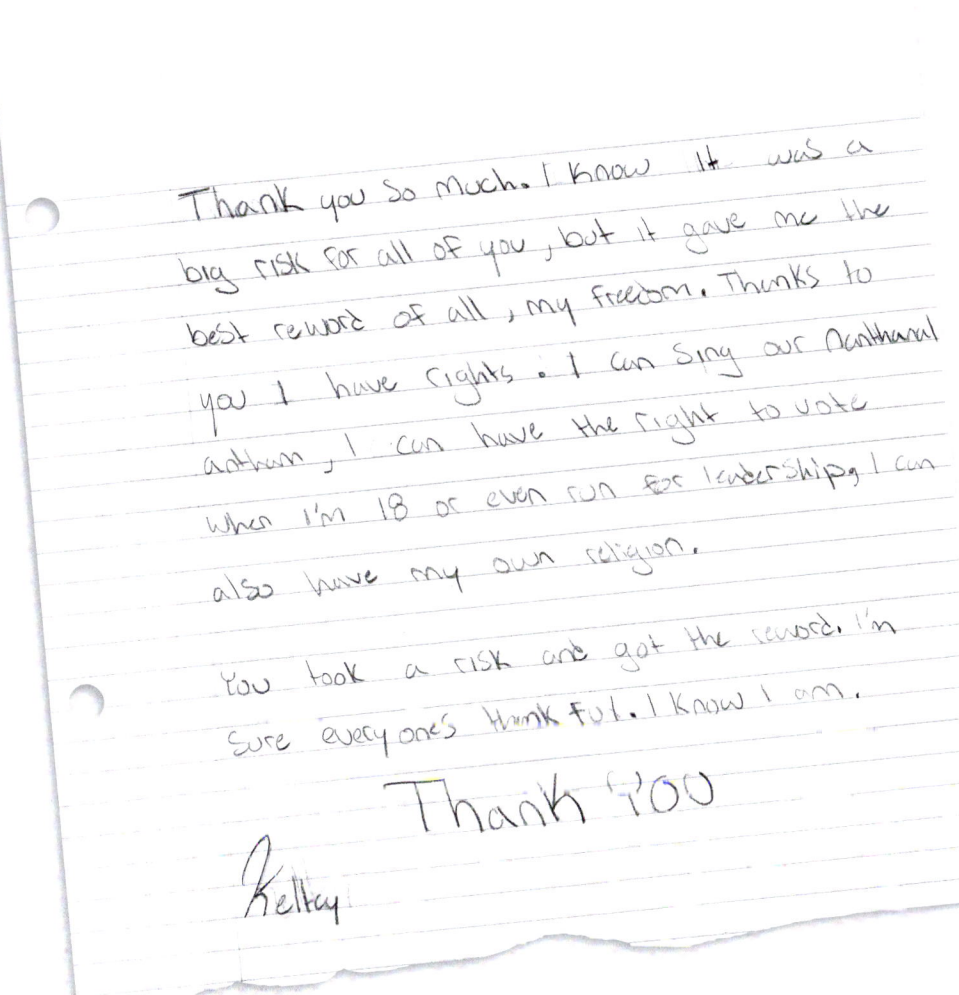

Donald Kohl recalls his days in the service of his country fondly. "It's where I learned about respect and love … and that helping others is always the right thing to do," he says.

# The Making Of A Man

If you need a hand,
he'll give you two

DONALD KOHL

**D**onald Kohl would never consider himself a hero. "Nothing special," he says of his wartime contribution to his country. Always more comfortable deflecting praise than accepting it, this delightful man insists he got more from the Second World War than he gave.

"It's where I learned about responsibility," he says. "I learned about respect and love … and that helping others is always the right thing to do."

They are lessons that would shape a young man's life and stick with him. In its barest, ugliest sense, war is about killing. In this special case, for this special man, it was more about rebirth.

"I'd love to do it all over again," he says.

By the age of 13, Donald Kohl was already working in the Ontario's tobacco fields in Simcoe. By 17, he was itching for a fight.

"Four of us made a bet regarding who they'd take," he says. "We headed to the air force recruitment office in Hamilton and I guess I won, because I was the only one they took." Size does matter. "I was a big boy. My friends called me the Jolly Green Giant."

His prize was a trip to England, all expenses paid. It did not please his parents or his new bride, Joyce. He already had one brother in the air force and another in the army. "I was the only one left at home, but I loved planes," he says. Like so many others, he wanted to do his part. Like so many others, it was the uniform that enticed him.

There were a lot of homesick boys on the ship taking them overseas, but there were no tears from him. "Young, baby-faced guys were crying, but I enjoyed it. I got sick a couple of times, but not like some of them. We played a lot of cards and I was fortunate enough (and big enough) to get a top hammock." That was the key to happiness. "The guys below wore a lot of puke."

He knew very little about navigation, but that didn't stop the powers that be from making him a navigator with the Dakota transport squad. "The night before D-Day, we towed gliders into France. We were always going somewhere."

The last days of the war were the most rewarding. "We dropped food for those poor, starving people in Holland," he says. "That did the heart good." It was dangerous work. "We came back full of holes a few times. Our plane was so slow. You could almost run faster, but I had faith. I did a lot of praying and forgot about fear."

 *"If anyone blew up a paper bag around me, I'd drop to the floor."*

He has great memories of the Beaver Club in London, for example. "The girls just loved the Canadians. They fought over us all the time and the Americans didn't like it one bit," he says. "You could pick up a girl any time, especially if you had pantyhose. They couldn't get them over there, but we could get anything we wanted if we had a pair."

One girl wanted to marry him, but there was just one problem. Joyce was at home. "I didn't keep any secrets from her when I got back," he says. "She understood. I wasn't a wild man like most of the guys."

When frightened mothers put their own safety ahead of that of their children as they ran for the air-raid shelters, Donald Kohl would pick up the children and carry them to safety. "I'd grab one under each arm," he says.

When Joyce sent care packages, all the chocolate went to the kids. "It was wonderful to see them smile," he says.

While he didn't return to Canada a beaten man, there were a few cracks in his armour. He was in hospital for almost a year because of his nerves. "If anyone blew up a paper bag around me, I'd drop to the floor," he says. "It took a long time to get over that."

Donald went to the University of Guelph, and then to a community college to receive his chef's papers. "I always loved to cook," he says. He was the head chef at the hospital in Orangeville for 25 years, most of them when Joyce was working there as a nurse. He also spent 15 years at the Nottawasaga Inn and opened Granny's Fish and Chips in the town of Shelburne.

Donald Kohl greets everyone with a warm smile. He has given up trying to hide the fact that he's bald … and beautiful.

His specialties to this day are soups and gravies, mincemeat pie and cheesecakes. "I make them and give them away," he says.

It was a wonderful marriage. Their secret? "Talk out grudges," he says. The results of their commitment to each other is two daughters, five grandchildren and four great grandchildren.

Today, he lives alone a weak-armed stone's throw from Royal Canadian Legion Branch 220 in Shelburne, in his own condo. Donald lost his dear wife to Alzheimer's and a stroke in 2002.

OK, he did keep one secret from her when he returned home from the war. He wore a toupee when baldness struck. He wore it for 30 years and no one knew.

"The grandkids wondered why I never went swimming," he laughs. Joyce didn't exactly chuckle the day she found his spare. "She came running into the living room, screaming for me to get a club, because we had a rat in one of my drawers."

He doesn't bother with it now. Donald Kohl, now in his 82$^{nd}$ year, has more important things to concern himself with than vanity.

"I spent some time sitting around feeling sorry for myself when I lost her," he says. "But I could only sit and look at the walls for so long. I had to get off my ass and do something."

He got up. And he hasn't sat still since. "If I feel bad, I go for a walk. I walk it off," he says. "I'm not a taker. If you want something done, I'm there. I joined almost every organization in town." He cooks for fellow seniors. If you need a ride to the doctor's office, call Donald. If you want to rent a hall at the Oaks Nursing Home, call Donald.

"I believe in charity and helping others," he says. "When I can help someone, it's beautiful. That's when I'm really living. If I could be in Africa, doing something for those starving people, I'd be there."

If you're a teacher in need of someone to talk to the kids, call Donald. "I love kids," he says. "They ask what happened in the war and I say it shaped my life."

In 2003, friend and fellow veteran Ken Wallace retraced his steps in Europe and returned home a driven man. Those who died are honoured, but so many others were wounded both physically and mentally, he thought. What about the living casualties?

"We never said thank you to all the chaps who got hurt. It tore me apart. I got to the point where I was feeling that nobody gives a damn about what these guys have done," he told *Legion Magazine*.

Instead of just getting mad, Wallace turned a negative into a positive. Donald Kohl and Eldon Henderson immediately jumped at the chance to help spearhead Shelburne's Lost Soldier Memorial.

The result of their efforts was the unveiling of a magnificent memorial in front of the town hall in September of 2004. "We hit the streets and the people came through," Donald says. "People are good, if you give them a chance."

There was enough money left over to restore the cenotaph constructed after the First World War, in 1923. He should be very proud, but Donald Kohl just smiles and shrugs. "I like to help," he says.

# It's A Mad, Mad World

'Sometimes it's best to look the other way'

BERT MADILL

Time has whittled away at the height and physique of the man, but his stature remains undiminished.

If you only judged Bert Madill by the company he keeps, the ever-present oxygen tank and the tube running to his nose would not begin to tell his story. He may not be going as strong as the 20-year-old who once ruled the skies, but he is far from a dead stop. There is no disputing the man's resolve.

At 84, he still calls himself Mad Bert, "the maddest of the Berts." And then he smiles. "I'm as nutty as anybody I know," he says. "I just wanted a signature phrase."

If he is mad at all, it's because he had to give up golf a couple of years ago. No anger. No bitterness. Definitely no malice. This recipient of the Distinguished Flying Cross during the Second World War wouldn't hurt a fly or a flea.

Or an elephant.

"Did you know that an elephant can carry as much as a three-tonne truck?" he says. "There was an edict that we were supposed to shoot them because the Japanese used them to carry supplies. I wouldn't do it. I couldn't do it. What did an elephant ever do to me? I didn't join the air force to shoot elephants."

There are some things a man can't bring himself to do. Even in wartime.

Lieutenant Bert Dennis Madill was stationed mostly in Burma. His enemy was the Japanese, but there were limits as to how far he would go.

Shooting elephants was beyond the limit. So was mortal combat when he caught the enemy with his pants down. Sometimes it's best to laugh and move on to fight another day. There are enough dark moments.

"I don't remember where we were, but I remember where he was – squatting, right in the middle of an open field, obviously doing his business." And it was serious business, apparently, because on the first fly-over, he didn't budge.

"I didn't have the heart to shoot him," says Bert. "We must have scared the s—t out of him, though. We flew over him one more time and I tipped my wings. He was still sitting there."

Same wing man, different reconnaissance mission. "We spotted this lone truck heading up a mountain road," Bert says with a chuckle. "It would have been a lot of fun, easy target practice, but ..."

They never got the chance. Coming around to line him up, the driver of the truck was literally scared to death. "He drove right off the road and crashed down the side of the mountain. So long, pal."

Bert was an Edmonton kid with a fascination of airplanes. At 17, he dropped out of high school and found a job downtown. He knew what he was going to do. The Royal Canadian Air Force recruitment centre was right around the corner.

Days after turning 18 in January of 1942, he enlisted. An only child, this did not go over well with mom and dad. She went into hysterics; he went ballistic. But there was no turning back. First stop, Brandon, Manitoba. Then Ottawa. Then England, for operational training in a Hurricane.

By November, he was en route to Bombay in the Pacific Theatre to join the 28th Fighter Squadron. "Two months on a troop ship," he says. "That was fun."

It took a while to get used to it when people actually started shooting back. That's the trouble with the enemy, he says. "No sense of humour."

Mad Bert had one, though. "You had to," he says. His favourite plane was the American-built Thunderbolt, 14,000 pounds of fury. A stork carrying a bomb in a blanket was painted on the nose, 'Birth Of The Blues' was written underneath.

Looking back, he chooses to remember the good times – the friends and follies, the madam in the brothel in Madras, South India. "She became my friend, someone I could talk to," he says. "Quite a gal. She ruled with an iron fist and I loved sitting at the bar, shooting the breeze with her."

Then there were the two pilots from the Indian Air Force. He was flying with them one day when the following conversation took place. Word for word, he swears, every last detail ...

"Yellow One, this is Yellow Two."

"Go ahead, Yellow Two."

"Yes, Yellow One, I have a bit of a problem here. I'm running low on fuel."

"That's OK, Yellow Two. Stick close to me. I got lots."

With that, Mad Bert Madill cackles like a kid. The friends and the foes. There was always somebody to laugh at.

Bert Madill, the maddest of the Berts, couldn't bring himself to shoot an elephant.

# Love At First Flight

The flag in his front yard honours those who fell

"You won't have any trouble finding the place," Jim Brownell says. "Just look for the Royal Canadian Air Force flag. I put it up every morning and I take it down every evening."

It is a labour of love, a tribute to fallen comrades. It is always an honour, never an inconvenience.

Sure enough. There it is, waving proudly in the breeze outside his beautiful home in Hanover, Ont. It is a flag that represents a standard of excellence for the man and his country.

As a young boy growing up in Port McNicholl, Ont., Jim had his head in the clouds. He and his brother read aviation magazines and built model airplanes. He recalls vividly his excitement the day a ski plane landed on the lake ice near his school.

"It was recess and I just took off running," he says. All he cared about was finding his dad and the $5 he needed for a ride. "I ran all the way downtown, then back to the plane. It was about two kilometers. I remember sitting on the knees of two women, but I didn't care. It was a tremendous feeling. I knew right then I was going to be a pilot."

In 1940, he found himself at a YMCA camp. "We weren't supposed to bring a radio, but I did. I heard the Battle of Britain on my radio. I remember vividly the description of the newspaper man who wrote, 'Brave men are dying and I don't know if it's ours or theirs.' "

Even now, 65 years later, those words echo in his head and bring a flood of tears. He apologizes, but there is no need.

Jim Brownell receives the Distinguished Flying Cross. Even as a young boy, he knew he would one day take to the sky. He wouldn't take no for an answer.

Although he dreamed of piloting a Spitfire, Jim Brownell had three choices when he got to England. It would be a bomber, a bomber or a bomber.

Jim Brownell didn't waste a second when he became old enough to join the service. He found himself at Manning Depot in Toronto, in the spring of 1941. It was the first of many stops on the way to war. It all could have ended in disgrace very quickly.

For some reason he still can't comprehend, he was issued a rifle and ordered to guard the entrance that faced the Toronto Island Airport. "It didn't even have a bolt," he says of his weapon. "What was I supposed to do, hit somebody over the head with it?"

Jim couldn't say no when a fellow came by with a horror story about his wife and child. He had to get out of camp and see them. "It was really sad, so I just let him go."

The fellow didn't make it 100 yards before the military police were on him. Both of them were arrested and Jim was to be brought up on charges the next morning. "I was duly frightened," he says.

It turns out a friend of his had another friend who made up the transfer rosters. Jim was told to have his bags packed by 3 a.m., with the tags turned in. Sure enough, the guy showed up and Jim joined the others being trucked to the train station, with the military police in hot pursuit. He was told to get into the middle rank of the middle file when the men were lined up so the culprit could be apprehended. "That's the closest you can come to being invisible," he says.

On the steps of the train, he thought the jig was up when an arm reached out and grabbed him. "I was thrown into a bathroom and told to keep the door locked. My heart still races when I think about it," he says. "I don't even know who saved me."

Next stop: the technical school in St. Thomas, Ont. "It was like a prison," he says. "We had this old Englishman teaching us. I remember him saying, 'I have six months to teach you snot-nosed kids everything I learned in 17 years.' You had to grow up fast."

He was a quick learner, too, finishing first in his class and earning a gold medal. And, more importantly, the perk that came with it – his choice of assignments. Winnipeg or Mont-Joli, Quebec. He chose Mont-Joli "because they had airplanes."

Not that he was allowed to fly them. "I swept hanger floors by the acre," he laughs. In Victoriaville, Que., he took and passed his math test but he was still told he was a bomb aimer. "Like hell I am," he said. His next stop was Three Rivers, Que., flying Fleet Finch planes equipped with skis. "I practiced landing in my own tracks," he says.

 *"Brave men are dying and I don't know if it's ours or theirs."*

In the spring of 1943, Jim found himself in Camp Borden, Ont., flying Harvard trainers. His dream was becoming reality, but there is danger in the air. "Don't kill yourself showing off before the Germans get a crack at you," he was warned.

By that summer, he was on his way to England from New York aboard the *Cythia*. "It was a disgusting thing," Jim says. "We couldn't keep up with the rest of the convoy and it eventually broke down. I'll never forget this huge battleship coming alongside to shield us." The trip back to New York was harrowing. "We had a balloon as an escort."

A train took them north to Montreal, then east to Halifax. And what was waiting for them? Just the *Queen Elizabeth*. "What a ship," he says. "It cruised at 36 knots."

He was stationed in Greenock. "I became a tea person," he says. "I learned that what looks like sugar isn't sugar, it's salt." England, however, wasn't his cup of tea. He wanted to go home, but not as badly as he wanted to fly. "Somebody always reminded me that I had volunteered."

You learn to do what you're told. "I was ordered to stand by a fire bucket on a roof until 3 a.m.," he says. When someone suggested dinner at a nearby hotel, he thought that sounded like a fine idea. Until the next morning when his name was called and he was paraded in front of the commanding officer.

"Young man," the officer said, "I have a piece of paper that could send you home in disgrace." Jim Brownell was immediately scared straight. War is a serious business.

In his dreams, he flew a Spitfire. In reality, he had three choices.

"I could fly bombers or bombers or bombers."

When Flying Officer Brownell reported to his camp in northern Scotland, he checked in with the CO and asked a simple question: Where can I go? "This guy, his name was Smith, didn't even raise his head," Jim says. "He said, 'You can go to hell.' I'll never forget that."

War is never mistake-free. "I was sitting on the runway preparing to take off one night when the girl in the tower told me to stay where I was, that there was a German night fighter in the area. After a while, she came back on the radio and told me it was OK to land. Hell, I hadn't even taken off yet."

Training on Oxfords, a twin-engine communications plane, Jim once again got top marks. When he climbed into his Lancaster bomber for his first of 51 missions, Jim Brownell had a total of four hours flying time in a bomber. "There was a shortage of pilots," he explains. "Most of our targets were in the Ruhr Valley. We called it Happy Valley."

 *"I was sitting on the runway preparing to take off one night when the girl in the tower told me to stay where I was, that there was a German night fighter in the area. After a while, she came back on the radio and told me it was OK to land. Hell, I hadn't even taken off yet."*

He recalls the night he was told to dump 500 gallons of fuel into the North Sea before landing. "I wrote my dad and asked how long that would last in his old Buick," he laughs.

Thirty-seven of his missions were as a Pathfinder, lighting targets for the main force that followed. It was harrowing, dangerous work, "but we never thought about getting shot down."

It was an incredible sight to see hundreds of bombers take off and form up. One night in particular, on Jan. 16, 1945, he did his job exceptionally well. His actions earned him the Distinguished Flying Cross.

It was near the city of Magdeburg, Germany. Ground markers had come up well short of the intended target. It was left to Jim and his crew to fly directly over a large enemy force that had taken cover in a forest and drop a primary blind marker that illuminated the area for four minutes as it drifted to earth. The raid was a success and they limped home full of holes courtesy of a German fighter.

Jim Brownell had respect for the enemy, but he does not regret his actions that led to so many lost lives.

That night, in the officers' mess, he met a pilot who had flown 104 missions. "The guy turned to a navigator who had 90 and said, 'Get some in.' There was a little drinking that night."

Jim could have stopped after 30 missions. "No way," he says. It was the time of his life. The boy became a man overseas, then returned to Canada and went back to high school.

"The tough part for me was coming home," he says. "I was a nobody." He became a sales clerk for five years, then a friend recommended him for a teaching job with the Toronto Board of Education. He spent 29 years teaching history and geography in Toronto before following his daughter north to Hanover.

Joan and Jim Brownell had four children. Today, they have nine grandchildren and three great grandchildren.

"I honour the men I met and the men who died," he says of the flag that flies proudly from a pole in his front yard.

—  🍁  —

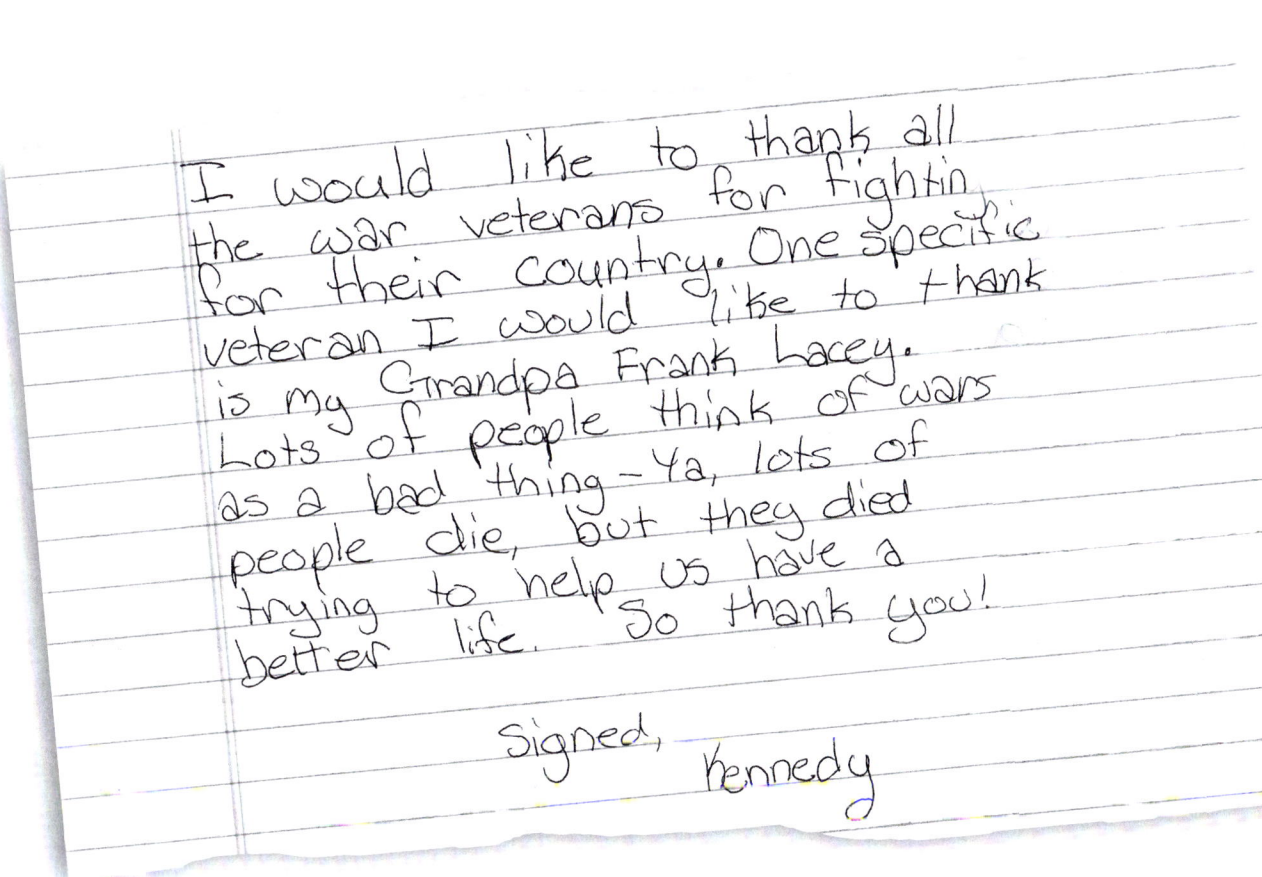

I would like to thank all the war veterans for fightin for their country. One specific veteran I would like to thank is my Grandpa Frank Lacey. Lots of people think of wars as a bad thing — Ya, lots of people die, but they died trying to help us have a better life. So thank you!

Signed,
Kennedy

# Just Call Him Lucky

He should have died that day,
and that day, and that day…

HUGH
RAYMENT

As a youngster growing up on the family farm near Viking, Alberta, Hugh Rayment was sure of only one thing – life stinks.

"My dad paid me 10 cents an hour to pull stinkweed," he laughs. "I learned how to work five minutes after I learned how to walk. By the time I was 14, I could run every piece of equipment."

Not that farm livin' was the life for him. "I never had any intention of becoming a farmer." Instead, he chose to help change the world.

Albert Rayment emigrated to Canada after the First World War. Although he was an architect, he chose to homestead in Central Alberta, spending the first winter in a tent. That must have been fun. It can be a little nippy in the middle of January. Or the middle of July, for that matter.

"It was basically a gopher ranch," Hugh says. It was especially tough for his mom. Every pot and pan in the place was being used to make moonshine. "There were bottles everywhere. I remember finding a neighbour passed out in the washtub."

Hugh was the third of seven children. When the Second World War broke out, his older brother Fred was first to join. He had been shot down over Germany and was a prisoner of war. That could have meant an exemption for Hugh, but he felt a sense of responsibility. You mess with one Rayment, you mess with them all.

He was only 18. His first choice was the air force. "My night vision was terrible." His second choice was the navy. "There was a three-month wait." Welcome to the army. "They threw me a uniform before I got through the gate."

By September of 1944, Hugh Rayment was a lean, mean fighting machine. He'll never forget the harrowing trip across the English Channel on a landing craft. "We were packed in there like sardines," he says.

And he'll never forget the smell. Literally and figuratively. "War stinks," he says. In France for only 48 hours, he was already a seasoned soldier. "To say the least, I was apprehensive about my future."

He learned quickly that the ditch was the first line of defence. "You get your nose into the dirt as far as you can," he says.

And, when luck smiles on you, you smile back. "We could hear a shell coming, so we ducked into a building and crawled under a counter," he says. "It was a direct hit but, when the smoke cleared, we looked up and there was a row of bottles – cognac and gin. We each grabbed one. It's amazing what fear can do to you but, thanks to the cognac, we spent the rest of the day laughing."

He should have died that day. Of the 30 men who went out, only 13 came back. He remembers throwing a grenade at an upstairs window and having it hit the wall and land at his feet. House-to-house fighting was the worst. He walked into a room one day and saw a potato masher coming at him. He dove into the hall. "I don't know how I survived that," he says. "After the thing exploded, I couldn't hear for three days."

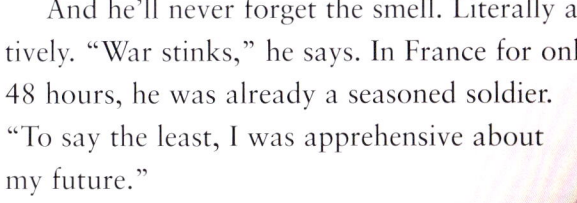

Hugh Rayment learned that good luck is as important as good sense when it comes to surviving war.

Hugh Rayment was one of the first Canadians to cross the Dutch border. He received a hero's welcome. And a fine dinner.

"The old girl had a big iron pot on the stove and was making rabbit stew," he says. "We all had a big bowl and the husband brought out the brandy and cigars. I always joked that I must have got the foot, because my name should have been Lucky."

He remembers one fire fight when the two sides were just metres apart separated only by a mound. "I could hear the Germans talking," he says. He remembers digging a foxhole and climbing into it as the rain pelted down at the same rate as the artillery shells. "The hole filled up with water." And his head filled up with terrible thoughts.

 *"The old girl had a big iron pot on the stove and was making rabbit stew. We all had a big bowl and the husband brought out the brandy and cigars. I always joked that I must have got the foot, because my name should have been Lucky."*

So many close calls and yet he was never seriously wounded. "Self preservation is a wonderful thing."

When it came to close shaves, he should have been a barber. At one point, a telegram was sent to his parents informing them he was missing in action. Passwords were important in the dark and the confusion of battle. Lost and on his own one night, he heard "Japanese" as he crawled through the mud. He was supposed to say "Jitters." Instead, he said, "Shut up. I'm a damn Canadian." That's a good way to get shot.

Hugh Rayment loves to laugh. Which is why he chuckles madly when he explains that he had a stone dug out of his forehead in 2004. His combat injuries were minor, but he did suffer mentally and physically. He was in Belgium when he broke down in late 1944.

"Battle fatigue," he says. "Or bomb happy. The bullets and shells are nothing compared to sleep deprivation. I can laugh about it now."

On New Year's Day, 1945, he woke up and couldn't get out of bed. "It felt like there was a knife stuck in my chest," he says. "My temperature was 105." He was diagnosed with double pneumonia. His weight plummeted from 140 pounds to 89 pounds. "I had no appetite. The flesh was just hanging off my bones."

The best part about being in a British hospital was the bottle of stout he received every day. He was there for three months before being transferred to a Canadian hospital near Dieppe, France. It was great to be home, so to speak, but he wasn't exactly receiving the finest treatment available. An orderly looked after him, but he received no medication. The nurses didn't even come by to check on him.

Bewildered and upset, he asked to see a padre. The padre told him about another chap he had counseled. The guy had gone on leave and returned with a venereal disease. Now he was really confused.

"What does that have to do with me?" he asked.

"You're in a VD ward," the padre said.

It wasn't until after the war that the real fun started. Then again, isn't that how it's supposed to work?

He befriended Col. St. Laurent and became his official driver in Nijmegen, Holland. He was also double-dutying as the bar steward at the officers' mess. As army life goes, it was a damn fine gig. One day, it occurred to him that he had been missing out on his daily ration. And, since there were six 20-litre bottles at the mess ... and he was in charge of the audits ... "Common sense said that I should have some," he says. "The next day at 10 a.m. seemed like a good time for a heist."

It goes without saying, but he says it anyway: "I had a lot of friends for a while." And, thanks to a couple of cans of paint, he also had his own jeep. A vehicle and endless rum. You can see this is going the wrong way.

Like the night he entered the roundabout going head on into a convoy of trucks. Either he was the only one in step or he was "sauced." Bet on the latter. "The MPs showed up and saved my life," he says. "A lot of fun and games."

Another night, he lost control and skidded right between two streetcars. Another night, the vehicle he was driving was struck by a train and carried 100 yards down the track. "Lucky," he says.

When Col. St. Laurent took his mutt to a dog training centre in Brussels, Belgium, Hugh was happy to drive him. "I had my own room in a ritzy hotel," he says. And since he had access to endless gasoline, he filled up jerry cans and sold them to various pub owners in exchange for a bottle.

This guy was ever luckier in peace than he had been in war. When Col. St. Laurent went home, his services were transferred to Col. Dickson. He drove a Packard staff car. In Paris.

"Never a dull moment," he says. "I have always tried to overlook the ugly part of war and think of the good times."

There was, not surprisingly, a rather large social function the night before he was to come home. "I had a lot of booze to get rid of," he explains.

He met this nurse, see. By the time he got home the next morning, he had 10 minutes to pack. And one minute to get both barrels from his commanding officer.

"You've got a lot of smartening up to do," he was told.

He did. By July of 1946, he was back at his pre-war job at the airport in Vancouver. He got his pilot's licence. He got a university degree.

He repaired appliances for 10 years at Eaton's in Edmonton. He started his own appliance service company. He didn't get rich, but life was more than comfortable. "I don't believe in failure," he says.

His biggest stroke of luck, as it usually is with men, was marrying a good woman. He and Elsie produced six healthy children, who went on to produce 12 grandchildren. And they went on to produce 13 great grandchildren.

"Life has been a ball," he says. Hugh Rayment is a Life Member of the Vernon, B.C. Legion. He still visits local schools to help today's youth better understand the sacrifices of war time.

It has been a good life, a very lucky life. It all goes back to a bowl of rabbit stew.

— 🍁 —

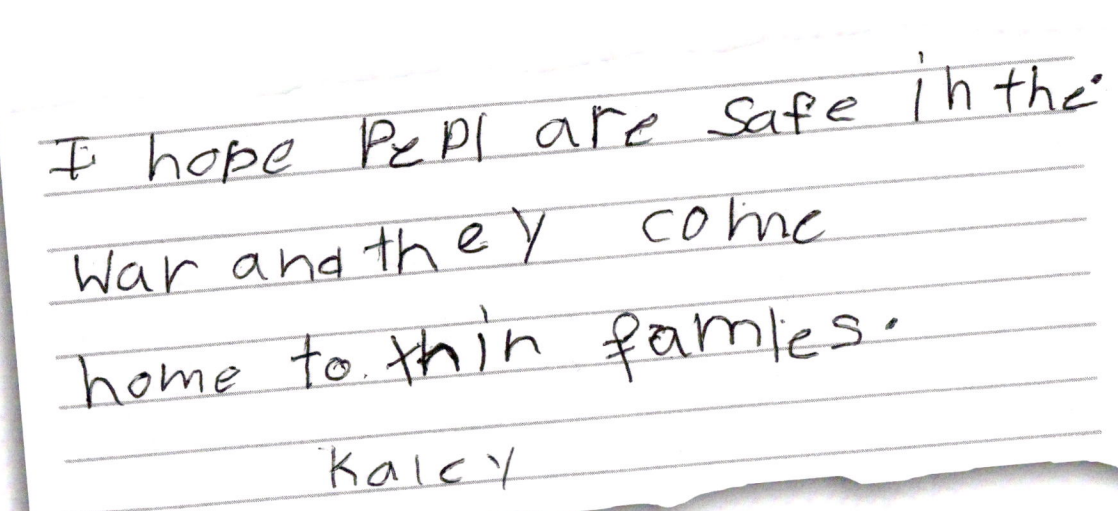

I hope pepl are safe in the war and they come home to thin famles.

Kaley

# More Power To Him

It's good to be lucky, and lucky to be good

CLIFF POWER

**I**t has been said that a person has to be good to be lucky and lucky to be good. If that fails, there's always cheating.

The question has to be asked after Cliff Power sends one victim after another away from the cribbage table beaten and skunked. Then again, there is no shame in losing to a three-time Royal Canadian Legion crib champion.

He smiles when the challenge is issued because he knows the outcome. Petty officer Clifford Samuel Power smiles often, almost always. And, he readily admits he has cheated before.

It was the night of Sept. 13, 1942, 900 kilometres east of Newfoundland, in the middle of the North Atlantic. He was in the stoke hole, aboard the destroyer *HMCS Ottawa*, when German U-boat 91 fired two torpedoes into the side of his convoy escort ship, the second one breaking her in two.

At that time, the Canadian navy boasted a fleet of 188 ships and provided almost half of the escorts for convoys between North America and Britain.

"I cheated death that night. I was a fortunate man to survive," says this wonderful 83-year-old native of the tiny Nova Scotia town of Mushaboom (pop. 250). When the torpedoes hit, shrapnel struck him in the stomach. As the ship was sinking, a mate tied him to a float and threw him overboard. "I never did find out who did it."

That act, along with the cold salt water, saved his life. "I would have bled to death," he says. He chooses not to remember the pain of losing one-quarter of his stomach, but he does recall the mental torture of bobbing in the water, waiting seven hours to be rescued. "It was horrible," he says. "All sorts of things go through your head."

Sixty-nine sailors were saved that night, but 113 souls were lost.

Cliff Power would spend 28 days in hospital. Upon his release, he was assigned to the corvette HMCS *Matapedia* and later served on the destroyer HMCS *St. Croix*. In total, he made eight trips across the Atlantic, helping to equip the war machine.

 *"He asked me to hold his beer, then put two of them up against a wall. He had paws like a gorilla."*

This is a man who sees the glass half full. Unless he's thirsty. Cliff met his wife Margaret, who was also in the service, during the Second World War. They were together 55 years until an aneurism took her four years ago. She was from land-locked Edmonton. He was a boy who grew up on the ocean in the Maritimes with one brother, Rod. And NINE sisters. His father Rueben was in the Merchant Navy for 38 years.

They moved to Edmonton after the war, "because Margaret said so," he laughs. He held all kinds of jobs. He was a farmer, a truck driver, a caterer and a miner. Mostly he was a father and husband. Cliff and Margaret raised three boys and two girls. He has eight living grandchildren and four great grandchildren.

"He coached us in baseball and hockey," says Bob, his eldest son. "He is a lifetime member of the Legion. He has been involved for 55 years as a volunteer and has run the Strathcona Branch shuffleboard league for 23 years." When Branch No. 150 moved to a new location in the spring of 2005, he did the ceiling. "Not bad for an old fart."

Except for the sinking of the *Ottawa* and the friends he lost, he has mostly good memories of his time in the service. "I was proud to serve my country," he says. "I have had a great life."

Cliff was only 17 when he went against his parents' wishes and joined the navy in November of 1939. "It was something I had to do," he says. He was young, so full of life and mischief.

Both he and brother Rod were in Halifax on V-E Day. That spelled trouble. The city fathers made it impossible to buy liquor, but the boys had some in reserve. Of course. "There was a tussle involving Rod and a Warrant Officer over a woman," he says. "When the guy went home, he called the cops and gave them his own address by mistake. He was so drunk when they arrived that they searched his house and found a case of gin hidden in the ashes of his stove. They ended up charging him."

There was time while on leave in Halifax when he and his mates were at the Red Triangle Club when the crew of a Russian ship walked in. "All women," he says. "They had a case of scotch. I was young." And so were they. Details are greatly overrated.

Leave doesn't mean leave of your senses. It only seems that way. You gotta have a winger. And it helps if he's a six-foot-six Cape Bretoner by the name of Orville Neville when the cops stop you for walking down the street with a beer in your hand.

"He asked me to hold his beer, then put two of them up against a wall," Cliff laughs. "He had paws like a gorilla." The police didn't stick around to wage much of a debate, correctly figuring that discretion was the better part of valour.

There was a tradition that sailors were given a shot of rum each day at 11 a.m. That didn't mean they had to drink it. Cliff and his mates opted to save theirs until it was truly worthwhile. But, since they were not allowed to take it on shore, they, improvised.

"We told a deck mate about our little predicament," he says of the seven bottles they had saved up. Mr. Helpful, they called him. The Halifax port was overrun by cats. May as well put 'em to use. The deck mate was stopped, of course, when he left the *Matapedia* with his kit bag. Inside, the MPs found a cat. The next time, a cat. The next time, a cat. The next time, they just waved him through. Inside were the seven bottles of rum.

Cliff Power was a fine sailor, but he's a better cribbage player.

# Madcap And Englishman

'It belongs to the guy behind me, sir.'

JIM KELLY

They didn't just break the mould when they made Jim Kelly. They smashed it to smithereens with a shovel, then ran over it with a tank. Then they backed up and ran over it again. Then they blew it up.

You don't take his word with a grain of salt. You need the whole salt mine, and even then you're not sure what you're dealing with.

"I've always been a bloody liar," he says.

Say what you will about this madcap Englishman who came to Canada after the Second World War, he has a lovely set of teeth.

"I have an arrangement with Mr. Jones at the Jones Funeral Home," he explains. "Whenever I lose my teeth or want to make a change, I just go and see him. He has a whole drawer full. We just get out a big bucket of disinfectant and …"

He pauses, presents his best straight face, then bursts into hysterics. "Noooooo," he says. "I really get the girls going with that one."

He was there on D-Day, landing with the predominantly Canadian force at Juno Beach as a member of the 35th Royal Marine commando unit. As horrible as it was, it would have been even worse if he hadn't stowed five bottles of whiskey in his backpack. He made it all the way through to the Netherlands before pneumonia and hearing loss brought about his discharge.

"Then I came home and committed suicide." Pause. "I got married."

Just kidding, of course. He lost his much better half, Louisa, to diabetes three years ago. Together, they had five children – four girls and a boy. He has 12 grandchildren and 14 great grandchildren.

"I hate Christmas," he says. But, again, of course, he's just kidding. He has spent a lot of Decembers dressing up as Santa Claus in Moose Jaw Sask., in order to put a smile on a child's face.

"Because there's nothing better than that," he says.

And there's nothing worse than war. Jim Kelly doesn't talk about many of the things he has seen and done. "Bloody awful," he says. Which is why you didn't wait for fun when the opportunity presented itself. Even if it didn't, he'd make his own.

One thing about Jim Kelly, at least he's honest. "I've always been a bloody liar," he says.

An impressive haul, but Jim Kelly would be the first to tell you he never won any awards or medals for good behaviour.

"I remember a night on leave when three of us went out. I know I got drunk because I ended up on a woman's bed and I still had my clothes on the next morning.

"We had gotten separated, of course. I saw one of the lads the next morning and I said, 'What the hell happened to you?' He said, 'I think I got married.'" Jim was appalled by the very idea. "Who to?" he asked.

"I think it was my sister," he said. "I got on the job and she kept screaming, 'Oh, brother.'"

It would be a better story if it could be said that the army brought about discipline and focus in him, but that wasn't exactly the case.

Or even remotely the case, for that matter. He was his own man which, at times, led to some rather childish escapades. Even confined to barracks, you would very rarely find him there.

There is an everlasting bond that develops between men who depend on each other for their very lives. When they're not trying to kill each other.

"When we were in battle, we were all brothers," he says. "When we weren't in battle, the battle royal was on. We had three guys who didn't drink, but I made damn sure they got their daily ration."

Whether it was in the bar or on the battlefield, he figured he was trained to fight so he may as well fight. You had to be ready to leave quickly when you went out with Jim. Things – very bad things – had a tendency to happen. It's only right that he had the riot act read to him on many occasion, because he admits to starting a few.

"The Polish guys were pretty good guys, but you had to watch them," he says. "You'd be dancing with a girl and they'd just walk right up and take her." At their peril, of course.

Jim laughs like a madman. Because he is one. Before heading to France, they had to get seven needles. The men were standing in a field, naked as jaybirds as the English officer made his way down the line. He stopped in front of one lad and gave him a slap in the face.

"Did that hurt?" he asked.

"No, sir."

"Why not?" the officer said.

"I'm in the South Battalion Duke of Wellingtons, sir."

"Good lad."

He continued down the line and stopped in front of another. This time, the officer punched the soldier in the kidney.

"Did that hurt?" he asked.

"No, sir."

"Why not?"

"I'm in the South Battalion Duke of Wellingtons, sir."

"Good lad."

The officer moved on and stopped in front of Jim Kelly. Looking down, he noticed some rather impressive equipment and gave it a whack.

"Did that hurt?" he asked.

"No, sir."

This surprised the officer a great deal. So he gave it another whack, one that can best be described as a helluva whack.

"Did that hurt?" he asked.

"No, sir."

"Why not?"

Jim smiled. "It belongs to the guy behind me, sir," he said.

His ears didn't hear very well and they weren't overly sympathetic, either. "This one lad sent a letter to his wife and a letter to his girlfriend. He put them in the wrong envelopes. We laughed about that for days. Talk about feast for famine."

Jim Kelly likes to give the impression he's crazy. Not so. He is 87 … going on 12. He is a proud man who knows right from wrong, even if he pretends otherwise.

"My mom was a widow with eight boys and three girls at home when I ran off to war," he says. "We made 10 shillings a month and I sent seven home to her so she could feed the family. She was a great lady. She brought us up right."

He followed his brother Peter to Canada and settled in Moose Jaw. He never left. "Canada is the greatest country in the world," he says proudly. "I'm a Canadian." And a master storyteller who has spent a lifetime brightening people's lives with his jokes and volunteer efforts. Although not necessarily Louisa's life.

"She called me James Albert when she was mad," he says. "She called me James Albert quite often."

He has done all kinds of things and had all kinds of jobs. He built runways in Goose Bay, Labrador and Iceland. In Moose Jaw, he worked for Canadian Pacific Railroad and was a night watchman and maintenance man for Eaton's. He also worked at the library. "They wanted a well-educated man," he says. "But they chose me instead."

Jim Kelly is a life member of the Royal Canadian Legion, Branch 59. For 15 years, he was commander of the colour party. He has been to more funerals than he can count. He speaks to children at schools, reliving his experiences and, I suspect, scaring the hell out of their parents.

His message? "Whatever you do, stick to it."

After our meeting, as I prepared to leave, I told him I was heading to Weyburn. "Where will you sleep?" he asked. When I told him I didn't know, he invited me back inside his tidy apartment and pointed at his couch. "Take that with you," he said.

Jim Kelly. Good to the last prop.

# Missed It By That Much

'I made the mistake of doing really well on my gunnery test.'

Ken Linklater

Ken Linklater had an advantage over most men when he signed up to fight for his country. When it came to dealing with the fallen, he had been there … done that.

"My dad was a funeral director," he says. "I had pretty much seen it all. I did some embalming. It wasn't unusual for me to go 72 hours behind the wheel of an ambulance or a hearse."

Born in Teeswater, Ont., the family moved to nearby Kincardine to take over the funeral home-furniture store when he was just a boy. You could buy a couch or you could buy the farm. You might say they had you coming and going.

War is a strange place to go to avoid dealing with death, but Ken looked at it as a great escape when he turned 18 on Jan. 21, 1941.

His dad had other ideas. "He wouldn't let me go," he says. Two older brothers were already overseas and his old man needed help. Sixteen months later, however, there was no stopping him. It wasn't exactly with his parents' blessing that he joined the Royal Canadian Air Force.

At least there was a method to his perceived madness.

"If I was going to get killed, I wanted it to be quick," he explains. "I didn't want to suffer in a muddy trench or drown in the middle of the North Atlantic." He had never been on a plane before and had no grand aspirations of becoming a pilot.

"I made the mistake of doing really well on my gunnery test," he says. That's how he found himself in a Lancaster bomber turret for 35 missions, most of them over Germany's Ruhr Valley, Stuttgart and Berlin.

Better late than never. Avid golfer Ken Linklater poses for a picture after his recent hole-in-one at the Kincardine Golf and Country Club.

Close calls? "Yeah, every day," he laughs. They were never shot down, but they were certainly shot up. In the 35 missions, the crew fought off 27 enemy fighter attacks. Their record was 196 holes in the old girl, including one in the gas tank.

"I wonder how many hits it could withstand before it fell apart," Ken laughs. Probably 197. "Luck plays a big part during a war. You never know when your number is up."

Case in point: one of their rare daylight missions. Because they were carrying one eight-tonne bomb, their Lanc could only climb to 14,000 feet. Ken was in the upper turret when he looked above and saw another plane drop it's bomb load. It was at that point that he said goodbye to himself.

"It was truly amazing," he says. "One of the bombs dropped straight down between the tail and the left wing of our plane. It missed us by a couple of inches."

Another time, the front turret was completely shot away, with Cecil Nugent inside. Somehow, the force of the explosion knocked him backwards. "I think I've been hit," Nugent said. Ken laughs. "Had he ever, but he didn't have a scratch on him."

The cruelty of fate. Cecil was lost back in Canada when the commercial plane he was in crashed during his honeymoon. Although all seven crewmen made it home, only Ken Linklater remains alive today.

Superstition played a big part. He ate onions before every flight. "I figured that if I was captured, I could just breath on them."

He knew first thing in the morning, when he walked into the mess, if a flight was planned for that night. "We got bacon and eggs, toast and coffee, if we were going out." And the rest of the time? "Terrible. There might be roast beef, but it was always cooked in mutton grease. It took me 50 years before I would even try rack of lamb."

Being a gunner in a Lancaster bomber was one of the most dangerous jobs you could have, but there were good times. Ken's luck certainly held. His prowess with a trigger was nothing compared to his uncanny knack with a pair of dice in his hand.

"Pretty good craps player," he understates. "I sent my pay home and lived off my winnings." Craps bought a lot of beer. And a car for the boys to get around in. "The roads were so narrow. That made things interesting a few times. I remember one night we were on bicycles for some reason and one of the guys rode straight into the statue in the middle of town. He was too drunk to get hurt. The air commodore called for a parade one morning and not one single Canadian showed up. They were going to put us in jail. As if that would have been punishment. They needed us."

Their barracks wasn't the Hilton, but he made the best of it. "By the time I came home, in early December of 1944, I had 14 blankets."

Although Ken and Reita had known each other for years, they became an item during a dance in 1947. "He still had his uniform on and he looked so nice," she says.

They were married two years later. He followed his dad into the funeral business, and together they raised two daughters. They have five grandchildren and two great grandchildren, a beautiful home and a passion for golf.

"I know he had lots of girlfriends," Reita chuckles, "because I found his address book."

Ken took his wife to England for a vacation in 1980. "I remember it was some sort of national holiday and all the kids kept coming up to Ken and asking for money," she laughs. "He wasn't giving them any so I had to remind him that some of them might be his grandchildren."

Ken Linklater chooses to recall the war years' good times. "I wouldn't have missed it for the world," he says.

# Champagne Breakfast

He wasn't a drinker,
but he quickly became one

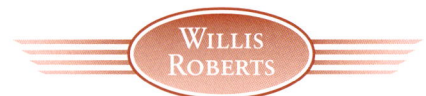

WILLIS ROBERTS

It could be suggested that Willis Roberts' decision to join the army instead of the navy or the air force was a no-brainer. Smarts was the one thing he had plenty of.

As a 20-year-old, he went straight from studying forestry engineering at the University of New Brunswick into the Canadian Officers Training Corps. (COTC) and emerged as a Lieutenant before he had even fired a shot in anger. And that's only for starters.

When you talk about long and distinguished careers, this man's life has been the equivalent of a marathon victory.

"I got sick if I even looked at a boat and the air force was something relatively new," he says. Plus, he liked mutton. Willis lives in a house just 2½ blocks from the home he grew up in, but that doesn't mean he has sat still.

He chose the artillery while at Camp Petawawa and went overseas with the 2nd Canadian Heavy Anti-Aircraft Regiment on the Australian meatpacker *Northumberland*. She carried 10 million dozen eggs and six million pounds of mutton. The voyage took 19 days.

Willis remembers being astounded by the number of ships in the convoy that left Halifax harbour. "I couldn't count them all," he says.

The trip was a sickening experience. Literally. "I was sick before we even made it out of the harbour," he laughs. "We had a contest to see who could throw it the farthest."

He wasn't a drinker, but he quickly became one. It was more a case of self defence than a great love of headaches. Through trial and error, he

234

discovered that brandy calmed his stomach. "Whenever I felt woozy, I headed for the bar," he says. "Booze is supposed to make you sick, but it had the opposite effect on me."

It might have been the brandy, but Willis Roberts doesn't remember where he disembarked. His first base was the monster known as Aldershot, but he was soon stationed at gun sites around London.

"We got one and chased a few others," he says of the German bombers that came in waves during the Battle of Britain. "A few had hot tails going home."

The men discovered quickly that if they weren't religious, it would be worth their while to become religious.

"You could go on these tours of churches and cathedrals," he laughs. "Beside every one of them was a pub. That's just how they do things over there. It's a great country. We'd make it to the church … if we had time. Our first parade over there on a Sunday, the various religions were asked to fall out one at a time for church. Soon there was only one guy standing there. He said he didn't have a religion."

So, while the others headed off to worship, his job was to clean the latrines. "It was a couple of weeks later that he went to the CO and asked if he could declare himself a Catholic on Sundays only."

There was fun, but the thing that stands out for Willis was the professionalism and honesty of his men. He knew each of them by name.

"You could leave a bottle of booze out and nobody would take it," he marvels. "If you wanted to be one of the men, one of the boys, you did what you were told and nothing else. As long as you were responsible. If someone got drunk and couldn't do his job, there was hell to pay."

They had been in England just a few months when the outfit became mobile. Problems arose if it stayed in one place too long. For example, there was a lineup at the padre's door every Monday morning after leave.

Willis Roberts, after receiving an honourary doctorate from the University of New Brunswick.

235

An officer and a gentleman. Willis Roberts has enjoyed a long and distinguished life.

"Guys get lonesome and the women are in the same mood," Willis laughs. "The lads kept wanting to get married. There would be five or 10 waiting to see the padre."

One of the men had a problem – he was already married. He wrote home to his wife, asking for a divorce. "No damn way, young fella," she wrote back. "What does she have that I don't have."

Willis laughs hysterically. "He wrote her back again," he says. "He answered her question. 'Nothing. But she has it over here.'"

There wasn't always honesty when it came to women. "The night before we went to Europe, a lot of the guys wrote letters to their girl. Some of them had to write five or six of them."

Willis Roberts landed July 1, 1944, in Beny-sur-Mer, France. It was three weeks after D-Day. "We fired 400 rounds the first night." By the end of the war, his regiment had fired more than 100,000 artillery shells on the march through France, Belgium, Holland and Germany.

As a battery commander, he had 325 men under him. "If one man was a hero, they were all heroes," he says. And most of them were pranksters, too. The guy who was always on time for parade would inevitably find his boots tied together. The best-dressed guy always knew where to find his suit when it rained – hanging outside.

"Laughing is important … as long as

you're not sitting by yourself with a stupid grin on your face," Willis says.

The stories of heartbreak and horror are endless. Which only makes the stories of inspiration that much more special. As a high-ranking officer in the field, Willis Roberts had his own batman, or personal servant. One of them was a 16-year-old boy who kept his shoes shined and his uniform pressed. His name was Abe. He couldn't read or write. And he wasn't much of a driver, either.

"The first time he came to one of those traffic circles they have over there, he went straight through the middle," Willis says.

He almost killed the boss, but a great bond developed. When Willis wrote home to his wife Joyce, telling her about this fine, young man, Abe and Joyce became friends. One was a teacher, the other a student. Through the mail, she sent him words to study. Then books. Within six months, he had progressed enough to send entire letters back to her.

Abe remained in the service of his country after the war, but he didn't meet Joyce until years later, when he was stationed at nearby CFB Gagetown in the '80s. Thanks at least partially to Joyce Willis, he had become a Regimental Sergeant-Major.

"Isn't that something!" Willis says without patting himself on the back. Full of goodness but not of himself, the man's pants are still perfectly pressed and his tie fits snug around his neck.

"He wears a tie every day," his daughter Regi says.

"I wouldn't feel right without it," he says.

Willis Roberts' war took him into Germany and lasted till the last hour. "The war ended at eight o'clock and we fired our last shell at seven," he says. His men fired 200 rounds the last day.

"These two clowns, my buddy Reg Samson and another guy, came to visit that night. I had this nice bottle of scotch and they had some rum. We were in the cellar of a house. They were drunk when they arrived and they were drunk when they left. The war was over. I told Abe to let me sleep until 11 a.m., but I knew he wouldn't."

At 7:20, Abe rousted him with word that there was a parade outside he had to inspect. "He said he would leave me a good, strong drink. It was champagne. When I went outside, there were 35 or 40 Germans standing there with their hands up. I went over and clicked my heals a couple times, then I went for breakfast."

It was a champagne breakfast like no other. When it came to the champagne, there was no end. The driver of the water wagon didn't come back with a single drop. Instead, he discovered the German navy's liquor depot and returned with 300 bottles of champagne.

"Have you ever eaten porridge with champagne?" Willis asks. "I ate sausages and eggs cooked in champagne."

What wasn't gone was divided up among the men. By 10 a.m., a shortage had developed and there was only one thing to do – go back for more. "Lackey was his name," Willis says. "He came back with 300 more bottles." And not a drop of water. By 2:30 in the afternoon, he was on his third important mission of the day.

Lackey was six-foot-six. Nobody was going to fight him for it. But there was a problem. The 2$^{nd}$ Division had discovered the depot and put a guard on the stash. Still, fate smiled. "The Sergeant of the guard was Lackey's brother. They had to wait until it was time to change the guard, but Lackey got re-stocked." This load included scotch and whiskey.

Willis still had 15 bottles of aiming juice when he got back to England. By August, he was on his way home, where he was promoted to Lieutenant-Colonel before leaving the service. He remembers the first sign he saw when his ship arrived back in Halifax. "Drink Canada Dry," he says. "I'm still at it."

Which reminds him. "Dammit ," he says, "I'm going to pour us a drink."

The other thing he remembers about his homecoming is that Joyce only shook his hand. "And she kissed that damn Reg Samson." He is the godfather of their oldest of two daughters. He lost Joyce six years ago. Now in his 89$^{th}$ year, he has five grandchildren and two great grandchildren

Willis Roberts went to work in surveying with the provincial government, mapping the entire province. He became the director of surveys for the province and president of the Canadian Land Surveyors. He started a school of surveying at the University of New Brunswick and received an honorary doctorate from UNB last year. In 1983, he was the recipient of the Canadian Geographical Society's outstanding personal achievement award.

A great soldier, but a greater man, he just recently started opening up about his experiences overseas.  He is now writing his own book. "I guess I'm proud," he says.

As for his accomplishments during the Second World War, he shrugs. "I was just a person who was in it."

# Acknowledgements

It started, as all life stories must, with a mother and a father. "You better sit down," I told them. "I want to be a writer." I was 14.

"And I want to be a rocket scientist," my father said. I needed 100% on my next English test to get my average up to 42. My math teacher, Mr. Chang, had recently pinned me against the blackboard by my throat. My geography teacher, Mr. Renzella, is the reason I cheer for whoever the Italians are playing.

It was the epitome of blind faith when they shipped me off to my cousin Brian and Sharon's home in Barrie, Ont., to attend Georgian college. Except on the mornings after pub nights. Because they paid the tuition, and for a million other reasons, I thank them first.

The support I have received during this process has been sometimes overwhelming. And sometimes not so much.

My friend Brian Lacey was impressed when I told him what I was up to. "Just think," he said, knowing full well he was asking a lot. "Then you'll have written more books than you've read."

He was the exception. As he usually is.

Edmonton Strathcona Legion Branch 150 president Ted Gazley was the first person I went to see. He loved the idea. Since that initial meeting, he and his wife Shirley have been a constant source of support and inspiration.

Ted introduced me to General Tim Grant, Commander of Land Forces Western Area. It was my plan, when I went to see him at CFB Edmonton, to ask him to write the foreword to this book. He said he'd be glad to, but he had a better idea.

"I know Rick Hillier pretty well," he said. "I think he's the man you want." Rick Hillier is General Rick Hillier, Chief of the Defence Staff. That's all. Just the most powerful and influential soldier in the country. As if.

I was somewhere between Moncton and Fredericton when my cell phone rang. "This is Annie Dicaire, correspondence officer for Gen. Hillier," the voice on the other end said. "I'm calling to inform you that Gen. Hillier would be honoured to write your foreword."

And suddenly I was crying in the face of danger. It can be hazardous to drive with tears streaming down your cheeks. Talk about instant credibility, an endorsement beyond my wildest imagination.

And to think he said thank you when he sent his wonderful words to me a few weeks later. Preposterous. Thank you, sir.

It's always fun to say thank you. Especially at a time like this. So many people played a part in this project. I know exactly where I'd be without them – flipping burgers.

So thank you to Gary and Grant Hill of Budget Edmonton for putting me behind a steering wheel instead of on the side of the road with my thumb out during my coast-to-coast tour of Canada.

And thanks to Phil Clarke of Moxie's Edmonton for seeing that I didn't starve to death on my journey.

Also to former Mayor of the City of Edmonton Bill Smith and Edmonton Oilers president Patrick LaForge for lying so eloquently when I asked them to write testimonials on my behalf for my website.

Thank you to Duncan Sinclair, Don Schick, Steve Robbins, Tony Olivieri, Stephen Droeske and my brother Bob Haskins and his wife Brenda. I am forever in your debt. OK, hopefully not forever.

My gratitude to each of the following: Bob Hannah, Paul Stanway, Dean and Melissa Pickup, Roger Dubuc, John Caputo, Craig Martin, Ken and Lori Chilibeck, my cousin Blaine Sutter and his wife Diane, Rob Simonowits, Tom Stoncel, Frank and Deb Pirker, Kim and Craig Tunbridge, Cindy Prodan and Terry Tietzen. Even if you don't know what you have meant to this book, I do. And to Kaley Bilyk, Kennedy Lacey and the Grades 5 and 6 students at Minchau Elementary School for their beautiful notes to Canada's heroes.

My love and thanks to my wife Tamara, sons Ryan, Sean and Jaden, and daughter Glenys. Without someone to share this with, what's the point? So thank you, also, to Emil and Irene Bilyk, Russ and Lanis, Blaine and Rhonda, Trevor and Kim, and Brianne.

Thank you to everyone who helped smooth the path at every Royal Canadian Legion I stopped at along the way.

My respect and admiration, always, for today's military men and women, and certainly their families, for putting themselves in harm's way so the rest of us don't have to. God bless you and Godspeed. You are today's heroes.

Lastly, and most importantly, thank you to yesterday's heroes. For your courage in 1941 and your candor in 2006. Meeting you has been one of the highlights of my life. I won't begin to tell you I know how you feel because, like Joe Dyck says, "You wouldn't believe me. Unless you were there."

In my mind, every year is the Year Of The Veteran.

# To order additional copies of this book, please contact:

Laughing In The Face Of Danger

TMH Marketing Inc.
PO Box 32092
2331-66 Street
Edmonton, AB
T6K 4C2

Phone: 780-642-7987

Fax: 780-642-7859

Email: scott@scotthaskins.ca

Web: www.scotthaskins.ca
(Printable order form available online)

## "If blood's yellow, I've been shot."